KT-221-718

TREASURY OF CHRISTMAS Crafts

TREASURY OF CHRISTMAS Crafts

EDITORIAL

Editor, Family Circle Books: Carol A. Guasti
Assistant Editor: Kim E. Gayton
Project Editor: Leslie Elman
Copy Editor: Laura Crocker
Book Design: Bessen, Tully & Lee
Editorial Assistant: Kate Jackson
Editorial Freelancers: Celeste Bantz, Kristen Keller
Typesetting: Alison Chandler, Caroline Cole, Maureen Harrington
Letter Art for Chapter Introductions: Lauren Jarrett
Illustrations: Excerpts from the book, Ready-To-Use Old-Fashioned Christmas Illustrations,
copyright ©1989 by Dover Publications, Inc.; edited by Carol Belanger Grafton.
Cover Photos: Winter Woods Wreath — Carin Riley; Quilt Basket Ornament — Taylor Lewis;
Country Dove Ornament and Corn Husk Tree-Top Angel — McGinn/Velez.

MARKETING

Director, Family Circle Books & Licensing: Margaret Chan-Yip
Direct Marketing Manager: Jill E. Schiffman
Fulfillment/Planning Coordinator: Carrie Meyerhoff
Administrative Assistant: Dianne Snively

Published by The Family Circle, Inc.
110 Fifth Avenue, New York, NY 10011

Copyright® 1990 by The Family Circle, Inc.

All rights reserved. No part of this book may be reproduced in any form or by any electronic means, including information storage and retrieval systems, without permission in writing from the publisher, except by a reviewer who may quote brief passages in a review.

Manufactured in the United States of America

10 9 8 7 6 5 4 3 2 1

Library of Congress Cataloging in Publication Data
Main entry under title:

Family circle treasury of christmas crafts.
Includes index.
1.Christmas.   2.Crafts.
I.Family Circle, Inc.   II.Title: Treasury of Christmas Crafts.

TT900. C4F36   1989   745.594'1   90-80374

ISBN 0-933585-16-0

Other Books By Family Circle

Best-Ever Recipes

The Best of Family Circle Cookbook series
(Pub. Dates: 1985 - 1989)

Busy Cook's Book

Good Health Cookbook

Make It Country

The Family Circle Christmas Treasury series
(Pub. Dates: 1986 - 1989)

Favorite Needlecrafts

Hints, Tips & Smart Advice

To order **FamilyCircle** books, write to Family Circle Books, 110 Fifth Avenue, New York, NY 10011.

To order **FamilyCircle** magazine, write to Family Circle Subscriptions, 110 Fifth Avenue, New York, NY 10011.

TREASURY OF CHRISTMAS
Crafts

Table of Contents

Introduction

hristmas and crafting always seem to go together. Somehow, we find the time to do a little bit extra for the holiday season. Those few quiet moments we have are devoted to creating something special—a quilt to commemorate a couple's first Christmas together, a woolly knitted sweater for a favorite niece or grandchild, a gingerbread house to surprise the kids. Nothing quite says Christmas like something homemade, and that is why we created this book.

Our collection of favorite Yuletide projects also includes a bevy of crafts for the home—indoors and out! There are wreaths fashioned from calico and cranberries, as well as elegant ones that glint with gold. You'll find whimsical ornaments, beautiful crèches, wonderful stockings, and tree skirts that lend the perfect burst of color under your tree.

There's something here for every crafter—quilting, knitting, crochet, sewing, even wood and paper crafts. If you're an experienced crafter, you won't have any trouble following our step-by-step instructions. If you're a beginner, or an older hand who needs a refresher course, our Craft Basics chapter will get you started. We've also provided beautiful color photos of the projects to guide and inspire you.

But perhaps the best part of this book comes long after the holidays are over. Through the blizzard of greeting cards and the whirlwind activities of the holidays, it's comforting to know that there will be tangible memories of the season. Those gifts that you make by hand will be treasured by loved ones long after this holiday has gone. They will be loving reminders of this Christmas, and a link to Christmases yet to come.

Greet the holidays with a room full of pretty patchwork.

The Holiday Home

et the glow of Christmas enter every room of your house. Whether you stitch up several items to carry through a theme, or just add a special touch here and there, we have the projects to make your house a holiday home.

Create pretty patchwork pieces for the bedroom, the kitchen and bathroom. Cheery checks and bright patches of color will fill your rooms with Christmas gaiety.

If you prefer to tuck a little seasonal magic into nooks and crannies, we have patchwork lace stockings, tiny teddy bears, fragrant potpourri and pomanders, table linens and potholders—even a quaint crèche made from twigs. All precious sights of the season.

And we offer you not one, but *two* gingerbread houses to bake. Our Sweet Tooth house has an A-frame shingled roof and weathervane. And our Hansel and Gretel cottage is a Swiss-style delight.

Create a Christmas wonderland in your home with these crafts, or give them away as very special gifts. The motifs and colors have been adapted for Christmas, but these projects are so lovely you can display them year-round. So dress your home in its holiday best, and set the scene for the most joyous season of the year.

ROOMS FULL OF CHRISTMAS

Patchwork Quilt; Patchwork Pillow, Pillow Shams and Ruffled Pillows (directions, page 6); Round Tablecloth (directions, page 6) and Square Tablecloth (directions, page 7).

A PATCHWORK BEDROOM

Bring a bright, holiday look into the bedroom with one or all of these patchwork projects.

PATCHWORK QUILT

AVERAGE: For those with some experience in quilting.
MATERIALS: Forty-five-inch-wide fabric: 4 yards of green, 3 yards of off-white and 1¼ yards of red; matching sewing threads; 6 yards of 44-inch-wide unbleached muslin, or a sheet, for quilt backing; masking tape; synthetic batting; quilter's pins; darner or milliner's needle; green quilting thread; between needle for hand quilting *(optional)*.

DIRECTIONS
(¼-inch seams allowed):
1. Cutting: On the green fabric, draw the following: two 9 x 81½-inch and two 9 x 78-inch borders, three 3½ x 60½-inch and eight 3½ x 18½-inch lattice strips, and twelve 3½-inch squares. Cut on the drawn lines. Draw twenty-four 4½-inch squares, and draw intersecting diagonal lines across them. Cut on the drawn lines (four triangles per square). **On the off-white fabric,** draw forty-eight each of 5⅜-inch, 5-inch and 3½-inch squares, and twenty-four 4¼-inch squares. Across the 5⅜-inch squares draw one diagonal, and cut on the drawn lines (two triangles per square). Cut out the 5-inch and 3½-inch squares. On the 4¼-inch squares draw intersecting diagonal lines, and cut out the four triangles. **On the red fabric,** draw forty-eight 5⅜-inch squares. Draw diagonally across each one, and cut out two triangles per square.
2. Quilt Block *(see* FIG. I, 1A*):* At a short edge, sew each green triangle to an off-white one to make a larger triangle. Sew two of these larger triangles together at the long edge (alternating the colors) to make a square. Repeat to make three more squares. Sew one of the patchwork squares, at the green edges, between two white squares. Repeat. Sew a green square between the remaining two patchwork squares at the white edges. Sew the three rows together to make the center of the quilt block *(see* FIG. I, 1A*)*. At the long edge, sew each red triangle to an off-white one to make a square. Then sew two of these squares together at the white edges. Repeat to make three more pairs. Sew two of these pairs to opposite edges of the green and white patchwork *(see* FIG. I, 1A*)*. Sew an off-white 5-inch square to each of the opposite ends of the two remaining pairs. Sew these two rows at opposite edges of the patchwork to complete the block.
3. Rows: Sew three quilt blocks alternately with two green 18½-inch lattice strips to make a horizontal row *(see* FIG. I, 1B*)*. Repeat three times. Sew these four rows alternately with three green 60½-inch lattice strips to finish the patchwork.
4. Borders: Sew a long border at each long edge of the patchwork *(see* FIG. I, 1B*)*. Sew a short border at the top and bottom edges.
5. Quilt Backing: Cut the muslin or the sheet in half crosswise (two 44-inch x 3-yard pieces) and sew them together at a long edge. Press.
6. Assembling: Spread the quilt backing, wrong side up, on the floor and tape down each corner. Spread the batting on top of the backing, smoothing it from the center out. Over the batting, spread the quilt top, right side up. With the quilter's pins, pin together the three layers, from the center outward, straight to each edge, and diagonally to each corner. Using the darner or milliner's needle, single lengths of off-white thread and long stitches, baste through all three layers from the center outward, straight to each edge and diagonally to each corner. Baste additional rows about 8 inches apart, stopping 1 inch from the raw edges.
7. Quilting: With the quilting thread, stitch in the ditch of the green lattice and border seams by hand with a between needle, if you wish, or by sewing machine.
8. Binding: Trim the quilt backing and batting ¾ inch inside the quilt top edges. Turn under the quilt top ¼ inch, then ½ inch, pin a hem at each edge, and stitch all around. Remove the basting.

FIG. I, 1A PATCHWORK QUILT
QUILT BLOCK

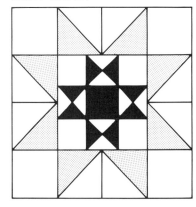

FIG. I, 1B PATCHWORK QUILT
QUILT LAYOUT

PATCHWORK PILLOW
(18 inches square)

AVERAGE: For those with some experience in quilting.
MATERIALS: Scraps of green, off-white and red fabric; matching threads; piping *(optional)*; 18½-inch square of fabric for pillow back; synthetic stuffing or 18-inch square pillow form.

DIRECTIONS
(¼-inch seams allowed):
1. Make a quilt block *(see Patchwork Quilt, Step 2, page 5, and* Fig. I, 1A*)* for the pillow front.
2. If you wish, stitch piping to the edges of the quilt block pillow front, right sides together and raw edges even, clipping the piping seam allowance at each corner.
3. Pin the pillow back to the pillow front, right sides together and raw edges even. Stitch around three sides and four corners. Turn the pillow right side out and stuff it or insert the pillow form. Turn in the open edges, and slipstitch the opening closed.

PILLOW SHAMS
(for queen-size pillows)

AVERAGE: For those with some experience in sewing.
MATERIALS FOR TWO PILLOW SHAMS: 2 yards of 54-inch-wide fabric; matching thread.

DIRECTIONS
(½-inch seams allowed):
1. Cut the fabric in half lengthwise, making two 27 x 72-inch strips. Stitch a ½-inch hem along each short edge. Fold the strips in half, hemmed edges together, and pin-mark down the center fold.
2. Spread out each strip, right side up, and fold one end 2½ inches beyond the pin-marked center line. Repeat at the opposite end, overlapping the first by 5 inches. Pin across the overlaps and along the raw edges.
3. Stitch ½ inch from the raw edges. Turn the pillow sham right side out, and press it.
4. Topstitch a border through both layers, 2 inches from each edge. Insert the pillow through the back opening.

RUFFLED PILLOW
(16 inches square)

AVERAGE: For those with some experience in sewing.
MATERIALS: ½ yard of 54-inch-wide fabric; 2 yards of piping *(optional)*; matching thread; synthetic stuffing or 16-inch square pillow form.

DIRECTIONS
(½-inch seams allowed):
1. From the fabric, cut two 17-inch squares and a 3-inch-wide ruffle strip, pieced as needed, to measure 96 inches long.
2. If you wish, pin piping around the pillow front, right sides together and raw edges even, clipping the piping seam allowance at each corner. Using a zipper foot, stitch the piping in place around the front.
3. Stitch the short ends of the ruffle strip together to make a loop. Narrowly hem one long edge. Mark the other long edge at the middle, then at the quarters. Pin the ruffle to the pillow top, over the piping, right sides together and raw edges even, with the ruffle's finished edge facing the pillow center, and a quarter mark at each corner. Make shallow pleats as you pin, to take up the extra fullness. Stitch, using the zipper foot.
4. Stitch the pillow front to the pillow back along the previous stitching, with the ruffle inside toward the center. Stitch around three sides and four corners. Turn the pillow right side out and stuff it or insert the pillow form. Turn under the open edges, and slipstitch the opening closed.

ROUND TABLECLOTH
(about 100 inches in diameter)

AVERAGE: For those with some experience in sewing.
MATERIALS: 6 yards of 54-inch-wide fabric; matching thread.

DIRECTIONS
(½-inch seams allowed):
1. Cut the fabric in half crosswise to make two pieces 54 inches wide and 3 yards long. Cut one piece in half, lengthwise, to make two pieces 27 inches wide. Stitch one narrow piece to each long edge of the wide piece. Press the seams open.
2. Fold the cloth in half, crosswise, seams matching. Fold it again, lengthwise, to make a 53-inch square with four layers. From the center fold, mark off a quarter circle with a 50-inch radius. Pin the marked line through all the layers and cut out along the pins; save all the scraps for appliqués. Narrowly hem the raw edge.

FIG. I, 2 TREE APPLIQUÉS

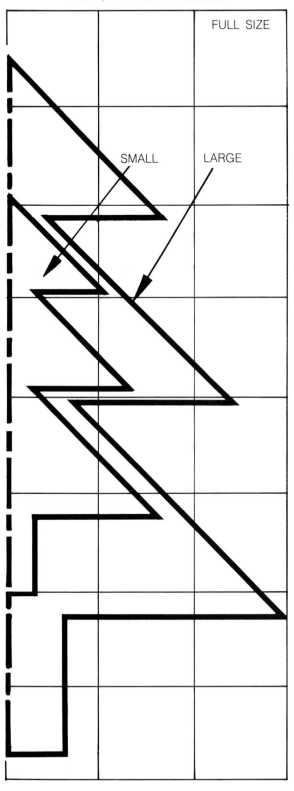

FULL SIZE

SMALL   LARGE

SQUARE TABLECLOTH
(53 inches square)

EASY: Achievable by anyone.
MATERIALS: 1½ yards of 54-inch-wide fabric; matching thread; fabric scraps for appliqués *(use scraps from the Round Tablecloth, page 6)*; dressmaker's carbon; tracing wheel; fusible interfacing; tracing paper.

DIRECTIONS:
1. Straighten the ends, if necessary, of the 54-inch square of fabric. Turn and stitch a ¼-inch hem at two opposite edges of the tablecloth, then hem the remaining edges of the tablecloth.
2. Trace the tree appliqué half-patterns in Fig. I, 2 onto folded tracing paper. Unfold the paper for the full-size patterns. Using the dressmaker's carbon and tracing wheel, trace four large trees and eight small trees onto the appliqué fabric. Pin the fabric to the fusible interfacing, and cut out both layers together.
3. Pin a large tree appliqué with interfacing, centered, at a corner of the tablecloth. Pin a small tree appliqué with interfacing on either side of the large tree appliqué *(see photo, page 4).* Fuse the appliqués with a hot iron. Repeat for the remaining three corners. When the appliqués are cool to the touch, zigzag stitch over the raw edges around the trees, if you wish.

A PATCHWORK KITCHEN

APPLIQUÉD POTHOLDERS
(9 inches square)

AVERAGE: For those with some experience in sewing.
MATERIALS: Red and green fabrics; matching threads; fusible interfacing; synthetic batting; paper for pattern.

DIRECTIONS
(¼-inch seams allowed):
1. Heart Potholder: Sew 1½-inch-wide strips of the red fabric to two opposite edges of a 7½-inch green fabric square. Trim the red edges flush with the green. Sew two more strips of the red fabric to the remaining green edges, and trim the edges.
2. Enlarge the heart pattern in Fig. I, 3 onto paper, following the directions on page 239. With the red fabric pinned to the fusible interfacing, cut out a heart. Pin the heart appliqué with interfacing to the center of the green square, and fuse them together with a hot iron. Machine stitch over the raw edges with a close zigzag (satin) stitch.
3. Cut a 1¼ x 5-inch red fabric strip. Turn under ¼ inch at each long edge, and press. Fold the strip in half lengthwise, long edges matching, pin and edgestitch. Fold the tab in half, and cross the ends. Pin the ends to one corner of the potholder top, right sides together and raw edges even, and stitch.
4. Baste two 9½-inch squares of batting to the wrong side of the potholder front. Pin a 9½-inch red fabric square to the potholder front, right sides together, with the hanger loop inside toward the center. Stitch around three sides and four corners. Turn the potholder right side out. Turn in the open edges, and slipstitch the opening closed. Topstitch ¼ inch around all the edges.

FIG. I, 3 HEART APPLIQUÉ

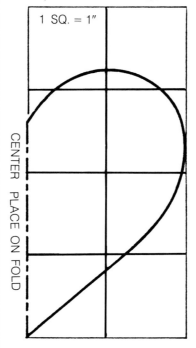

1 SQ. = 1″

CENTER PLACE ON FOLD

5. Diamond Potholder: Follow the directions for the Heart Potholder, Steps 1 to 4, using a 4½-inch fabric square placed on the diagonal instead of the heart appliqué.
6. Tree Potholder: Follow the directions for the Heart Potholder, but omit Step 1, using a 9½-inch red fabric square for the potholder front. Use the large tree appliqué in Fig. I, 2 *(page 7)*, cut from green fabric, instead of the heart appliqué, and place the tree appliqué on the diagonal as shown in the photo on page 9.

OVEN MITT

AVERAGE: For those with some experience in sewing.
MATERIALS: 9½ x 24 inches of red checked fabric; matching thread; synthetic batting or polyester fleece interlining; paper for pattern.

DIRECTIONS
(¼-inch seams allowed):
1. Baste the batting or fleece to the wrong side of the fabric. Topstitch diagonal parallel lines, to connect the corners of the square checks, across the fabric. Repeat the topstitching in the opposite direction, at right angles to the first stitchlines.
2. Enlarge the pattern in Fig. I, 4 onto paper, following the directions on page 239. Cut out a front and a back for the mitt.
3. Sew the two halves of the mitt right sides together, leaving the wrist edge open. Double stitch at the base of the thumb, and clip the seam allowance to the stitchline. Turn up a ½-inch hem at the wrist edge, and stitch. Turn the mitt right side out.

FIG. I, 4 OVEN MITT

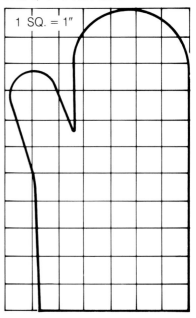

1 SQ. = 1″

CAFÉ CURTAINS

AVERAGE: For those with some experience in sewing.
MATERIALS: Fabric; matching thread; curtain rod.

DIRECTIONS
(¼-inch seams allowed):

1. Install the curtain rod, and measure the distance from the rod to the window sill. Cut two pieces of fabric that length and the full window width; using the pair will give the curtains double fullness. Cut two 3¼-inch-wide ruffle strips, pieced as needed, each strip twice as long as the width of one curtain piece. Hem the short ends of each strip.

2. Stitch a narrow hem at each side edge of each curtain. At each top edge, turn down ¼ inch, and press. Then turn down 2 inches, press, and stitch along the bottom folded edge. Measure 1 inch from the top, and stitch along this line to make the rod casing for the curtain.

3. Stitch a ¼-inch hem on one long edge of each ruffle. Stitch a gathering row ¼ inch from each remaining raw long edge. Place a ruffle piece on top of a curtain piece, right sides together, the raw top edge of the ruffle matching the raw bottom edge of the curtain. Make the outside ends flush and pin them together. Pull up the gathers to fit the width of the curtain, distributing the fullness evenly. Pin the gathered ruffle in place, and stitch over the gathering line. Turn over the ruffle and press it downward.

Appliquéd Potholders; Oven Mitt; Café Curtains

A PATCHWORK BATHROOM

HOLLY HAND TOWELS

AVERAGE: For those with some experience in sewing.

MATERIALS: Red and green fabric scraps for appliqués; 3-inch-wide strip of red fabric; red sewing thread; fusible interfacing; purchased white guest towel; dime; paper for pattern.

DIRECTIONS:

1. Trace the holly leaf pattern in FIG. I, 5 onto paper. Pin the green fabric to the fusible interfacing. Cut out three holly leaves from the fabric and interfacing. Using the photo as a placement guide, fuse the leaves to the towel. For each holly berry, trace around the dime on the red fabric. Cut out the berries along with a layer of fusible interfacing, and fuse the berries to the towel.

2. Cut the red fabric strip 1 inch longer than the width of the towel. Turn under one long edge of the strip ¼ inch, and press. Edgestitch the strip to the bottom edge of the towel; the strip should extend ½ inch on each long edge of the towel. Turn under the short ends of the strip, and hem them flush with the towel's long edges. Blind stitch the top edge of the strip to the towel.

Holly Hand Towels; Hearts & Gingerbread Garland

HEARTS & GINGERBREAD GARLAND

AVERAGE: For those with some experience in sewing.

MATERIALS: Green and red fabric scraps; green sewing thread; fusible interfacing; 1 yard of ¼-inch-wide green satin ribbon; paper for patterns.

DIRECTIONS:

1. Trace the heart and gingerbread boy patterns in Fig. I, 5 onto paper. Using the green fabric for the gingerbread boys and the red fabric for the hearts, trace as many shapes as desired. Pin each fabric scrap with the traced shapes to another scrap of the same color fabric, wrong sides together, with a layer of fusible interfacing between them.

2. Cut out the shapes through all three layers and, using a hot iron, fuse the layers of each shape.

3. Arrange the hearts and gingerbread boys alternately in a row, with the arms of the gingerbread boys overlapping the hearts by about ¼ inch. Stitch the overlaps securely.

4. Cut the green satin ribbon into two equal pieces. Fold one piece of ribbon in half, lap the fold over one end of the garland, and stitch the lap securely. Repeat with the second piece of ribbon at the other end of the garland.

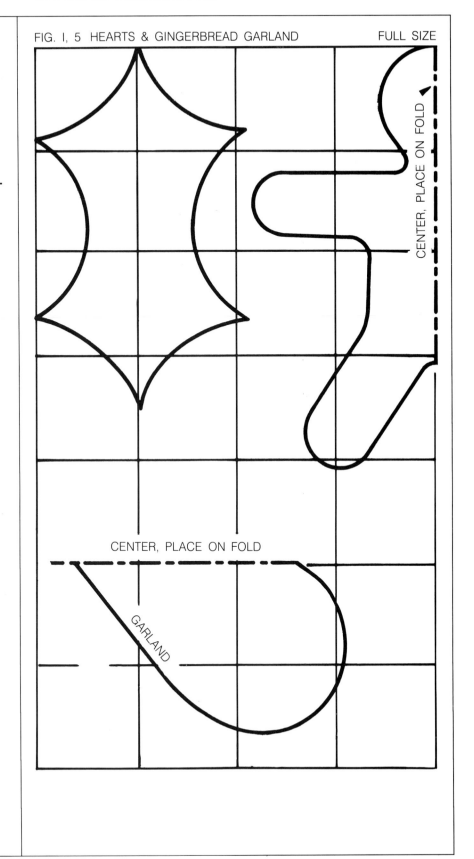

FIG. I, 5 HEARTS & GINGERBREAD GARLAND   FULL SIZE

CENTER, PLACE ON FOLD

CENTER, PLACE ON FOLD

GARLAND

Country Kitchen Curtains; Holly Wood Wreath

COUNTRY KITCHEN CURTAINS

This tulip motif has a Pennsylvania Dutch feeling that complements any country decor.

AVERAGE: For those with some experience in sewing.

MATERIALS: Muslin; black pencil; scrap paper; masking tape; 7-inch square of Mylar®; black fine-point permanent felt-tip pen; single-edge razor blade or sharp-pointed craft knife; paper toweling; acrylic paints: red and green; 2 stencil brushes; newspaper; iron.

DIRECTIONS:

1. Curtains: Measure the distance from the curtain rod to the sill. Cut two muslin pieces that length and the full window width. Stitch a ¼-inch hem at the side edges, and a 1½-inch hem at the bottom. Cut a top facing strip for each curtain that is 3 inches wide by the width of the curtain.

2. Tabs: Cut twelve tabs, each 5 x 2½ inches. Fold each tab in half, to 5 x 1¼ inches, and stitch ¼ inch from the long raw edges. Turn the tabs right side out, and press. Fold each tab in half, to 2½ x 1¼ inches, and pin each to the top edge of a curtain, right sides together and all raw edges even. Place one tab flush with each side edge and four tabs, equally spaced, between. Pin the facing on top, and stitch ½ inch from the top edge of each curtain over the tab ends. Turn the facing to the wrong side, with the tabs facing upward. Turn under the lower edges of the facing, and slipstitch it in place.

3. Stencil: Enlarge the designs in FIG. I, 6 with the pencil onto paper, following the directions on page 239. Tape the paper patterns under the Mylar, and trace the designs onto the Mylar with the black pen. Place the Mylar on top of a cutting board and carefully cut out the designs using the razor blade or craft knife.

4. Cover the flower designs with masking tape when painting the green leaves; cover the leaves when painting the red flowers. Tape the stencil to the curtains, placing the motifs as you wish *(see photo for placement suggestions)*. Place paper toweling under the curtains where you will be stenciling. Do not thin the paint. Pick up a small amount of paint with one of the stencil brushes, and brush off the excess paint in a circular motion on newspaper. Holding the brush straight up, stencil the design on the curtains. Use a separate brush for each paint color. After the stenciled designs have dried, set the paint by pressing the designs with a hot, dry iron.

FIG. I, 7 HOLLY WOOD WREATH

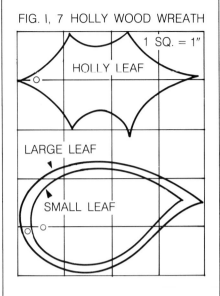

1 SQ. = 1"

HOLLY LEAF

LARGE LEAF

SMALL LEAF

HOLLY WOOD WREATH

A simple, sturdy decoration you'll enjoy for years to come.

AVERAGE: For those with some experience in woodworking and crafts.

MATERIALS: ⅛ x 3-inch lattice or ⅛ x 3 x 24-inch strips of "Midwest" micro-cut cherry wood (available at art supply or craft stores); 8 feet of ⅛-inch heavy wire; No. 20 wire; flexible tie wire; green floral tape; paper for patterns; sandpaper; drill; flat latex paint: red and 3 shades of green; paintbrush; one hundred ½-inch-diameter wooden beads; graphite paper; stylus or old ballpoint pen.

DIRECTIONS:

1. Cut the heavy wire in half. Overlap the ends of one piece to make a 15-inch-diameter circle. Fasten the overlap with tie wire. Repeat to make a second circle. Tape the two circles together with floral tape.

2. Enlarge the patterns in FIG. I, 7 onto paper, following the directions on page 239. Using the graphite paper and stylus or old ballpoint pen, trace the patterns onto the lattice or cherry wood. Cut out about two dozen each of the three sizes of leaves. Sand the edges, and drill a small hole near the base of each leaf. Insert a 6-inch length of No. 20 wire into each hole, and twist the ends together tightly to make a stem. Wrap the stems with floral tape.

3. Paint the leaves green, using the darkest shade for the holly. Paint the beads red. Insert a 6-inch length of No. 20 wire through each bead, and twist the wire ends tightly. Twist five or six berries together to make a clump. Make 18 clumps.

4. Wrap the leaf stems around half the wreath. Changing direction, wrap the other half. Wire the berry clumps to the wreath. Add a loop of No. 20 wire to the back for a hanger.

FIG. I, 6 CURTAIN STENCIL   1 SQ. = 1"

CUT OUT
SHADED AREAS

ALL THROUGH THE HOUSE

Patchwork Lace Stocking; Sweet Hearts; Beary Christmas (directions, page 16);
Home Sweet Home Sampler (directions, page 18).

PATCHWORK LACE STOCKING

A beautiful way to use all the bits of lace you've saved over the years.

AVERAGE: For those with some experience in sewing.

MATERIALS: ½ yard of dark brown fabric; 1 yard of muslin; ½ yard of synthetic batting; 15-inch strip of beading lace; assorted lace scraps; ⅔ yard of ⅜-inch-wide brown ribbon; paper for pattern.

DIRECTIONS
(½-inch seams allowed):

1. Enlarge the pattern in Fig. I, 8 onto paper, following the directions on page 239. Cut out two stockings from the muslin, one from the brown fabric and one from the batting.

2. Baste together one muslin, the batting and the brown stockings.

FIG. I, 8 PATCHWORK LACE STOCKING

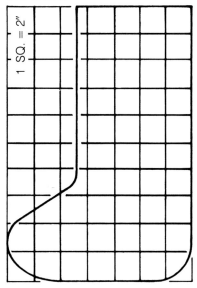

3. Stitch down the lace scraps side by side in horizontal rows on the brown stocking, starting with one row of beading lace at the top *(see photo)*. Beginning at the curve, stitch down lace scraps in vertical rows. Thread the ribbon through the beading lace at the top of the stocking.

4. Place the remaining muslin stocking against the right side of the patchwork lace stocking. Stitch around the edges, leaving the top open. Clip the curves, turn the stocking right side out, and press carefully.

5. Fold down the top edge, turn under the raw edge, and slipstitch. Stitch a brown ribbon loop to the top back of the stocking for a hanger.

SWEET HEARTS

Stuff these pretty hearts with potpourri to make charming sachets.

EASY TO AVERAGE: Tatting requires some experience in crocheting.

MATERIALS: Medium-weight unbleached linen or muslin; matching thread; paper for pattern; tracing paper; dressmaker's carbon *(optional)*; tracing wheel *(optional)*; black fine-point permanent felt-tip pen; acrylic paints; small, stiff paintbrush; sewing needle; synthetic stuffing, or potpourri *(recipes, page 16)*; purchased or tatted lace edging.

Note: *To make your own tatted lace edging, you need heavy crochet cotton; tatting shuttle; size 6 steel crochet hook for joining ring. Instructions for tatting are at right.*

DIRECTIONS
(¼-inch seams allowed):

1. On the pattern paper, draw freehand a large heart that is 6½ or 7½ inches high and wide. Cut out the heart pattern. Using the pattern, draw two hearts on the linen or muslin. Decorate the fabric before cutting out the hearts.

2. To decorate the heart, choose a picture you like (perhaps a child's drawing), and trace it onto the tracing paper. Transfer the drawing to a fabric heart using dressmaker's carbon and a tracing wheel. Or, if the drawing shows through when placed underneath the fabric, draw it directly onto the fabric. Using the black permanent pen, outline the design with a broken line to simulate stitches. Paint on colors with thin washes of acrylic paint so the black outlines show through. Apply the paint with an almost dry brush to prevent the paint from spreading beyond the outlines; practice drawing and painting on scrap pieces of your chosen fabric to perfect the technique.

3. When the paint is dry, cut out the heart pieces ¼ inch beyond the heart outlines and sew them, right sides together, leaving a 2-inch opening for stuffing. Turn and stuff with stuffing or potpourri. Blind stitch the opening closed *(see Embroidery Stitch Guide, page 240)*. Blind stitch the lace edging all around the heart.

SIMPLE TATTED LACE EDGING
Abbreviations: ds — double stitch, p — picot, j — join. Picots in this edging are ½-inch spacing. Make a ring of 5 ds, p, 5 ds, p, 5 ds, p, 5 ds, close ring. * Leaving ½ inch of thread between rings, make another ring of 5 ds, j to last picot of previous ring, 5 ds, p, 5 ds, p, 5 ds, close ring. Repeat from * until you have the number of rings desired. Cut the thread, and whipstitch the end to the back of the last ring.

LAVENDER POTPOURRI

EASY: Achievable by anyone.
MATERIALS: 2 cups of dried lavender leaves; 1 cup of dried lavender flower buds; ½ cup of dried rosemary leaves; ½ cup of dried cornflowers or other blue flower; 1 teaspoon of orris root powder; ½ cup of dried purple berries: bayberry or juniper *(optional)*; lavender oil.

DIRECTIONS:
Mix together the lavender leaves and buds, rosemary, cornflowers or other blue flower, and the orris root powder. If you wish to display the potpourri in an open bowl, add dried purple berries for more bulk and color. To renew the fragrance when it fades, add 1 or 2 drops of the lavender oil. Display the potpourri in an uncovered decorative container as a room freshener, or use it to fill Sweet Hearts *(directions, page 15)* and scented hot pads.

NEW ENGLAND SPICE POTPOURRI

EASY: Achievable by anyone.
MATERIALS: 2 cups of dried rose geranium leaves; 1 cup of dried sweet woodruff leaves; ¼ cup of whole cloves; ¼ cup of whole allspice; ⅛ cup of freshly grated cinnamon; 7 whole nutmegs; ½ cup of dried berries: pink pepper tree, juniper, bayberry or firethorn *(optional)*.

DIRECTIONS:
Mix together the rose geranium, woodruff, cloves, allspice, cinnamon and nutmegs (cloves are a natural preservative, so no additional fixative is needed). If you wish to display the potpourri in an open bowl, add dried berries. To renew the fragrance, slightly crush a nutmeg. Display the potpourri in a decorative container.

HERBS AND SPICE POTPOURRI

EASY: Achievable by anyone.
MATERIALS: 1 cup of dried rosemary leaves; 1 cup of dried peppermint leaves; ½ cup of dried lemon thyme; ¼ cup of whole allspice; 1 teaspoon of orris root powder; 1 cup of dried red berries: holly, firethorn or sumac *(optional)*; holly berry or bayberry oil.

DIRECTIONS:
Mix together the rosemary, peppermint, lemon thyme, allspice and orris root powder. If you wish to display the potpourri in an open bowl, add dried red berries. To renew the fragrance when it fades, add 1 or 2 drops of the holly berry or bayberry oil. Display the potpourri in a decorative container, or use it to fill Sweet Hearts *(directions, page 15)* and scented hot pads.

BEARY CHRISTMAS

Stuff a tiny calico heart with potpourri or scented wax chips, and slipstitch it to the front of the bear.

AVERAGE: For those with some experience in sewing.
MATERIALS: ⅛ yard of unbleached muslin or linen, or dark brown or camel-color print or solid-color fabric; scrap of light brown or camel-color fabric; matching threads; synthetic stuffing; embroidery floss: black and brown; embroidery needle; ribbon; paper for patterns.

DIRECTIONS
(¼-inch seams allowed):
1. Enlarge the pattern pieces in FIG. I, 9 onto paper, following the directions on page 239. Cut out all the pieces as indicated on the pattern, adding a seam allowance to each piece, from the muslin or linen, or other fabric. Use the light brown or camel-color scrap for the Foot Pads. Arrows on patterns indicate grain lines.
2. Place two Ear pieces right sides together. Sew around the curve, leaving an opening at the bottom. Clip the curve. Turn and press. Turn the open edges to the inside of the Ear, and slipstitch the opening closed. Repeat for the other Ear.
3. Sew the Body pieces, right sides together, leaving an opening at the top. Clip the curves, and turn. Stuff up to the Head opening until the Body is very tight and hard. Make a running stitch ¼ inch around the top of the Body. Draw up the stitches tightly until the opening is closed. Slipstitch the opening closed.
4. Sew two Leg pieces right sides together. Leave an opening at the foot, clip the curves and turn. Stuff the Leg tight and hard up to the foot opening. Turn under the edges of a Foot Pad, and slipstitch it in place on the bottom of the Leg. Repeat for the other Leg.

5. Sew two Arm pieces right sides together, leaving an opening on the back side of the Arm. Clip the curves, and turn. Stuff the Arm until it is tight and hard, and slipstitch it closed. Repeat for the other Arm.
6. Matching the points on the pattern with right sides together, sew the Gusset to the Head on both sides, from the base of the Head, point A, to point B. Clip the curves. Then sew from the front of the Head, point C, all the way up through point B and the Gusset, which is now folded in half. This forms the point of the nose. Clip the curves, turn, and stuff the Head tightly. Run a double thread ¼ inch below the open edge all around. Pull up tight, and slipstitch the opening closed.
7. Mark the eyes, mouth and ears on the Head. Run a thread with a large knot through the center of the right eye and out through the right Ear line. Pull tight. Repeat until you have a dimple for the eye and Ear. Slipstitch the Ear in place. Repeat for the left eye and Ear. Using the embroidery needle and black floss, embroider the eyes and mouth. Position the Head onto the Body, and slipstitch it in place. Embroider the front and back sides of each paw with the brown floss. Then attach the Arms and Legs to the body as indicated on the pattern by the stars. Slipstitch the Arms and Legs in place.
8. Tie the ribbon in a bow around the bear's neck.

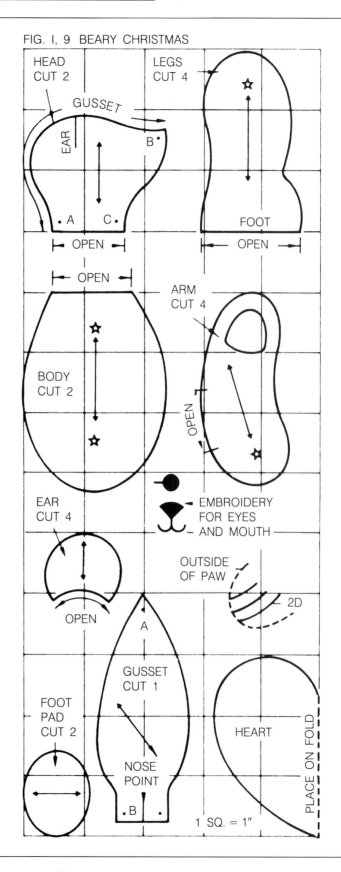

FIG. I, 9 BEARY CHRISTMAS

Christmas is a good time;
a kind, forgiving, charitable time;
the only time I know of,
in the long calendar of the year,
when men and women seem by
one consent to open their shut-up
hearts freely, and to think
of other people below them
as if they really were
fellow passengers to the grave,
and not another race of creatures
bound on other journeys.

— Charles Dickens

HOME SWEET HOME SAMPLER

A treasured gift for new homeowners.

CHALLENGING: Requires more experience in embroidery.

MATERIALS: ⅛ yard of small navy calico print; ¼ yard of medium-size navy calico print; ½ yard of white broadcloth; 6-inch-diameter circle of purple calico print; 3 x 5 inches of green calico print; 2¾ x 5 inches of blue calico print; 1 x 2¾ inches of light brown calico print; red, green, brown, black and white solid color fabric scraps; ⅜-inch-wide navy solid color ribbon or border fabric; ½ yard of synthetic batting; fusible interfacing; embroidery needle; embroidery floss *(see list below)*; sewing machine with zigzag attachment; four 14-inch-long stretcher bars; adhesive tape; staple gun and staples; paper for pattern.

Embroidery floss:	**10.** Medium Brown
1. Red	**11.** Black
2. Dark Red	**12.** Orange
3. Dark Green	**13.** Blue Gray
4. Medium Green	**14.** Light Gold
5. Medium Blue	
6. Purple	Embroidery stitches:
7. Dark Pink	A — French knot
8. Curry Yellow	B — Chain stitch
9. Aqua	C — Satin stitch

DIRECTIONS:

1. Enlarge the embroidery pattern in FIG. I, 10 onto paper, following the directions on page 239, and transfer the pattern to a 16-inch square of white broadcloth.

2. Following the diagram, embroider the design around the center. Cut out the calico pieces for the center circle, the sky, sun and ground cover, using the photo on page 14 as a color guide. Secure the calico pieces to the picture with the fusible interfacing, following the diagram, and zigzag stitch around each piece.

3. Cut out the solid color pieces for the house, barn, tree and wheelbarrow, using the photo as a color guide. Secure them to the picture with the fusible interfacing, following the diagram, and zigzag stitch around each piece. Embroider the windows, doors, flowers, and so on, following the diagram and using an outline stitch.

4. Cut a 4 x 44-inch strip of the small navy calico print, fold under one edge ¼ inch, and sew the folded edge to the picture, mitering the corners. Center the ⅜-inch-wide navy ribbon or border fabric over the edge of the navy calico border, and stitch it down, mitering the corners.

5. Cut a piece of white broadcloth and a piece of batting the same size as the picture. Lay the picture, right side up, on top of the batting and backing, and baste all three layers together. Quilt in the ditch around the navy calico border strip, and around the inside and outside edges of the purple calico circle in the center.

6. Make a frame from the four stretcher bars. Cut pieces of batting wide enough and long enough to encircle each side of the frame, and hold the pieces in place on the back of the frame with tape. Cut a piece of the medium-size navy calico print fabric the same width as the batting. Starting with one inside corner, staple the fabric to the back of the frame, pull the fabric over the front and around to the back, and staple the fabric to the back outside edge of the frame. Fold the fabric at a right angle for the corner. Continue stapling to the inside edge, then the outside edge of the frame, ending with a folded corner.

7. Center the picture in the frame, turn both over carefully, and staple the picture to the back of the frame, working from one side to the opposite to stretch the picture until it is taut. Trim the edges of the picture close to the staples.

FIG. I, 10 HOME SWEET HOME SAMPLER

1 SQ. = 1"

Sunshine Potpourri, Pomanders and Cinnamon Stick Centerpiece & Place Cards (directions, page 22);
Spice Nuggets (directions, page 23).

SUNSHINE POTPOURRI

EASY: Achievable by anyone.
MATERIALS: 2 cups of dried thyme leaves; ½ cup each of dried white flower petals (rose, daisy, cosmos, clematis, statice) and dried yellow flower petals (rose, marigold, acacia, freesia, goldenrod, nasturtium, poppy); ⅓ cup of tiny flower heads or florets (Queen Anne's lace, yarrow, baby's breath); ¼ cup of chamomile flower heads; ¼ cup each of dried lemon verbena leaves and dried mint leaves; ⅛ cup of orris root chips or 1 teaspoon of orris root powder.

DIRECTIONS:
Mix all the ingredients together and display the potpourri in a decorative container. To layer the potpourri for display, do not mix the ingredients. Place the ingredients in separate layers in a glass jar or bowl. Store the potpourri in a container with a tight-fitting lid.

POMANDERS

EASY: Achievable by anyone.
MATERIALS: Oranges; lemons; limes; whole cloves; pencil; skewer; light tack hammer; rind peeler *(optional)*; orris root powder; ribbon *(optional)*.

DIRECTIONS:
1. Outline the design you wish on each fruit rind with the pencil.
2. Using the skewer, poke pilot holes along the design. Insert one clove into each hole and tap with the tack hammer. Or, if you wish, use a rind peeler to remove the rind, following the design lines, and insert the cloves in the cut-away areas. Or cover the entire rind of the fruit with cloves.
3. Roll the finished pomander in the orris root powder to help preserve it. The fruit will darken and shrink a bit as it dries. If you wish, display the dried pomanders by grouping them in baskets. Or tie them individually with ribbon, leave a ribbon loop at each top, and hang the pomanders on your Christmas tree or from the edge of a shelf or mantel.

CINNAMON STICK CENTERPIECE & PLACE CARDS

EASY: Achievable by anyone.
MATERIALS: Approximately twenty-seven 16-inch-long cinnamon sticks for centerpiece; twelve 4-inch-long cinnamon sticks for each place card; assortment of dried flowers (larkspur, statice, lavender, rosebuds or blooms); pine cones; 2-inch-wide pale green velvet ribbon; ¼-inch-wide pale green velvet ribbon; 1-inch-wide pale green grosgrain ribbon; ¾-inch-wide pale green grosgrain ribbon; tacky glue; floral tape.

DIRECTIONS:
1. To make the centerpiece, wrap four 16-inch-long cinnamon sticks together with floral tape; don't cut the tape.
2. Add the rest of the 16-inch sticks by holding a few sticks at a time against the original sticks, and winding the tape around the entire bundle. Try to maintain a somewhat flat bottom, so the centerpiece won't roll when it's placed on the table.
3. Insert the flowers by dipping their ends in glue and placing them among the cinnamon sticks. Glue pine cones among the flowers.
4. Wrap the 2-inch-wide velvet ribbon around the bundle and tie it in a bow. Add a bow of 1-inch-wide grosgrain ribbon on top of the velvet bow. Glue a few small flowers and cones to the knot portion of the bow.
5. Make the place cards in same way as the centerpiece, using the 4-inch-long cinnamon sticks, and the ¼-inch and ¾-inch-wide ribbons.

SPICE NUGGETS

EASY: Achievable by anyone.
MATERIALS: 1- and 1½-inch-diameter Styrofoam® balls; powdered spices of your choice: spices that work well include ginger, cinnamon, allspice, nutmeg, cloves, *fines herbes,* orris root, sandalwood, frankincense and dried, diced orange peel (for a kitchen theme, try ground thyme, sage, oregano, basil or parsley); craft glue; water; nonaerosol hair spray; berries, sprigs of artificial greenery, tiny bows, pine cones, shiny beads *(optional).*

DIRECTIONS:

1. Coat each ball in a mixture of equal parts of craft glue and water. Allow the excess mixture to drain for a minute.
2. Sprinkle each ball with a powdered spice to coat the ball evenly. Let the ball dry for two hours. Spray the spice ball with the nonaerosol hair spray to prevent flaking. If you wish, decorate the spice balls with berries or sprigs of artificial greenery. Or attach tiny bows, pine cones or shiny beads as accents.

KISSING BALL

AVERAGE: For those with some experience in crafting.
MATERIALS: Boxwood or other evergreen clippings; block of oasis (available at floral supply stores); chicken wire; pieces of heavy gauge wire; coat hanger; No. 18 wire; cranberry strings and clusters of lady apples *(optional)*; wax spray *(optional)*; wooden floral pick; red velvet ribbon.

DIRECTIONS:

1. To make the core, wrap the block of oasis with the chicken wire, bending the wire to cover every side of the oasis. Twist small pieces of heavy-gauge wire through the chicken wire to hold the chicken wire's edges in place. Soak the oasis in water, and hang it from the coat hanger until the excess water drips off.

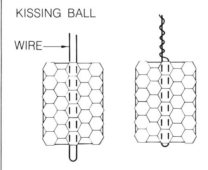

KISSING BALL

WIRE ⟶

OASIS BLOCK COVERED
IN CHICKEN WIRE

2. Cut a 4-foot length of the No. 18 wire, and bend it in half. Push the wire through the bottom of the oasis *(see illustration, above)* so the wire's U-shaped end rests against the oasis bottom. At the oasis top, twist the wire together. Then twist the wire ends

Kissing Ball

to a length to reach a ceiling hook.
3. Hang the core from the coat hanger so the core is at eye level in your work space. Cut the boxwood or other evergreen clippings, and push the pieces into the oasis. Trim the pieces, if necessary, to form a round shape. Add cranberry strings and clusters of lady apples, if you wish. Spray the ball with wax, if you wish.
4. Attach a piece of wire to the floral pick. Fold a 12-inch length of the red ribbon in half, and cut fishtail ends. Twist the wire attached to the floral pick around the folded end of the ribbon, and push the pick into the bottom of the ball. Attach a loop of red ribbon to cover the hanger.

Yuletide Heart Potholder; Christmas Tree Potholder

YULETIDE HEART POTHOLDER

These seasonal potholders also can be used as festive hot pads.

AVERAGE: For those with some experience in sewing.
MATERIAL: Two 12-inch squares of red pindot cotton fabric; one 9-inch square of bright green heart print

cotton fabric; one 3½-inch-tall heart cut from bright red heart print cotton fabric; one 12-inch square of synthetic batting; 1½ yards of ½-inch-wide white lace; ¼ yard of ½-inch-wide white picot satin ribbon.

DIRECTIONS:
1. Cut the lace into four 12-inch pieces, and arrange the pieces on the

red pindot potholder front to form a 6½-inch square. Stitch the lace in place. Press under the edges of the green fabric square 1 inch on all four sides. Place the green square in the center of the lace square. Topstitch the green square in place.
2. Place the potholder front on the back, right sides together. Place the batting on the wrong side of the

potholder back. Stitch a ⅝-inch seam around the edges, leaving 3 inches open. Turn, press, and topstitch ¼ inch around all the edges.
3. Place the red fabric heart in the center of the green square. Blanket stitch *(see Embroidery Stitch Guide, page 240)*, or machine appliqué, around the heart. Stitch 1 inch in from the green edge all around, forming a quilted square around the heart.
4. Make a bow from the ribbon, and stitch it to the upper left hand corner.

CHRISTMAS TREE POTHOLDER

AVERAGE: For those with some experience in sewing.
MATERIALS: Two 12-inch squares of green-dot white cotton fabric; one 5-inch square of dark green print cotton fabric; one 12-inch square of synthetic batting; ⅔ yard of ½-inch-wide white lace; small green pompon; ¼ yard of ¼-inch-wide red satin ribbon; tracing paper.

DIRECTIONS:
1. Cut the lace in half, place the halves on two opposite outside edges of the white potholder front *(see* Fig. I, 11A*)*, right sides together; baste in place.
2. Place the white squares right sides together. Place the batting on the wrong side of the back piece. Stitch a ⅝-inch seam around the edges, leaving 3 inches open. Clip the corners, turn, and press. Topstitch ¼ inch around all the edges. Topstitch again 1 inch in from the edges.
3. Trace the half-pattern in Fig. I, 11B onto folded tracing paper; open for the full pattern. Using the pattern, cut out a tree from the green fabric. Center the tree on the potholder, with the pompon on top. Blanket stitch *(see Embroidery Stitch Guide, page 240)*, or machine appliqué, around the tree.
4. Make a bow from the ribbon, and stitch it to the upper left hand corner.

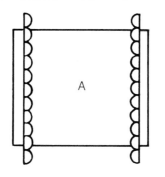

FIG. I, 11A CHRISTMAS TREE POTHOLDER LACE PLACEMENT

A

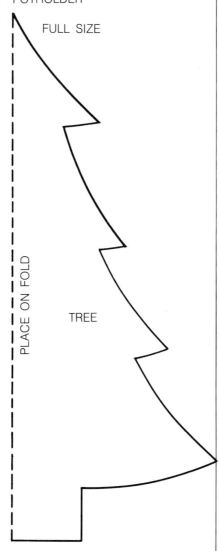

FIG. I, 11B CHRISTMAS TREE POTHOLDER

FULL SIZE

PLACE ON FOLD

TREE

GIVE A FESTIVE EDGE TO GUEST TOWELS

Trim solid-color purchased hand towels with washable ribbons or lace in an attractive arrangement. Measure the length of the woven band on each towel; add up the total for the yardage of ribbon needed. Edgestitch the ribbon to each towel band, turning under the cut edges at each end.

EYELET & ORGANDY

Beribboned beauties to make for your home or as very special gifts.

EYELET PLACE MAT

AVERAGE: For those with some experience in sewing.

MATERIALS: Forty-four-inch-wide fabric: ½ yard of eyelet, and ½ yard of cotton blend lining (will make two place mats); 2 yards of ¾-inch-wide green picot satin ribbon; 1 yard of ½-inch-wide red satin ribbon; ½ yard each of ⅜-inch and ⅝-inch-wide green satin ribbon; ½ yard of ⅝-inch-wide red satin ribbon; matching threads.

DIRECTIONS:

1. Cut one 13 x 19-inch rectangle each from the eyelet and the lining. Using FIG. I, 12 as a guide, pin and edgestitch the ribbons to the front of the eyelet.
2. Pin the eyelet to the lining, right sides together, and stitch a ½-inch seam all around, leaving an opening at the bottom for turning. Trim the corners, and turn the place mat right side out. Press, and slipstitch the opening closed.
3. Edgestitch the green picot satin ribbon to the outside edges of the place mat, mitering the ribbon at the corners.

EYELET PILLOW

AVERAGE: For those with some experience in sewing.

MATERIALS: Forty-four-inch-wide fabric: ½ yard of eyelet, and ½ yard of cotton blend lining; 1 yard each of ½- and ⅝-inch-wide red satin ribbon; 1⅔ yards of ⅞-inch-wide green satin ribbon; 2 yards of 2¾-inch-wide ruffled eyelet; matching threads; synthetic stuffing.

DIRECTIONS:

1. Cut four 15-inch squares, two from the eyelet, two from the lining. Using the photo as a guide, pin the ribbons to an eyelet square. Pin the eyelet square to a lining square. Edgestitch the ribbons to the pillow front, then stitch around the edges of the front.
2. Stitch the second eyelet square to the remaining lining square. Pin and baste the eyelet ruffle to the pillow front, right sides together, easing in an extra pleat at each side of each corner. Stitch together the short ends of the eyelet ruffle. Pin the pillow back to the front, right sides together, with the ruffle inside. Stitch, using the basting as a guide and leaving an opening at the bottom for turning. Trim the corners, turn the pillow right side out, and press. Stuff the pillow, and slipstitch the opening closed.

ORGANDY PILLOW

AVERAGE: For those with some experience in sewing.

MATERIALS: Forty-four-inch-wide fabric: 1 yard of white organdy, and ½ yard of white cotton blend lining; 3¾ yards of ½-inch-wide red picot satin ribbon; 2 yards of ⅝-inch-wide red satin ribbon; 1 yard each of ⅞- and ⅝-inch-wide green satin ribbon; matching threads; synthetic stuffing.

DIRECTIONS:

1. Cut four 15 x 17-inch rectangles, two from the organdy, two from the lining. Cut three 4 x 44-inch strips of organdy for a ruffle.
2. Pin each organdy rectangle to a lining rectangle.
3. Pin the ribbons to the organdy pillow front, using the photo as a guide, and edgestitch them in place.
4. Stitch the three strips together along their short edges to form a loop. Fold a long edge ½ inch to the front; press. Edgestitch the red picot ribbon over the folded edge of the ruffle.
5. Run two rows of gathering stitches on the unfinished long edge of the ruffle. Pull up the gathers in the ruffle to fit the pillow front, easing in extra fullness at the corners. Baste the ruffle to the pillow front, right sides together. Pin the pillow back to the pillow front, right sides together, with the ruffle between. Stitch, using the basting as a stitch guide and leaving an opening at the bottom for turning. Trim the corners, turn the pillow right side out, and press. Stuff the pillow, and slipstitch the opening closed.

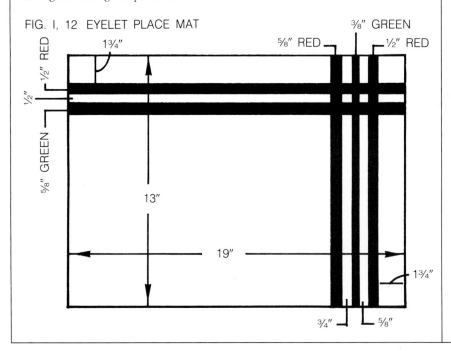

FIG. I, 12 EYELET PLACE MAT

⅜" GREEN
⅝" RED
½" RED
½" RED
½"
⅝" GREEN
1¾"
13"
19"
1¾"
¾"
⅝"

ORGANDY APRON

AVERAGE: For those with some experience in sewing.

MATERIALS: ½ yard of 44-inch-wide white organdy; 3 yards of 1½-inch-wide red satin ribbon; 2½ yards of ⅝-inch-wide red satin ribbon; 2 yards of ½-inch-wide red satin ribbon; 1½ yards of ¾-inch-wide green picot satin ribbon; ½ yard each of red and green ⅜-inch-wide satin ribbon; ½ yard of ½-inch-wide green satin ribbon; 1½ yards of ⅝-inch-wide green satin ribbon.

DIRECTIONS:

1. Press the fabric. Using the photo as a guide, pin the ribbons to the fabric, beginning 10 inches in from the side edges for the verticals and 2¾ inches from the bottom for the horizontals. Edgestitch the ribbons.

2. Fold under a ½-inch hem on the sides of the apron, press, and stitch. Fold ½ inch to the front of the apron along the bottom edge, and press. Fold under the ends of the green picot ribbon, and edgestitch it over the apron's folded raw edge.

3. Run two rows of gathering stitches at the top edge of the apron.

4. Cut off a 13-inch strip of the 1½-inch-wide red ribbon, and press the ends under. Mark the center of the apron, and of the short piece and remaining long piece of 1½-inch-wide red ribbon.

5. Pin the center of the long piece of red ribbon to the center front (right side) of the apron. Pin the center of the short piece of ribbon to the center back (wrong side) of the apron, pressed ends facing inward, with the raw edge of the apron between the layers of ribbon. Pull up the gathers so the apron fits inside the length of the short ribbon, distributing the fullness evenly. Pin the ribbons together, encasing the apron top edge and the gathering rows. Topstitch around the "waistband," and press.

Eyelet & Organdy set: apron, pillows, tablecloth, place mat and napkin.

ORGANDY TABLECLOTH

AVERAGE: For those with some experience in sewing.

MATERIALS: 1¼ yards of 44-inch-wide white organdy; 5 yards each of ⅝-inch and ⅞-inch-wide green satin ribbon, ½-inch-wide red satin ribbon, and ½-inch-wide red picot satin ribbon; matching threads.

DIRECTIONS:

Cut a 44-inch organdy square. Using the photo as a guide, pin the ribbons to the cloth 3 inches, 4½ inches and 6¼ inches from the tablecloth edges. Edgestitch the ribbons in place. Press the tablecloth edges ½ inch to the front all around. Edgestitch the red picot ribbon over the folded raw edges of the tablecloth, mitering the ribbon at the corners.

BERIBBONED NAPKIN

EASY: Achievable by anyone.

MATERIALS: 17-inch square of white polyester/cotton fabric (½ yard will make two napkins); 2 yards each of ¼-inch-wide red satin ribbon and ½-inch-wide green picot satin ribbon; matching threads.

DIRECTIONS:

Pin the red satin ribbon 1½ inches from each napkin raw edge, and edgestitch the ribbons. Press the napkin raw edges ½ inch to the front. Edgestitch the green picot ribbon over the folded raw edges of the napkin, mitering the ribbon at the corners. Press the napkin.

TWIG CRÈCHE

(8 x 16 x 13 inches)
The nativity crafted in a rustic style.

AVERAGE: For those with some experience in woodworking and crafts.

CRÈCHE

MATERIALS: ¼ x 8 x 16-inch plywood; various size twigs *(see Cutting Directions)*; straw; brown wood stain; four ¾-inch screws; hot glue gun; round file; saw; screwdriver.

DIRECTIONS:

1. Select the twigs, and cut off the branches. At the points where the twigs will be joined, file a slightly concave shape to give the glue a better surface. Cut the twigs to size *(see Cutting Directions)*.

2. Stain the A bottom brown. When the stain has dried, attach each B post to the A bottom, inserting the screws through the A bottom into the B posts *(see FIG. I, 13A, page 30)*.

3. Hot glue the C beams to the tops of the B posts. Hot glue the C1 cross beams between and at the ends of the C beams. Glue the D diagonal braces in place *(see FIG. I, 13A, page 30)*. Glue the E and E1 braces to the B posts, 3½ inches above the A bottom.

4. Cut the F rafters' center angles 30°. Glue the front F rafters together at the center, and then to the top of the B/C posts/beams. Glue the front H trusses between F and C *(see FIG. I, 13A, page 30)*. Repeat at the back. Glue the G roof beams between and to the F rafters.

5. Place the structure face down. Run a bead of glue along the back edge of the A bottom, the E brace, and the back C beam. Place the J back wall twigs in the glue, and butt them against each other to form the back wall. When the glue has dried, stand the crèche upright and cover the floor of the crèche with the straw.

CRIB

MATERIALS: Various size twigs *(see Cutting Directions)*; grapevine tendrils or straw; saw; two ¾-inch brads; hammer; hot glue gun.

DIRECTIONS:

1. Select the twigs, cut off the branches, and cut the twigs to size *(see Cutting Directions)*.

2. Lay one A leg on top of another, and cross them 1⅜ inches from one end. Drive a ¾-inch brad through the two A legs to form an "X." Repeat for the other set of legs. Glue the B ridge to the top of the A legs where they cross *(see FIG. I, 13B, page 30)*. Before the glue sets, adjust the top of the legs to be 3¼ inches apart.

3. Lay a bead of glue along the top of the legs and place the C side sticks in place, butted against each other, to form the crib sides. When the glue has dried, place the grapevine tendrils or straw in the crib as a mat.

LAMB

MATERIALS: Various size twigs *(see Cutting Directions)*; saw; drill and ¼-inch drill bit; hot glue gun.

DIRECTIONS:

1. Select the twigs, cut off the branches, and cut the twigs to size *(see Cutting Directions)*. One half inch from each end of the A body, drill two ¼-inch-diameter holes about ¼ inch deep at 30° angles for the legs. Drill a ¼-inch-diameter hole slanted about 10° forward for the neck. Drill a ¼-inch-diameter hole about ⅜ inch from one end of the D head.

2. Glue the B legs to the A body *(see FIG. I, 13C, page 30)*. Glue the C neck to the D head and then to the A body. Glue the E ears to the side of the D head, and the E tail to the A body.

CUTTING DIRECTIONS

CRÈCHE	Code	Pieces	Size
	A (PLY)	1	¼ x 8 x 16-inch Bottom
	B (TW)	4	½-inch-dia. x 9-inch Posts
	C (TW)	2	⅜-inch-dia. x 16-inch Beams
	C1 (TW)	2	⅜-inch-dia. x 7-inch Cross beams
	D (TW)	4	⅜-inch-dia. x 5¼-inch Diag. braces
	E (TW)	1	⅜-inch-dia. x 15-inch Brace
	E1 (TW)	2	⅜-inch-dia. x 7-inch Braces
	F (TW)	4	½-inch-dia. x 10-inch Rafters
	G (TW)	5	⅜-inch-dia. x 7-inch Roof beams
	H (TW)	4	⅜-inch-dia. x 2¾-inch Trusses
	J (TW)	63	⅛-inch-dia. x 10-inch Back wall
CRIB	Code	Pieces	Size
	A (TW)	4	¼-inch-dia. x 3½-inch Legs
	B (TW)	1	¼-inch-dia. x 4-inch Ridge
	C (TW)	18	⅛-inch-dia. x 4-inch Sides
LAMB	Code	Pieces	Size
	A (TW)	1	¾- to ⅞-inch-dia. x 3¼-inch Body
	B (TW)	4	¼-inch-dia. x 2-inch Legs
	C (TW)	1	¼-inch-dia. x ¾-inch Neck
	D (TW)	1	⅝-inch-dia. x 1-inch Head
	E (TW)	3	⅛-inch-dia. x ⅝-inch Ears/Tail

Twig Crèche

CRÈCHE FIGURES

MATERIALS: One yard of unbleached muslin; matching sewing thread; ecru buttontwist thread; synthetic stuffing; twine; strands of burlap or yarn; coat hangers; wire cutters; masking tape; paper for patterns; glue.

DIRECTIONS:

1. For Mary and Joseph Wire

Bodies: For each figure, make an armature piece from the coat hangers, using a 10-inch length for the arms, and a 9-inch length for the body. Wrap the sharp ends of the wires with masking tape. Shape the bottom end of each body wire to resemble an egg dipper. Bend Mary's body wire so the figure will be kneeling.

2. Mary and Joseph Head/Body

Pattern: Draw an oval 2½ inches wide and 3 inches high on paper for the head pattern. Erase the bottom of the oval, and extend the lines downward 3 inches to make the body pattern. Draw a straight line across the bottom. Cut out the paper pattern.

3. Sleeve Pattern: Draw a triangle with a 6½-inch base and 14-inch sides on paper. Measure 5½ inches from the center bottom, and draw a straight line across the triangle at that point. Cut out the triangle and cut along the line to remove the upper point. Use the remaining lower portion of the triangle for the sleeve pattern.

4. Child Body and Head: Draw and cut a paper body pattern 2½ inches

wide and 3¼ inches long. Using the pattern, cut out a body from the muslin. Sew ⅜-inch seams on the side and bottom edges and turn right side out. Sew a gathering row along the top edge. Stuff the body firmly, and gather the neck edge. Cut, gather, and stuff a 3-inch muslin circle for the child's head. Flatten the circle, with the gathering at the back, and sew the head to the body at the neck. Sew twine loops to the head for hair.

5. Mary and Joseph Head/Bodies: Using the patterns, cut two head/body pieces each from the muslin. Seam each piece ½ inch all around, leaving an opening for turning. Trim the seams and turn the pieces right side out; stuff the heads firmly. Place each

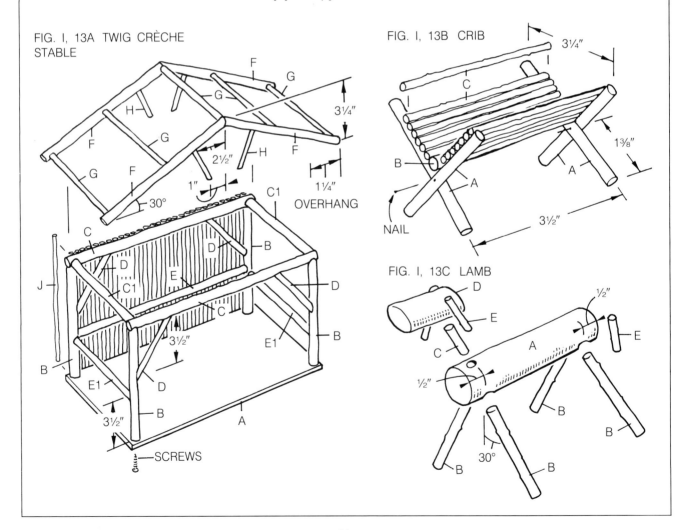

FIG. I, 13A TWIG CRÈCHE STABLE

FIG. I, 13B CRIB

FIG. I, 13C LAMB

head on the straight end of a body wire, and wrap buttontwist thread tightly around the wire under the chin to secure the head. With the heads in place, Joseph is about 10 inches tall and Mary is about 8 inches tall.

6. Sleeves: Using the pattern, cut four sleeves from the muslin. Seam the long edge of each sleeve ½ inch, and turn it right side out. For each figure, slip a sleeve onto each of the wire arms and sew the sleeves ½ inch below the chin to the body front and back, raw edges turned under.

7. Tunics: Cut a 10 x 14-inch piece of muslin on the bias for Joseph's tunic. Sew a ½-inch seam along the short sides. Fold under the top edge ½ inch, gather it tightly, and tack it to the waist. Hem the tunic. Repeat for Mary's tunic, using a 9 x 12-inch piece of muslin.

8. Mary's and Joseph's Hair: Glue strands of burlap or yarn across Joseph's head from front to back. Trim the ends evenly. Repeat for Mary's hair, stitching for a center part.

9. Joseph's Beard: Fold 4-inch-long strands of burlap or yarn in half, stitch or glue them onto Joseph's face, and trim the beard.

10. Joseph's Coat: Cut a 7 x 21-inch piece of muslin on the bias. Drape the coat over Joseph's head and across the shoulders, making tucks in the back to form a hood. Tack the coat to the head, shoulders and back. Turn under the bottom edges of the tunic and the coat to make the figure stable.

11. Mary's Veil: Cut a 19-inch-diameter muslin half-circle. Turn under the raw edges and stitch. Turn under the straight front edge, and center it on Mary's head. Tack together the folded veil edges at the chin.

12. Child's Swaddling: Cut a 7-inch square of muslin, fold it diagonally, and wrap it around the Child with the point up behind the head. Pin the ends in the back.

❋ ❋ ❋ ❋ ❋ ❋ ❋ ❋ ❋ ❋ ❋ ❋ ❋

EVER GREEN:
KEEPING NATURAL MATERIALS FRESH FOR THE HOLIDAYS

Woody Greens: Hammer the stems to crush the bark and fibers, and place the stems in water immediately. Combine 2½ gallons of lukewarm water with 1 (liter) bottle of lemon-lime soft drink, or ½ cup of sugar, or 1 cup of corn syrup. Mix the ingredients well, and place the mixture in a bucket. Place the stems in the bucket until you are ready to use them.

Magnolias: Soak the cut stems in 2 gallons of hot water mixed with 3 tablespoons of laundry bleach until you are ready to use the flowers. To shine the leaves, rub on vegetable oil with a soft cloth. Keep fresh indoor arrangements, such as woody greens and magnolias, in a cool place and far away from radiators, fireplaces, and other sources of heat.

Roping: Keep it in a cool place. Spray roping and other cut greens with water every other day; spray boxwood roping with "Wilt Proof."

Evergreens: Spray the greens with acrylic floor wax to trap moisture inside them. Be careful not to get acrylic wax on furniture or other wood surfaces.

Leafy Greens: To add a glossy finish to the leaves, spray or rub on "Green Glow," "Plant Shine" or "Leaf Polish."

Fruits: Purchase fruits as green and firm as possible, and refrigerate them immediately.

* *Whole fruit, except citrus: Dip the fruit in a bowl of "Klear." Push a piece of No. 22 or 23 wire through the fruit, and suspend the fruit from a coat hanger to drip dry.*

* *Halved fruit: Dip the cut side into melted paraffin. Let the paraffin dry, repeat the dipping, and dry the paraffin completely.*

Pineapple Wreath: To mount a whole or half pineapple on a wreath or Styrofoam® plaque, first wrap heavy-gauge wire around the pineapple, just below its leaves. Push the wire through the plaque and around wooden floral picks or toothpicks, or twist the wire around the back of the wreath. Twist the ends of the wire up and around the hanger at the top back.

Nuts and Pine Cones: Dip nuts in "Klear," and let them dry. Drill a hole about ½-inch-deep into the tops of nuts or into the backs of pine cones. Insert heavy floral wire, and apply a drop of glue with a hot glue gun at the opening. Let the glue dry completely. Attach the wire end to a wreath or decoration. Nuts, pine cones, and dried fruits are reusable if kept in airtight plastic bags containing moth flakes. Store in a cool, dry place.

GOOD ENOUGH
TO EAT

Sweet Tooth Gingerbread House

SWEET TOOTH GINGERBREAD HOUSE

AVERAGE: For those with some experience in baking and cake decorating.

MATERIALS:

1   batch Gingerbread Dough
    (recipe, page 34)
    Red and blue hard candy
    balls
2   batches Royal Frosting
    (recipe, page 34)
    Sliced natural almonds
    Candy pebbles
    Assorted candies: chocolate
    mints, tiny pastel mints,
    Life Savers®, Smartees,
    pastel candy sticks, candy
    dots on paper, or your
    own selection
    Green and red food
    colorings
    Sugar ice cream cones
    Silver dragées
    Gummie bears
    Swedish fish candy
⅓   cup granulated sugar, plus
    additional for snow
    10X (confectioners'
    powdered) sugar

Brown paper; two 16 x 12 x ⅛-inch foam core boards (available at art supply stores); hammer; heart and other-shape canapé cutters *(optional)*; sharp paring knife; 1- to 2-inch gingerbread man cookie cutter; shirt cardboard; paper toweling; 2 pastry bags; aluminum foil; toothpicks.

DIRECTIONS:

1. Prepare the Gingerbread Dough: Refrigerate the dough for at least 3 hours, or overnight.

2. Patterns: Enlarge the patterns in FIG. I, 14 *(page 35)* onto brown paper, following the directions on page 239. Using the paper patterns, cut out the house and entrance pieces from one of the foam core boards. Cut out the chimney pieces from the cardboard.

3. Preheat the oven to moderate (350°). Roll out the gingerbread dough, one quarter at a time, to a ⅛-inch thickness on a well-floured pastry cloth or board.

4. House Walls: Using the foam core board pattern pieces and the sharp paring knife, cut out the house front and back walls, and 2 house side walls. Place the pieces 1 inch apart on large baking sheets.

5. Entrance Walls: Using the foam core board pattern pieces and paring knife, cut out the entrance front wall and 2 side walls. Cut out the door piece from the front wall piece and, using a star-shaped canapé cutter or the sharp paring knife, cut out the window in the front door. Use a toothpick to add the details to the front door *(see photo)*. Place the pieces on a separate baking sheet. Reroll the trimmings, and set them aside.

6. Bake the house and entrance pieces, one baking sheet at a time, in the preheated moderate oven (350°) for 12 minutes, or until the gingerbread pieces are firm.

7. Stained Glass Windows: Crush the red candy balls with the hammer. Arrange the crushed candy in the door and window openings. Return the baking sheets to the oven and bake for 3 minutes more, or until the candies melt. Cool the gingerbread pieces on the baking sheets for 3 minutes. Loosen the gingerbread pieces from the baking sheets with a long knife. Slide the pieces onto wire racks, and cool them completely.

8. House Roof: Cut the rerolled gingerbread dough into 10 x 1-inch strips. Arrange the strips 1 inch apart on a baking sheet. Make a shaggy edge on each strip by making ½-inch-long cuts close together along one long edge. Bake the strips in the preheated moderate oven (350°) for 10 minutes, or until they are firm. Cool the strips on the baking sheet on a wire rack for 5 minutes. Loosen the strips with a

long spatula, and slide them onto the wire rack to cool completely.

9. Shutters, Fence and Gingerbread Men: Roll out the remaining gingerbread dough and cut out 8 shutter pieces. Place them on a baking sheet, matching 4 pairs. Cut out heart shapes from them with a canapé cutter or the tip of the paring knife. Make the fence by cutting the dough into 4 x 6-inch rectangles and making decorative tops with canapé cutters or the paring knife. Make vertical cuts at ¾-inch intervals for the fencing. Arrange the pieces on a baking sheet. Cut out the gingerbread men with the gingerbread man cookie cutter. With the paring knife, cut out the letters N, S, E and W ¾ inch tall. Bake the pieces in the preheated moderate oven (350°) for 8 minutes, or just until they are firm. Cool the pieces.

10. Assemble the House: Prepare 1 batch of the Royal Frosting. Spread a thin layer of frosting on the back of all the house gingerbread pieces and press them gently, but firmly, onto the matching house foam core board pattern pieces. Allow the frosting to dry for at least 1 hour. Join the house front wall to 1 house side wall with frosting on the second foam core board. Hold the edges in place for 5 minutes, or until the frosting sets. Join the house back wall and the remaining house side wall to the front two with frosting. Allow the frosting to firm up for 30 minutes.

11. Assemble the Entrance: Assemble the entrance front and side walls following the directions in Step 10, and join the pieces with frosting. Attach the front door to the front entrance piece, piping frosting around inside door edges to keep it in place. Allow the entrance to dry for at least 1 hour. Attach it to the house front with frosting.

12. Assemble the House Roof: Cut a 9 x 14-inch piece from the cardboard, and fold it in half crosswise to make two 9 x 7-inch sections. Spread some frosting along the top edges of the house front, back and side walls. Arrange the cardboard roof over the points of the tall walls, and allow the frosting to firm up for 30 minutes. Spread frosting on the cardboard roof. Working from the bottom up and using the photo as a placement guide, arrange the gingerbread roof strips on the cardboard roof, overlapping the edges slightly to look like shingles.

13. Assemble the Entrance Roof: Cut a 1 x 8-inch piece from the cardboard, and fold it in half crosswise to make two 1 x 4-inch sections. Secure the cardboard roof on top of the entrance front with frosting. Spread the entrance roof with frosting, and cover it with the sliced almonds (see photo, page 32).

14. Assemble the Chimney: Spread the side edges of the cardboard chimney pieces with frosting, and assemble them to make a box shape. Spread the outside of the box with frosting, and cover it with the candy pebbles. Allow the chimney to firm up for 30 minutes. Attach the chimney to the top of the roof with frosting.

15. Decorate the House: Using the frosting as "glue" and the photo as a placement guide, decorate the house with the assorted candies.

16. Trees and Wreaths: Prepare a second batch of the Royal Frosting, and tint part of it bright green with the food coloring. Tint a small amount deep pink with the red food coloring. Cover all the frosting with damp paper toweling. Invert the ice cream cones, spread some green frosting over them, and sprinkle them with the silver dragées. Top the trees with the Gummie bears. To make the wreaths, fit a pastry bag with a small star tip, and fill the bag with the remaining green frosting. Pipe out 1-inch-diameter wreaths onto aluminum foil. Allow the wreaths to dry. Fit a second pastry bag with a writing tip, and fill the bag with

the pink frosting. Pipe pink frosting bows onto the wreaths. Glue the wreaths onto the front door and the windows with the green frosting remaining in the first pastry bag.

17. Weathervane: Melt the ⅓ cup of granulated sugar very slowly in a small, heavy skillet. Cut 2 toothpicks in half, and dip the tips of each half in the sugar syrup. Attach a cookie letter to the pointed tip of each half, and attach the other tip to a whole toothpick inserted into the peak of the roof. Stick the Swedish fish candy on top of the weathervane.

18. Icicles: Break the blue candy balls with the hammer, and melt a few at a time in a small, heavy skillet. Pour the melted candy from the tip of a spoon over the edge of the roof to form icicles. Cut two 2 x 6-inch pieces of cardboard. Frost the back of the gingerbread fence pieces with white frosting, and attach them to the cardboard pieces. Allow the frosting to dry. Arrange the gingerbread men and the fence on the base, using the photo as a guide. Spread additional granulated sugar on the base, and sprinkle the 10X (confectioners' powdered) sugar on the roof.

GINGERBREAD DOUGH

Bake at 350° for 8 to 12 minutes.

1	cup vegetable shortening
2	cups molasses
½	cup warm water
8	cups all-purpose flour
3	teaspoons ground ginger
1	teaspoon salt

1. Melt the shortening in a large saucepan. Stir in the molasses and the water, blending them well.
2. Stir in the flour, ginger and salt until the mixture is smooth. Chill the gingerbread dough until it is firm enough to roll, for at least 3 hours, or overnight.

ROYAL FROSTING

Makes 1¼ cups.

2	egg whites
½	teaspoon cream of tartar
3	cups sifted 10X (confectioners' powdered) sugar

1. Beat the egg whites with the cream of tartar in a small bowl with an electric mixer at high speed until the mixture is foamy.
2. Beat in the 10X (confectioners' powdered) sugar gradually until the frosting stands in firm peaks, and is stiff enough to hold a sharp line when cut through with a knife. Keep the frosting covered with damp paper toweling and plastic wrap.

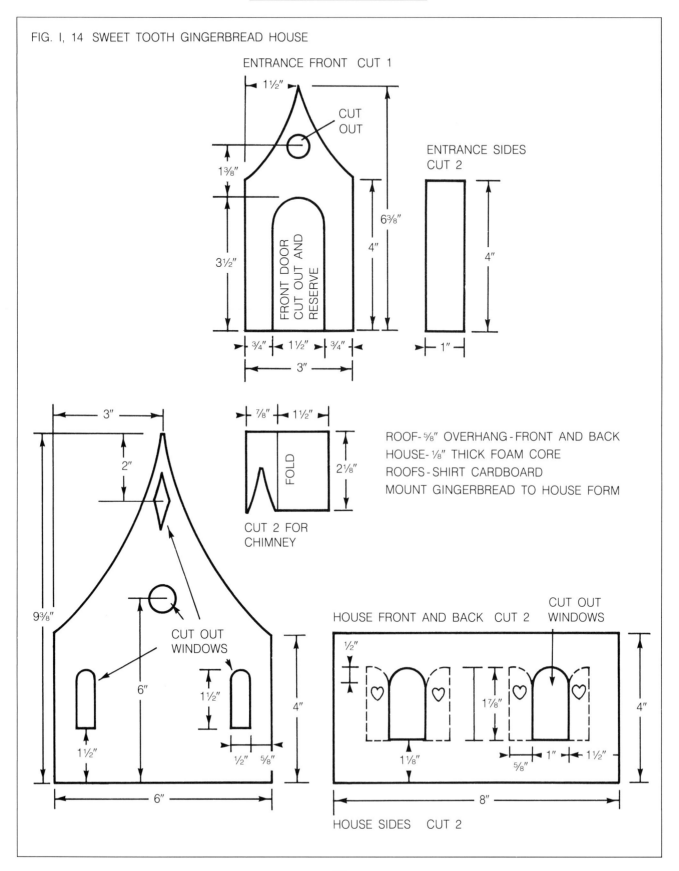

FIG. I, 14 SWEET TOOTH GINGERBREAD HOUSE

ENTRANCE FRONT CUT 1

CUT OUT

ENTRANCE SIDES
CUT 2

FRONT DOOR CUT OUT AND RESERVE

CUT 2 FOR CHIMNEY

ROOF-⅝" OVERHANG - FRONT AND BACK
HOUSE-⅛" THICK FOAM CORE
ROOFS-SHIRT CARDBOARD
MOUNT GINGERBREAD TO HOUSE FORM

CUT OUT WINDOWS

HOUSE FRONT AND BACK CUT 2

CUT OUT WINDOWS

HOUSE SIDES   CUT 2

*T*he children were nestled all
snug in their beds,
*While visions of sugar-plums
danced through their heads.*

— Clement C. Moore

HANSEL AND GRETEL GINGERBREAD HOUSE

A snow-covered cottage straight out of the classic fairy tale.

AVERAGE: For those with some experience in baking and cake decorating.

MATERIALS:

- 5 batches Gingerbread House Dough (recipe, page 43) Flour
- 1 package (30 tablets) menthol or other pale-color cough drops
- 5 batches Decorator Frosting (recipe, page 43) Red, green, black, brown, yellow and pale pink food coloring pastes
- 6 five-inch red and white peppermint candy sticks
- 2 to 3 bags (6½ ounces each) sliced natural almonds
- 1 bag (8 ounces) red cinnamon jelly disks
- 35 red and white peppermint swirl candies
- 1 box (7½ ounces) pumpernickel snack sticks OR: plain bread sticks broken into 2½-inch-long pieces
- 1 container (4 ounces) small red cinnamon candies
- 1 box (4 ounces) sugar ice cream cones

Extra-wide, heavy-duty aluminum foil; plastic wrap; ruler; pencil; lightweight glossy cardboard; scissors; graph or typing paper; carbon paper; 2-inch gingerbread girl and boy cookie cutters *(optional)*; sharp paring knife; serrated knife; ½-inch heart-shape aspic cutter *(optional)*; pastry bags; 20 x 24 inches of ¼- to ½-inch-thick plywood; fine-tip watercolor brush; semigloss polyurethane spray *(optional)*.

DIRECTIONS:

1. Prepare the Gingerbread House Dough: Prepare 1 batch of the Gingerbread House Dough. Line two 15½ x 12-inch baking sheets with aluminum foil, wrapping the foil edges under. Place the baking sheets on a damp cloth to prevent them from sliding when rolling out the dough. Place half the dough on each baking sheet. Using your hands, shape one of the dough halves into a rectangle and flatten it slightly. Roll it out to a 14½ x 11½-inch rectangle that is about ¼ inch thick. Cover the rolled dough with plastic wrap, and refrigerate it for at least 30 minutes. Repeat with the second half of the dough.

2. Patterns: While the dough chills, use the ruler and pencil to draw the patterns for the House, Figures and, if you wish, Fence on the cardboard. Label each pattern piece, and cut it out. All directions given for right and left sides assume you are looking at the front of the House.

a. House Back: Draw a 12 x 11½-inch rectangle, and label one 12-inch side Top. On the Top, mark 6 inches in from the sides to the center. Mark 4½ inches down from the Top corner on each side. Draw lines from the Top mark to the marks on each side to form the Roof peak; each line should be 7½ inches long. Cut out the House Back pattern.

b. House Front: Trace the cardboard House Back onto a second piece of cardboard, and cut out the second piece. For the Door, mark 1 inch in from the bottom left side. Make another mark 4¾ inches from the bottom left side. Mark a point 2½ inches up from the bottom, and 1 inch in from the left side. Mark another point 2½ inches up from the bottom and 4¾ inches from the left. Connect all the marks to make a 2½ x 3¾-inch rectangle. Now, measuring in 1⅞ inches from either side, mark the center point on the top

Hansel and Gretel Gingerbread House

and bottom lines. Draw a 5-inch line starting from bottom center mark and extending through the top line center mark. Draw 2 curved lines connecting the top point with the left and right

sides of the rectangle to form a rounded Door top. Cut out the Door in one piece and label the pattern. This will serve as a pattern for the Front Door and the Fireplace Oven Doors.

c. Front Window: Make a 2½ x 2-inch rectangle on graph or typing paper, and cut it out. Place the paper Window pattern on the House Front 2 inches in from the right side and 2½ inches up from the House bottom. Trace and cut out the Front Window, reserving the paper Window pattern.

d. House Left Side: Cut out a 9½ x 7-inch cardboard rectangle, and label one 9½-inch side Bottom. Center the paper Window pattern 2½ inches up from the Bottom. Trace and cut out the Left Side Window.

e. House Right Side: Cut out another 9½ x 7-inch cardboard rectangle, and label one 9½-inch side Top. For the Right Side Window, cut out a 2 x 1½-inch rectangle from graph paper. Position the paper pattern on

the upper left corner of the House Right Side, with a short side of the window pattern 1¼ inches down from the Top and a long side 1¼ inches in from the left side. Trace and cut out the Right Side Window.

f. Roof: Cut out two 11¼ x 9-inch cardboard rectangles. Label one Right Roof and the other Left Roof. Label one long side of the Right Roof, Bottom. Cut out a 3¼ x 2½-inch rectangle from graph paper. Place a short side of the paper pattern 1¾ inches in from the right edge of the Right Roof, with a long side of the pattern even with the Roof's Bottom edge. Trace and cut out 3 sides of the paper pattern from the Roof for the Fireplace Chimney to fit.

g. Fireplace Chimney: Cut out a 12 x 6-inch rectangle from graph paper. Fold it in half lengthwise. Label the 2 short sides Top and Bottom. Keeping the paper folded and starting at the Top, draw an 8-inch line 1¼ inches from and parallel to the center fold. Mark a point on the side opposite the fold, 3¼ inches up from the Bottom. Draw a line to connect that point with the lower end of the 8-inch line; the line will slant slightly. Cut along the lines through both thicknesses of paper. Unfold the paper, and trace the shape onto cardboard. Cut out the cardboard pattern and label it Fireplace Chimney Front. Cut out two 8 x 2-inch cardboard

rectangles; label each Chimney Side. Cut out two 3¼ x 2-inch cardboard rectangles; label each Fireplace Side. Cut out two 2-inch cardboard squares; label each Fireplace Top Side. Cut out a 4 x 2½-inch cardboard rectangle, and label it Chimney Back. Using the cardboard Door pattern, trace the top curved half onto a second piece of cardboard. Cut out the second piece, and label it Fireplace Oven Doors.

h. Balcony: Cut out a 12 x 1¾-inch cardboard rectangle, and label 1 long side Top Balcony Front. Measure and mark 1 inch up from a bottom corner. Measure and mark 1 inch over from the top corner of the same side. Draw a line between the 2 marks. Cut along the line to remove the corner. Repeat with the other top side corner. Draw and cut out two 1 x ½-inch cardboard rectangles and label each Balcony Side. Draw and cut out a 12 x 1-inch cardboard rectangle, and label it Balcony Base.

i. Front Door: Trim ¼ inch all around from the cardboard Door pattern; the Front Door pattern must be smaller than the Front Door opening because gingerbread dough spreads slightly when baked. Label the new Front Door pattern; it should be 4½ inches high and 3¼ inches wide.

j. Shutters: Draw and cut out a 2 x ¾-inch cardboard rectangle, and label it Shutter.

k. Large Flower Box: Fold a small piece of graph paper in half. Draw a 1½-inch line perpendicular to the center fold. Measure ¾ inch away from the line, and draw a 1¼-inch line from the center fold parallel to the first line. Connect the ends of the 2 lines. Cut out along the lines, unfold the paper, and trace the shape onto cardboard. Cut out the cardboard pattern, and label it Large Flower Box.

l. Small Flower Box: Follow the directions for the Large Flower Box, making the top line 1 inch and the bottom line ¾ inch.

m. Left Roof Front Trim: Draw a 7½ x 6½-inch rectangle on graph paper. Label one 7½-inch side Top. On the left side, measure down 5¼ inches from the Top and mark the point. Draw a line from the mark to the Top right corner. You should have a 9-inch diagonal line. On the right side, measure 1¼ inches down from the Top and mark the point. Draw a line from the mark to the bottom left corner. You should have a 9-inch line parallel to and about 1 inch away from the first line. Draw the Left Roof Front Trim scallop design *(see photo, page 37)* between the 2 parallel lines, with the scallop resting on the bottom line. Cut out the paper pattern, and trace it onto cardboard. Cut out the cardboard pattern; label it Left Roof Front Trim.

n. Right Roof Front Trim: Reverse the Left Roof Front Trim cardboard pattern on a second piece of cardboard. Trace the pattern onto the second piece, cut out the second pattern; label it Right Roof Front Trim.

o. Figures: Using carbon paper, trace the full-size Hansel, Gretel and Witch patterns in FIG. I, 15 *(page 42)* onto cardboard. If you do not have 2-inch gingerbread girl and boy cookie cutters, trace Girl and Boy Fence patterns in FIG. I, 15 onto cardboard. Cut out and label all the patterns.

3. Prepare the Gingerbread for the House: Preheat the oven to moderate (350°). Dust the cardboard House patterns lightly with flour. Remove the baking sheets of dough from the refrigerator. Arrange as many House patterns as possible on the dough, leaving ½ inch between them. Using the sharp paring knife and a ruler edge as a guide, carefully cut out the House Back, House Front, House Left and Right Sides, Right and Left Roofs, Fireplace Chimney Front, Chimney Sides, Fireplace Sides, Fireplace Top Sides, Chimney Back, Fireplace Oven Doors, Balcony Front, Balcony Base, Balcony Sides, Front Door, Small Flower Box, and Left and Right Roof Front Trims. Cut out 2 Large Flower Boxes. Cut out 8 Shutters. Carefully remove the cardboard patterns and all excess dough, leaving the aluminum foil on the baking sheets. Press together all the excess dough and reserve it, refrigerated in plastic wrap.

4. Using the sharp paring knife, cut out the windows on the House Front and House Left and Right Sides, being careful not to cut into the aluminum foil. Add the cutouts to the reserved dough. Fill the window openings with crushed menthol or other pale-color cough drops.

5. Using the sharp paring knife, score the upper half of the House Front, Balcony Front and Front Door to look like wood planking *(see photo)*. If you wish, use a ½-inch heart-shaped aspic cutter to cut heart shapes out of the Balcony Front.

6. Bake the House pieces in the preheated moderate oven (350°) for 15 minutes, or until the edges of the dough begin to brown and the pieces are set. Remove the trays to wire racks. Cool the pieces completely before removing them from the trays.

7. Continue making dough as needed, rolling it out on foil-lined baking sheets, cutting it out, and baking it until all the House pieces are completed. Store the baked pieces, loosely covered, at room temperature. *Do not refrigerate* the baked pieces.

8. Prepare the Gingerbread for the Figures and Fence: Let the reserved dough warm to room temperature for 1 hour. Roll it out on foil-covered baking sheets to a ⅛-inch thickness. Cover the rolled dough with plastic wrap, and refrigerate it for at least 30 minutes.

9. Lightly dust the Hansel, Gretel and Witch patterns with flour. Place the patterns on the dough ½ inch apart. Cut out the figures with the sharp paring knife. Use 2-inch girl and boy cookie cutters or the cardboard patterns to cut out 20 each of the Girl and Boy figures. Cut out a small heart using a ½-inch heart-shaped aspic cutter or cardboard pattern. Remove the excess dough. Bake the figures in the preheated moderate oven (350°) for 6 minutes.

10. Prepare the Gingerbread for the Bricks: Again press together the excess dough, and roll it out on a foil-covered baking sheet to a ¹⁄₁₆-inch thickness. Cover the rolled dough with plastic wrap, and refrigerate it for 30 minutes. Cut out about twenty 1 x ¼-inch rectangles for bricks. Bake the bricks in the preheated moderate oven (350°) for 2 minutes. Cool the baked gingerbread pieces.

11. Attach the Balcony Base: Make 1 batch of Decorator Frosting; make additional batches as needed. Always keep the frosting covered with plastic wrap or damp paper toweling to keep it from drying out. Frost the lower half of the House Front to resemble stucco. To place the Balcony Base, mark a point in the frosting on the right side 1 inch below where the Roof begins to slant upward. Repeat on the left side. Draw a line to connect the 2 marks. Spread frosting on the back edge of the Balcony Base, and press the Base firmly in place on the line in the stucco. Let the frosting dry overnight.

12. Tint about 1 cup of frosting red with the red food coloring paste. Spoon the red frosting into a pastry bag fitted with a medium writing tip. Use it to outline the Girl and Boy pieces, Shutters, Fireplace Oven Doors, small gingerbread heart, and the bottom edge of the Left and Right Roof Front Trims. Decorate each Fireplace Oven Door with a heart in the center, and 2 hinges on the curved side. Pipe a heart in the center of

each upper quarter of the Front Door. If heart cutouts were made on the Balcony Front, outline them. If not, pipe hearts on every other scored line. Pipe 2 diamonds on each scored line that doesn't have a heart. Pipe a heart in the center of each Shutter. Pipe a tiny heart in the center front of each Flower Box.

13. Fill a pastry bag fitted with a medium writing tip with 1 cup of white frosting. Make a fleur-de-lis design above and below the heart on each Shutter, and at either side of the heart on each Flower Box *(see photo, page 37).* Outline each Window. Make pane dividers on the Front and Left Side Windows by piping 2 horizontal lines and 3 vertical lines. Pipe 2 horizontal and 1 vertical line on the Right Side Window.

14. Attach the Shutters and Flower Boxes: Using frosting for glue, attach a Shutter to both sides of each window; 2 Shutters should remain for the window above the Balcony. Attach a Large Flower Box under the Front and Left Side Windows. Attach the Small Flower Box under the Right Side Window. Let frosting dry overnight.

15. Assemble the House: Use white frosting to glue the House Front, House Back, and House Left Side and Right Side together. If necessary, use soup cans to hold the walls in position. Let the frosting dry overnight.

16. Assemble the Fireplace Chimney: Place the Fireplace Chimney Front face down on a table. Spread frosting along the edge of the right side. Press the edge of an 8 x 2-inch Chimney Side, then a

2-inch square Fireplace Top Side, and finally a 3¼ x 2-inch Fireplace Side into place. Repeat on the other side. Use soup cans to hold the pieces in place, if necessary. Let the frosting dry. Attach the Chimney Back with frosting to the upper portion of the Chimney, making all the edges even at the top. Let the frosting dry. Frost the entire Fireplace and Chimney to look like stucco. Before the frosting dries, attach the Fireplace Oven Doors to the Fireplace Chimney Front, centering them evenly along the bottom. Let the frosting dry.

17. Attach the Fireplace Chimney: Place the House on the plywood base, and secure it with frosting. Slide the upper portion of the Fireplace Chimney into the cutout in the Right Roof to check for fit. If the Fireplace Chimney is too large to fit, carefully enlarge the opening in the Right Roof with the serrated knife. The Fireplace Chimney should fit loosely; almond Roof shingles will cover any gaps. Frost all the top edges of the House, and fit the Right and Left Roofs in place. When the frosting has dried, frost the back edges of the Fireplace Chimney and fit it into place on the House Right Side, sliding it into the Right Roof cutout.

18. Attach the Balcony: Frost the 1-inch side edges and ½-inch bottoms of the Balcony Sides, and attach them to either side of the Balcony Base, with the 1-inch sides against the House and the ½-inch sides against the Base. Frost the bottom edge and side edges of the Balcony Front, and press it into place

on the Balcony Base against the Balcony Sides. The Balcony Base should extend beyond the Balcony Front to hold flowers. Frost the backs of the remaining 2 Shutters and attach them in closed position to the center of the upper half of the House Front, above and behind the Balcony Front *(see photo, page 37)*.

19. Use frosting to attach a candy stick to a House corner; the stick will not reach the Roof. Repeat with the other corners. Gently cut the remaining 2 sticks into 4 pieces long enough to fit in between the top of the candy sticks and the Roof; line up the swirls in the candy sticks when possible. Using a pastry bag fitted with a medium writing tip, pipe a white decorative edge along each side of all the candy sticks to finish the corners.

20. Attach the Roof Trims: Frost the front of the Right Roof. Place the Right Roof Front Trim against the frosting. Repeat with the Left Roof and Left Roof Front Trim. Brace the underside seam with a little extra frosting, if necessary. Let the frosting dry.

21. Attach the Roof Shingles: Starting at the bottom of the Left or Right Roof and working up, frost a small section of Roof and gently press the sliced natural almonds into the frosting for shingles. Continue working up the Roof, overlapping rows slightly to look like shingles. Repeat on the opposite Roof.

22. Frost the entire base with white frosting to look like snow. When the section in front of the Front Door is frosted, immediately press red cinnamon jelly disks into the frosting in rows of 4 to make the footpath. Unwrap the peppermint swirl candies, apply dabs of frosting to their backs, and attach them around the base of the House Front and House Left Side.

23. Use the pumpernickel snack sticks or plain bread sticks to make a log pile under the Right Side Window. Use a dab of frosting to secure each log to the base and to the other logs. Frost the backs of the Bricks, and place them in a random pattern on the stucco Fireplace Chimney and House Front.

24. Tint a batch of Decorator Frosting light green with the green food coloring paste. Place about ½ cup of the light green frosting in a pastry bag fitted with a medium leaf tip. Pipe leaves in the 3 Flower Boxes and along the Balcony ledge. Squeeze the remaining light green frosting back into the bowl, cover the bowl with plastic wrap, and reserve. Use dabs of white frosting to attach red cinnamon candies to the leaves. Using white frosting in a pastry bag fitted with a medium writing tip, pipe groups of 2 or 3 white berries near the red cinnamon candies.

FIG. I, 15 HANSEL AND GRETEL GINGERBREAD FIGURES   FULL SIZE

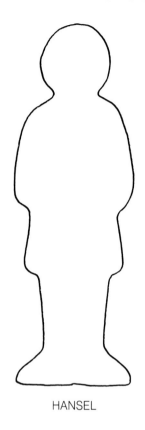

HANSEL

GRETEL

WITCH

GINGERBREAD BOY

GINGERBREAD GIRL

25. Make the Trees: Add more green food coloring paste and just a little black food coloring paste to the reserved light green frosting to make dark green frosting. Place the dark green frosting in a pastry bag fitted with a large leaf tip. To make a large tree, stack 3 sugar ice cream cones, using a little frosting to hold them together firmly. Pipe a row of leaves, tips downward, around the bottoms of the cones. Continue piping rows above, slightly overlapping them to resemble evergreen branches. Let the frosting dry. To make a small tree, use the serrated knife to cut off ¼ to ½ inch from the open end of each of 3 cones. Stack the shortened cones and pipe on branches as for the large tree. Let the frosting dry. Make 2 large and 4 small trees.

26. Attach the Fence: Attach the Girl and Boy Fence figures alternately to the base with dabs of frosting to make the Fence around the House.

27. Thin about 2 cups of white frosting with a little water. Using a spoon, carefully drizzle thinned frosting over the Roof peak, front Roof edges, log pile and trees for a snow and icicle effect. Let the frosting dry.

28. Frost the Figures: Add a little more water to the thinned frosting. Use the very thinned frosting to frost Hansel, Gretel and the Witch; the frosting should be a thin, smooth glaze on the figures. Let the frosting dry.

29. Decorate the Figures: Tint ¾ cup of white frosting brown. Place the brown frosting in a pastry bag fitted with a medium writing tip. Using the photo on page 37 as a guide, outline the 3 figures. Thin the red, yellow, brown and pale pink food coloring pastes with a little water. Using the photo as a guide, paint the clothing, skin coloring and features on the figures with the fine-tip watercolor brush; you may want to practice painting on paper first. Attach the small gingerbread heart to Gretel's

hands, and 3 small red cinnamon candies to Hansel's hands.

30. Attach the Witch and Front Door: Check to be sure the Front Door fits into the door opening. If necessary, trim the Front Door with the serrated knife to fit. Cut the Front Door into 4 parts, 2 upper doors and 2 lower doors *(see photo)*.

Frost the bottom of the Witch, and press it against the top back side of the lower left Door. Let the frosting dry. Frost the outside edges of the lower right, left and upper right Doors. Place the Doors in the doorway, and let the frosting dry. Frost the edges of the bottom left corner of the upper left Door, and place it in the doorway in the open position so the Witch can be seen; the upper left Door should rest partially on the lower left Door *(see photo)*. Support the upper left Door with a small can until the frosting dries.

31. Attach Hansel and Gretel: Use dollops of white frosting to position Gretel in front of the right front corner of the House, and Hansel alongside the footpath beyond the Fence. Position the trees around the House *(see photo)*.

32. To Preserve the Gingerbread House: Wrap the House tightly in plastic wrap, and store it in a cool, dry place. Or, if you wish, spray the House with semigloss polyurethane spray. Let the polyurethane dry completely and store the House, tightly covered, in a cool, dark place.

GINGERBREAD HOUSE DOUGH

Bake house pieces at 350° for 15 minutes, figures for 6 minutes, and bricks for 2 minutes.

5	cups unsifted all-purpose flour
1½	teaspoons ground cinnamon
1	teaspoon ground ginger
¼	teaspoon ground nutmeg
1	cup dark corn syrup
¾	cup (1½ sticks) margarine
¾	cup firmly packed dark brown sugar

1. Stir together the flour, cinnamon, ginger and nutmeg in a large bowl.
2. Heat together the corn syrup, margarine and brown sugar in a 2-quart saucepan over medium heat, stirring occasionally. Let the syrup mixture cool.
3. Stir the cooled syrup mixture into the flour mixture until they are well blended. Knead the dough with your hands until it is pliable, smooth, and an even color. Do not refrigerate the dough before rolling it out.

DECORATOR FROSTING

Makes 2½ cups.

1	box (1 pound) 10X (confectioners' powdered) sugar
3	egg whites
½	teaspoon cream of tartar

Beat together the 10X (confectioners' powdered) sugar, egg whites and cream of tartar in a medium-size bowl with an electric mixer at low speed until blended. Beat the frosting at high speed for 7 minutes, or until a knife drawn through it leaves a path. Keep unused frosting covered with plastic wrap or damp paper toweling.

A tree overflowing with the charm of American Country (directions, pages 52-55).

O' Christmas Tree

et a different tone for the holidays this year with a theme tree. For a Christmas out of Dickens, we have an opulent tree decorated with costumed girl and boy dolls, typical ornaments of the Victorian era in England. Simply styled, colorful ornaments such as our Christmas ducks and raffia cones bring the quaint beauty of American Country to any home. Delight your little ones with a tree full of knitted bears, snowmen and kittens. Or fill a room with holiday cheer—with a little help from St. Nicholas.

If you prefer to add only one or two new trims to the tree, don't miss our ornaments to stitch and craft. Create a miniature orchestra from balsa wood, or a star from pine cones. Use marzipan paste to sculpt smiling elves to dangle from the tree or use as table decorations. Crochet a little stuffed bear or lacy angel. Use scraps of fancy fabrics to make "crazy quilt" ornaments. And there's so much more!

Grace the top of your tree with our Cornhusk Angel. Or create a country-style Raffia and Calico Star. As a finishing touch, try a tree skirt with teddy bears, colorful calico patches or rustic cross stitch on burlap.

From cheerful and childlike to historic and elegant, we offer you a treasure trove of decorations for this Christmas, and for years to come.

VICTORIANA

Recreate the glory of a Dickensian Christmas. Tiny white lights give a candlelit look to your tree. Girl and boy dolls, candlewick ornaments and bunches of baby's breath tied with red ribbon complete the theme.
Use candlewick ornaments to decorate your banister, too. Stuff a few ornaments with potpourri to add a wonderful scent to any room in the house.

TOUCHES OF VICTORIANA

Use lots of lace, doilies, satin and velvet all over the house.

Look for antique dolls and old-fashioned toys at flea markets, and display them under the tree or on the mantelpiece.

Buy antique Christmas cards or facsimiles. Use them to make place cards, elegant ornaments and mantel decorations.

Wrap gifts in satin or moire fabric. Decorate them with lace ribbon and baby's breath.

Make quick trims from bows of velvet or satin ribbon, pieces of lace, bunches of baby's breath, strings of artificial pearls, and gilded nuts.

GIRL AND BOY DOLLS
Materials given are enough to make one boy doll and one girl doll.

AVERAGE: For those with some experience in sewing and crafts.

MATERIALS: Modeling compound; toothpick; 2 small screw eyes; extra-fine sandpaper; No. 0 artist's brush; acrylic paints: flesh, brown, red and black; rouge; eye shadow; satin finish spray varnish; mock wool fiber; hats and ribbon bows *(optional)*; ¼ yard of muslin; 4½ x 12 inches of fabric for girl's skirt; fabric scraps for other clothes; tacky glue; pins or string; matching threads; button thread; synthetic stuffing; 4 inches of narrow elastic; lace or other trim *(optional)*; paper for patterns; hanging wire.

DIRECTIONS
(¼-inch seams allowed):

1. Heads: For each doll, roll a 1½-inch-diameter ball of the modeling compound between your palms until it is smooth. Pinch up a little nose and two brows with your thumbnails. Form a chin and cheeks. Using the toothpick, make a small mouth opening and draw the lips. Press more modeling compound to the base of each Head, and shape it into a neck and shoulders, ending in a "lip" over which the muslin body can be drawn *(see* Fig. II, 1A, *page 48).* Push a small screw eye into the top of each Head for a hanger.

2. Shoes: Mold a ½-inch-diameter ball of the compound into a Shoe about 1 inch long, ¼ inch high, and ½ inch wide at the heel *(see* Fig. II, 1A). Depress a circle for the leg to fit into. Using the toothpick, make two little holes within the circle to sew through. Make four Shoes.

3. Baking and Coloring: Bake the Heads and Shoes in a preheated moderate oven (350°) until they are light brown; let them cool. Sand the surfaces smooth with the extra-fine sandpaper. Using the artist's brush and acrylic paints, paint the Heads flesh color. Paint the eyes and eyebrows brown, and the lips red. Add the rouge and a touch of the eye shadow. Paint the Shoes black. After the paint has dried, spray five or six light coats of the satin finish spray varnish on the Heads and Shoes to get a translucent "waxed" effect.

4. Girl's Wig: Tear or cut off 8 inches of the mock wool fiber, and sew a "part" at the side or center. Add braids, curls, pigtails or a bun, following the package directions. Distribute the hair over the Head, and glue the hair to the Head; use pins or string to hold the hair in place while the glue dries. Add a hat or hair ribbon bows, if you wish. Keep the screw eye accessible.

5. Boy's Wig: Tear or cut off 4 inches of the wool, and "part" it or tie it at the center. Attach the hair to the Head following the directions in Step 4. When the glue has dried, trim the boy's hair.

6. Bodies: Enlarge the patterns in Fig. II, 1B, *(page 49)* onto paper, following the directions on page 239. From the muslin, cut one pair of Body pieces and two pairs of Arm pieces for each doll. Stitch together each pair of Body pieces and Arm pieces, except at the straight top edges. At the raw edge of each Body, stitch a ¼-inch hem and draw a piece of button thread through it. Turn and stuff the Body, and insert a Head. Pull up the thread snugly over

Girl and Boy Dolls (directions, page 47); Candlewick Heart and Bell (directions, page 50)

stitch. Clip the neck edge, turn it under and stitch, over lace or another trim, if you wish. Hem the sleeves and the bottom edge of the shirt.

10. Assembling: Dress each Body. Stitch and glue the Shoes to the legs. Fasten an 8-inch length of hanging wire to each screw eye for a hanger.

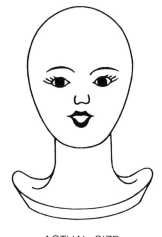

FIG. II, 1A GIRL & BOY DOLLS

ACTUAL SIZE

SHOE

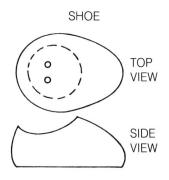

TOP VIEW

SIDE VIEW

the lip at the base of the neck, and tie the thread ends. Glue the Body to the neck to secure them. Turn and stuff the Arms. Turn in the raw ends and slipstitch the Arms closed. Sew two Arms, at the top edges, to each Body.

7. Skirt: Stitch together the short ends of the 4½ x 12-inch piece of fabric. Hem both long edges. Run a thread through one hem, and pull it up to fit the girl doll's waist.

8. Pants: Cut a pair of Pants pieces

(see FIG. II, 1B*)*, and stitch them together except at the top and bottom edges. Turn under ½ inch at the top edge, and stitch the 4-inch piece of narrow elastic to the wrong side, stretching the elastic as you sew. Hem the bottom edges.

9. Shirt/Blouse: Cut two pairs of Shirt pieces *(see* FIG. II, 1B*)*. Stitch each pair together at the sleeve and side edges. Cut the center opening at the back or front, turn under the raw edges, and

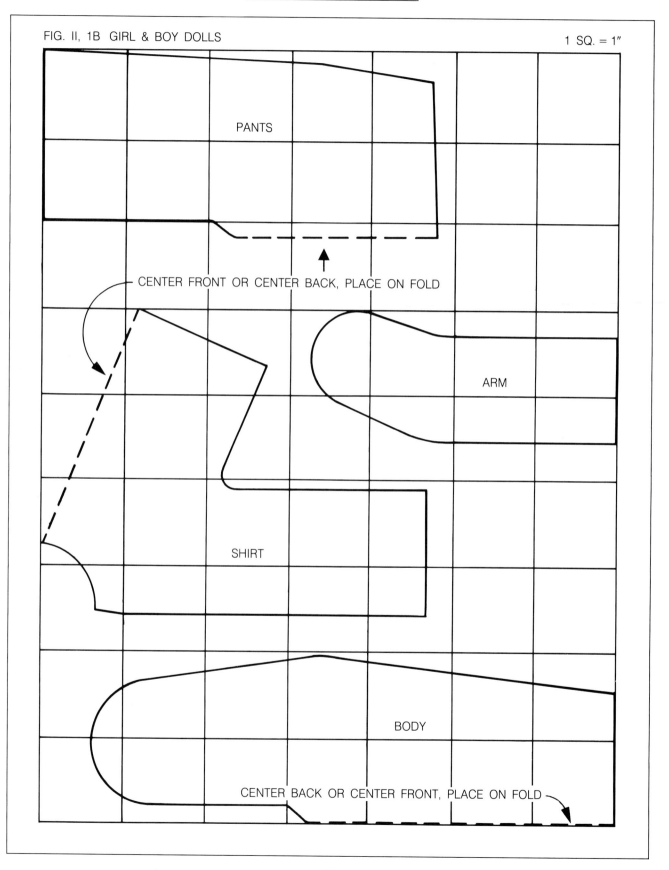

FIG. II, 1B GIRL & BOY DOLLS

1 SQ. = 1″

PANTS

CENTER FRONT OR CENTER BACK, PLACE ON FOLD

ARM

SHIRT

BODY

CENTER BACK OR CENTER FRONT, PLACE ON FOLD

CANDLEWICK HEART AND BELL

AVERAGE: For those with some experience in embroidery and sewing.

MATERIALS: Scraps of muslin and lace edging; matching sewing thread; candlewicking thread and needle; embroidery hoop; synthetic stuffing; tailor's chalk; paper for patterns.

DIRECTIONS
(¼-inch seams allowed):
1. Embroidering: Trace the full-size patterns in FIG. II, 2 onto paper. Trace each shape twice onto the muslin for the front and back. *Do not cut out the shapes.* Place the muslin in the hoop. Lightly mark a design on the muslin shapes with the tailor's chalk *(see photo, page 48, or improvise a design)*; leave the seam allowances empty. Using the candlewicking thread and needle, work French knots on the design *(see Embroidery Stitch Guide, page 240)*. Wash the muslin, and press it on the wrong side.

2. Assembling: Cut out the embroidered muslin shapes. Stitch the lace edging to one muslin shape (front), right sides together and raw edges even. Stitch the muslin back to the front, right sides together, leaving a 1-inch opening. Turn the ornament right side out, stuff it, and slipstitch the opening closed. Sew a thread loop at the center top for a hanger.

FIG. II, 2 CANDLEWICK HEART AND BELL   FULL SIZE

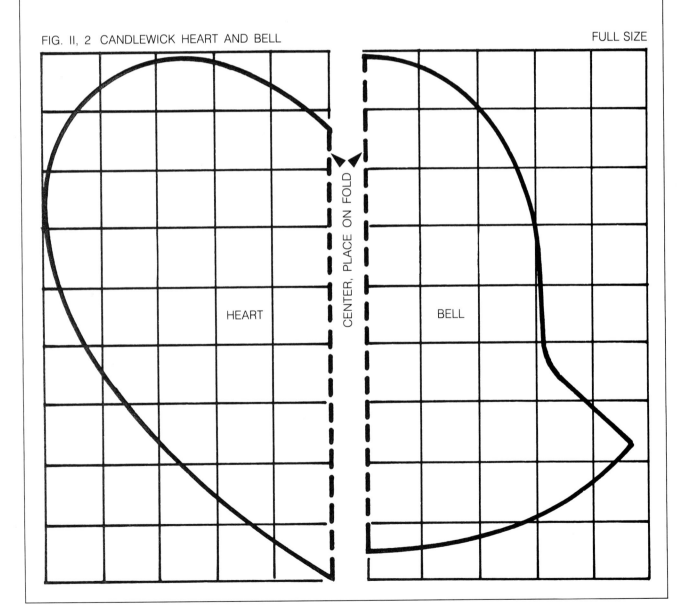

HEART

CENTER, PLACE ON FOLD

BELL

Tree Top Muslin Star

TREE TOP MUSLIN STAR

(*about 12 inches wide*)

AVERAGE: For those with some experience in embroidery and sewing.
MATERIALS: See Materials for Candlewick Heart and Bell, page 50.

DIRECTIONS
(*¼-inch seams allowed*):
1. Draw the star point pattern in Fig. II, 3. Draw a complete star by tracing the pattern five times around the center, with the inside edges matching.
2. Trace the complete star shape twice onto the muslin for the front and back. *Do not cut out the shapes.* Place the muslin in the hoop. Using the shaded area of the pattern as a placement guide, lightly mark a design on the muslin shapes with the tailor's chalk (*see photo, above, or create a design*); leave the seam allowances empty. Embroider and assemble the star, without lace edging, following the directions in Candlewick Heart and Bell, Steps 1 and 2 *(page 50)*.
3. Sew a double lace ruffle as shown.

FIG. II, 3
TREE TOP
MUSLIN STAR

3¼"

6½"

3¼"

STAR CENTER

DID YOU KNOW . . .

When Prince Albert wed Queen Victoria, he brought many German Christmas customs with him to England, including that of the Christmas tree. The tree at Buckingham palace was decorated with gingerbread cookies, candy, fancy cakes, ribbons, toys and dolls, and had an angel with outstretched wings at the top.

AMERICAN COUNTRY

*This pretty angel is simple and charming—the hallmarks of
American Country.*

BASKETS FULL OF BEAUTY

If you have an assortment of baskets in varying shapes and sizes, use them to create a country-inspired Christmas display. You can fill the baskets with just about anything: pine cones, berries, glass ball ornaments, winter fruits, candy, potpourri, greenery. Then decorate them with colorful ribbons. If you group the baskets in one area — a sideboard, mantel, coffee table or windowsill — use a variety of ribbons in complimentary colors and/or patterns. Or, if you prefer, place the baskets all through the house, and decorate them with the same type of ribbon to create a recurring theme.

SATIN ANGEL ORNAMENT

EASY: Achievable by anyone.
MATERIALS: ¼ yard of white satin fabric; ¼ yard of ¼-inch-wide white satin ribbon; ¼ yard of fusible interfacing; two 4-inch squares of lace or lace fabric; ¼ yard of flexible trim; one 25-mm round wooden bead with center hole; one ⅞-inch-diameter gold-colored ring; iron; white thread; paper; compass; glue; pins.

DIRECTIONS:

1. Fuse together the lace squares following the fusible interfacing manufacturer's directions. Cut out two 6-inch squares from the satin fabric. Place the satin squares wrong sides together, with a matching piece of fusible interfacing between them. Fuse together the satin squares.

2. Cut a 2 x 6-inch satin fabric strip. Cut a 1 x 6-inch strip of fusible interfacing. Center the interfacing strip on the wrong side of the satin strip, and fold the long edges of the satin over the interfacing to the center of the strip. Fuse together the satin strip. Fold the strip in half, right sides together, and sew the short ends together using a ¼-inch seam allowance. The resulting band will form the arms of the angel.

3. Using the compass and a piece of paper, draw a 4¾-inch-diameter circle. Divide the circle into quarters, and cut out one quarter of the circle. On the quarter circle, measure 1¼ inches from the center point along each straight edge, and mark these two points. Draw a line connecting these two points. Cut along the line and discard the smaller triangle; the remaining piece is the angel body pattern. Cut out an angel body from the fused satin square. Place the satin ribbon along one straight side of the satin body piece, starting at the wide bottom edge of the body piece and leaving 5½ inches of ribbon free at the narrow top edge of the body piece.

Glue the ribbon in place.

4. Fold over the free end of the ribbon so that about ¼ inch of the ribbon end is inside the body piece, and the ribbon forms a loop. Glue the ribbon end in place.

5. Glue the trim to the wide bottom curved edge of the body piece. Gently form a cone shape with the body piece, overlapping the straight edges by ¼ inch and keeping the narrow edge with the ribbon on top. Pin the body piece in place, and glue the straight edges of the body together. When the glue has dried completely, remove the pins.

6. Position the arm piece on the top portion of the body piece so that the arm seam is center front, and the glued edge of the body is center back *(see photo)*. Glue the arm piece to the center back of the body piece, and let the glue dry completely.

7. Glue the arm piece seam to the center front of the body piece. Thread the ribbon loop through the wooden bead. Glue the bottom of the bead to the top of the body piece.

8. Position the gold-colored ring on the ribbon loop about ¼ inch above the bead. Glue the ring in place.

9. Cut out a 3½ x 3¾-inch paper rectangle. Fold the rectangle in half lengthwise, and draw a half-heart shape along the fold using the entire piece of paper. Cut out the shape, and open it to make a pattern for the angel's wings. Cut out the wings from the fused lace square.

10. Center the wings along the center back seam of the body piece, and glue the wings in place.

Watermelon Wedge

WATERMELON WEDGE

AVERAGE: For those with some experience in needlework.

MATERIALS: Two 4-inch-diameter plastic needlepoint canvas circles; one 8 x 43-inch plastic needlepoint canvas mesh strip; polyester rug yarn: 5 yards of Bright Pink, 3 yards of Lime Green, and 3 yards of Dark Green; twelve 5-mm black beads; black sewing thread; metallic thread; tapestry needle; sewing needle.

DIRECTIONS:

1. Cut each circle in half along one side of the center mesh. Retain the halves with the center mesh; discard the remaining halves.

2. Cut the canvas strip into the following shape: 25 holes in the top row, centering the count on the strip. Increase 3 holes on each end in the

next row (31 holes). The third row has 37 holes, the 4th and 5th rows each have 43 holes, the 6th has 37 holes, the 7th has 31 holes, and the 8th has 25 holes. Leave all the edge meshes unworked.

3. Using the rug yarn and tapestry needle, work the half circles in interlocking gobelin stitch over two meshes *(see Embroidery Stitch Guide, page 240)*; use Lime Green in the outermost row and Bright Pink in the remaining rows. Compensate where necessary. Work the centers in horizontal long stitches. Work the canvas strip in tent stitch using Dark Green. Backstitch between the three meshes at each end.

4. Using the sewing needle and black thread, evenly space and sew six beads between the third and fourth rows on each half circle.

5. Join the half circles along their

straight edges by overcasting with Lime Green and Bright Pink. Join the rind strip to the half circles by overcasting with Dark Green.

6. Attach a length of metallic thread along the straight edge of the wedge, and tie the thread ends together to make a loop for a hanger.

Tasseled Raffia Cone

TASSELED RAFFIA CONE

Tuck some baby's breath or miniature candy canes into these pretty cones.

AVERAGE: For those with some experience in crafts.

MATERIALS: 4¼-inch-diameter plastic needlepoint canvas circle; 5 grams of natural-color matte artificial raffia; 5 grams of red artificial raffia; red sewing thread; tapestry needle; large sewing needle.

DIRECTIONS:

1. Hide all raffia ends by working stitches over the ends. Using doubled red raffia and the tapestry needle, overcast the edge of the circle, inserting the needle into the second row of holes.

2. Using a single strand of the natural-color raffia, and working from left to right, overcast all the interior rows. This gives a slanting stitch on the face of the work, and a vertical stitch on the reverse side. Finish the center with cross stitches.

3. Curl the circle into a cone, and sew it in place with the red thread and sewing needle.

4. Make a 2-inch-long tassel by taking ten 4-inch lengths of the red raffia, tying them at the center, folding them at the tie point, and tying them again ½ inch below the fold. Sew the tassel to the point of the cone.

5. Make a 7½-inch-long braid with three strands of the red raffia. At each end, knot the braid and leave ½ inch of unbraided raffia extending to make a tiny tassel.

6. Sew the braid's knots to opposite sides of the cone top for a hanger.

FIG. II, 4 FESTIVE DUCK

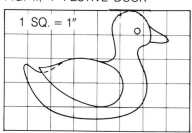

Festive Duck

FESTIVE DUCK

EASY: Achievable by anyone.
MATERIALS: Two 9 x 12-inch pieces of white felt; ¼ yard of fusible interfacing; thick acrylic paint: yellow and black; fine artist's brush; white glue; green chenille stem; small yellow silk flower and leaf; ½ yard of red curling ribbon; paper for patterns.

DIRECTIONS:

1. Enlarge the duck and wing patterns in FIG. II, 4 onto paper, following the directions on page 239.

2. Fuse the felt with the interfacing, following the package directions. Cut out three duck shapes and two wing shapes from the fused felt.

3. Glue two duck shapes together. Cut a 6-inch-long piece from the chenille stem. Glue the third duck shape to the first two, with 2 inches of the chenille stem piece inserted between them in position for the leg. Let the glue dry. Glue one wing to each side of the body. Let the glue dry completely.

4. Make the eye with a dot of black paint, and paint the bill and the cut edges of the bill yellow *(see FIG. II, 4)*. Let the paint dry completely.

5. Tie the ribbon into a knot around the duck's neck. Curl the free ends of the ribbon by pulling them firmly and quickly over the edge of a dull knife or scissor blade.

6. Glue the flower and leaf over the knot. Fasten the ornament to a tree branch by twisting the chenille stem around the branch.

GINGHAM AND LACE

Snowy lace and blue and white gingham create a lovely Yuletide tree. For an antique look, use ecru-colored lace and fill in with bows and dried flowers.

LACE CHAINS

To make the lace chains shown in the photo at left, start with ¹⁄₂-inch-wide "daisy" lace (1 yard of lace will make ¹⁄₄ yard of finished chain), and a container of fabric stiffener solution (see General Directions, at right).

Cut the lace into 6¹⁄₂-inch lengths. Dip the lengths in the fabric stiffener solution. Squeeze out the excess solution, and pat the lace between pieces of paper toweling.

Form one length of lace into a circle, overlapping the ends. Repeat, slipping the next length through the first circle, and overlapping the ends. Continue making linked circles until you reach the desired length.

Gently lay the chain on a piece of plastic wrap, and let it dry completely. If necessary, reinforce the overlapped ends with dots of craft glue.

WHITE LACE ORNAMENTS

EASY: Achievable by anyone.
GENERAL MATERIALS: Fabric stiffener; paper toweling; stiff paper; plastic wrap; transparent tape; glue gun and glue sticks, or thick craft glue.

GENERAL DIRECTIONS:
Make a solution of 3 parts fabric stiffener to 1 part water. Dip the doily into the fabric stiffener solution. Shape the doily, cover the shape with plastic wrap to keep the shape from sticking, and let it dry. When the shape is dry, decorate the ornament as indicated in the individual directions.

NOSEGAY CONES
MATERIALS: General Materials; 4-inch-diameter purchased white lace doily; ¹⁄₃ yard of ¹⁄₈-inch-wide gold-edged white ribbon; wrapped fancy candies, or silk flowers.

DIRECTIONS:
1. Cut a 4-inch-diameter circle out of stiff paper. Form the circle into a cone, and tape it in place. Trim the bottom edge so the cone will sit upright.
2. Dip the doily in the fabric stiffener solution. Squeeze out the excess solution, and pat the doily between pieces of paper toweling. Gently smooth out the doily to its original circle shape, then fold it in half, matching the curved edges exactly.
3. Shape the folded doily around the tip of the paper cone, making a neat point and overlapping the straight edges of the doily slightly to form an asymmetrical cone. Cover the doily with plastic wrap and let dry overnight.
4. Gently remove the plastic wrap from the cone. Cut an 8-inch length of the ribbon, and tie it into a small bow. Glue the bow to the front of the cone. Cut a 4-inch length of the ribbon, form it into a loop, and glue it to the top back of the cone for a hanger. Fill the cone with the candies or silk flowers.

LACE ROSETTE
MATERIALS: General Materials; 4-inch-diameter purchased white lace doily; 4 inches of ¹⁄₈-inch-wide gold-edged white ribbon.

DIRECTIONS:
1. Dip the doily in the fabric stiffener solution. Squeeze out the excess solution, and pat the doily between pieces of paper toweling.
2. Spread out a piece of plastic wrap. Gently smooth out the doily to its original circle shape. Gently pleat each curve in the doily's outer edge, pinching the center of the doily into a point. Keep the doily round as you work. Let the doily dry overnight.
3. Gently remove the plastic wrap from the rosette. Form the ribbon into a loop, and glue it to the back of the rosette for a hanger.

LACE FAN
MATERIALS FOR TWO FANS:
General Materials; 6-inch-diameter purchased white lace doily; ²⁄₃ yard of ¹⁄₈-inch-wide gold-edged white ribbon.

DIRECTIONS:
1. Carefully cut the doily in half. Dip the doily halves in the fabric stiffener solution. Squeeze out the excess solution, and pat the halves between pieces of paper toweling.
2. Spread out a piece of plastic wrap. Gently smooth out the doily halves. Fold the raw edge of each half ¹⁄₈ inch to the back, and press down. Pinch each half into pleats at the curves along its outer edge. Let the doily halves dry overnight.
3. Gently remove the plastic wrap from the fans. Cut the ribbon into two 8-inch and two 4-inch lengths: Tie each 8-inch length into a small bow, and glue a bow to the base of each fan. Form each 4-inch length into a loop, and glue a loop to the top of each fan for a hanger.

O' COME LITTLE CHILDREN

Children will love these little knitted creatures! Use brightly colored yarns (perfect for using up leftover skeins) to make the "knit-wits" figures. Hang them on the tree, and fill in with bright red ribbon bows. For more sparkle, string multi-colored lights on the tree.
Make extra figures to use as gift trims, and tie the boxes with matching yarn.

OTHER THEME TREES

Baby Tree: *Decorate a small tree with booties, baby's breath, silver spoons, drinking cups and little plastic toys. Wrap the bottom of the tree in a baby blanket, and intersperse pastel ribbon bows all over.*

Kitchen Tree: *Use wooden and metal spoons, cookie cutters, small wire whisks, and other pretty, small kitchen utensils tied to the tree with kitchen twine. Use a checkered tablecloth as a tree skirt.*

Fruit 'n Nut Tree: *Use quick-bonding glue or a glue gun to affix ribbon loops to nuts in the shell. Hang the nuts from the tree, along with tiny red apples and fresh kumquats tied with bright bows.*

KNIT-WITS
(3½ inches tall)

AVERAGE: For those with some experience in knitting. Directions are given for eight different knitted ornaments.

MATERIALS FOR EACH ORNAMENT: About 24 yards of leftover baby- or fingering-weight yarn in colors of your choice: we used White (A), Gray (B), Orange (C), Tan (D), Beige (E), Black (F), Red (G) and Green (H); embroidery floss: small amounts for facial features; 1 pair each size 1 and size 2 (for Stocking only) knitting needles, OR ANY SIZE NEEDLES TO OBTAIN GAUGE BELOW; tapestry needle; embroidery needle; synthetic stuffing; cardboard (for Santa only); crochet hook *(optional)*.

GAUGE: On size 1 needles in Stockinette Stitch (st st), 9 sts = 1 inch; 12 rows = 1 inch.

Note: When changing colors, pick up the color to be used under the color previously used, twisting the yarns on the wrong side to prevent holes in the work. Carry the unused colors loosely on the wrong side of the work.

GENERAL DIRECTIONS:

1. Assembling: Leave a 12-inch length at the beginning and the end of the work. At the cast-on edge of the work, thread the tapestry needle with the 12-inch length and pull through each loop. ***Do not*** gather up yet.

2. Neck: With matching yarn and the tapestry needle, pick up the front loop ***only*** of each stitch on the 25th row. ***Do not*** gather up yet. With right sides facing and with matching yarn, sew the two long edges together from the head to the toe. *Note: If applicable, first sew the ears and across the head.* Turn right side out and stuff loosely. Gather the yarn at the cast-on edge, and sew the opening closed. Gather the yarn at the neck and tie securely.

3. Legs *(see photo)*: With matching yarn and the tapestry needle, at the center front, work a running stitch up from the base for 8 rows, working through both thicknesses.

4. Arms: Work a running stitch ⅜ inch in from the side edges and 8 rows up from the base for 10 rows, working through both thicknesses. Add a 2½-inch hanging loop of yarn or wire to the top of the ornament.

5. Facial Features: With the embroidery floss and embroidery needle, work cross sts for the eyes and long sts for the nose and mouth. If applicable, add the whiskers.

6. Scarf: Cast on 4 sts and work in st st (k 1 row, p 1 row) in the colors of your choice for 7 inches. Bind off.

GRAY KITTEN

1. With size 1 needles and A, cast on 32 sts. In st st (k 1 row, p 1 row), work 4 rows A, 16 rows B.

2. Bib, Row 21: K 15 B, 2 A, 15 B. **Row 22:** P 14 B, 4 A, 14 B. **Row 23:** K 13 B, 6 A, 13 B. **Row 24:** P 12 B, 8 A, 12 B. Cut A. **Next 10 Rows:** Work in st st with B.

3. Ears (attach 1 yard of A for each ear), Row 35: K 7 B, 2 A, 14 B, 2 A, 7 B. **Row 36:** P 6 B, 4 A, 12 B, 4 A, 6 B. **Row 37:** K 5 B; with A k 4, p 1, k 1; k 10 B; with A k 1, p 1, k 4; k 5 B. **Row 38:** P 4 B; with A p 5, k 2, p 1; p 8 B; with A p 1, k 2, p 5; p 4 B. **Row 39:** K 3 B; with A k 6, p 3, k 1; k 6 B; with A k 1, p 3, k 6; k 3 B. **Row 40:** P 2 B; with A p 7, k 4, p 1; p 4 B; with A p 1, k 4, p 7; p 2 B. **Row 41:** Bind off 1 B st, k 1 A and bind off remaining B st; with A k 6, p 5; with B bind off 3 sts, p 1 A and bind off remaining B st; with A p 4, k 7; with B bind off last 2 sts — 24 sts. **Row 42 (left ear only):** With A p 2 tog, p 5, k 3, k 2 tog. Turn. **Row 43:** With A k 2 tog, bind off to last 2 sts, k 2 tog and pull yarn through. **Row 42 (right ear):** With A k 2 tog, k 3, p 5, p 2 tog. **Row 43:** Work same as Row 43 for left ear.

4. Tail: With B, cast on 4 sts. Work in st st for 2 inches, ending with a p row. With A, work 2 rows, turn; (k 2 tog) twice, turn; p 2, turn; k 2 tog.

5. Finishing: Follow the General Directions, Steps 1 to 6.

WHITE KITTEN

Work the same as for the Gray Kitten with A only.

STRIPED KITTEN

With size 1 needles and A, cast on 32 sts. In st st, work 4 rows A, (3 rows C, 1 row A) 5 times, 10 rows C. **Rows 35 to 43:** Rep Rows 35 to 43 as for Gray Kitten, substituting C for B.

PANDA

1. With size 1 needles and F, cast on 32 sts. In st st, work 8 rows F, 12 rows A, 4 rows F, 4 rows A.

2. Eyes, Row 29: K 12 A, 2 F, 4 A, 2 F, 12 A. **Next 3 Rows:** In st st, work 11 A, 4 F, 2 A, 4 F, 11 A. **Row 33:** Rep Row 29. **Row 34:** With A, p across.

3. Ears (attach 1 yard of F for each ear), Row 35: K 6 A, 4 F, 12 A, 4 F, 6 A. **Row 36:** P 5 A; with F p 4, k 2; p 10 A; with F k 2, p 4; p 5 A. **Row 37:** K 4 A; with F k 5, p 3; k 8 A; with F p 3, k 5; k 4 A. **Row 38:** P 3 A; with F p 6, k 4; p 6 A; with F k 4, p 6; p 3 A. **Row 39:** K 3 A; with F k 3, (sl 1, k 1, psso) twice, p 3; k 6 A; with F p 3, (k 2 tog) twice, k 3; k 3 A — 28 sts. **Row 40:** P 3 A; with F p 2, (p 2 tog) twice, k 2; p 6 A; with F k 2, (p 2 tog through back of second st) twice, p 2; p 3 A — 24 sts.

Row 41: With A bind off 2 sts, k 1 F, pass A st on needle over, (sl 1, k 1, psso and pass first F st on needle over) twice. Bind off 2 F and 5 A, k 1 F, pass A st on needle over, (k 2 tog, pass st on needle over) twice. Bind off 2 F and 3 A sts. Gather ears and fasten off.

4. Finishing: Follow the General Directions, Steps 1 to 6.

TEDDY BEAR

1. With size 1 needles and D, cast on 32 sts. Work in st st for 26 rows.

2. Muzzle, Row 27: K 14 D, 4 E, 14 D. **Next 3 Rows:** In st st, work 13 D, 6 E, 13 D. **Row 31:** Rep Row 27. **Next 3 Rows:** With D, work in st st.

3. Ears, Rows 35 to 41: With D **only,** rep Rows 35 to 41 of Ear for Panda.

4. Finishing: Follow the General Directions, Steps 1 to 6.

SANTA

1. With size 1 needles and F, cast on 32 sts. In st st, work 6 rows F, 4 rows G, 2 rows A, 12 rows G, 8 rows E, 2 rows A, 6 rows G. **Do not** cut yarn, but continue with G to end.

2. Hat, Row 41: K 3, (k 2 tog, k 6) 3 times, k 2 tog, k 3 — 28 sts. **Row 42:** P 3, (p 2 tog, p 5) 3 times, p 2 tog, p 2 — 24 sts. **Row 43:** K 2, (k 2 tog, k 4) 3 times, k 2 tog, k 2 — 20 sts. **Row 44:** P 2, (p 2 tog, p 3) 3 times, p 2 tog, p 1 — 16 sts.

Row 45: K 1, (k 2 tog, k 2) 3 times, k 2 tog, k 1 — 12 sts. **Row 46:** (P 1, p 2 tog) 4 times — 8 sts. **Row 47:** (K 2 tog) 4 times. **Row 48:** (P 2 tog) twice; k last 2 sts tog.

3. Finishing: Follow the General Directions, Steps 1 to 5.

4. Pompon for Hat: Wind A yarn around two fingers at least six times, tie tightly at the center and sew to the top of the Hat.

5. Beard: Wind A yarn 20 times around a 3 x ¾-inch piece of cardboard. Working at one edge of the cardboard, make a buttonhole stitch in each loop to hold the loops together. Slip the loops off the cardboard. Sew to the face, below the mouth, curving the sides upward.

SNOWMAN

1. With size 1 needles and A, cast on 32 sts. In st st, work 34 rows A, 6 rows H. **Do not** cut yarn; continue H to end.

2. Hat: Rep Rows 41 to 48 of Hat for Santa.

3. Finishing: Follow the General Directions, Steps 1 to 6.

4. Pompon: Work same as pompon for Santa.

STOCKING

1. With size 2 needles and double strand of A, cast on 24 sts. Work in st st for 10 rows. Change to size 1 needles and in st st work (6 rows G, 6 rows H) twice, then 2 rows G.

2. Heel, Next Row: With G k 8, turn; p 8, turn; k 7, turn; p 7, turn; k 6, turn; p 6, turn; k 5, turn; p 5, turn; k 4, turn; p 4, turn; k 3, turn; p 3, turn and k to end of row. **Next Row:** With G p 8, turn; k 8, turn; p 7, turn; k 7, turn; p 6, turn; k 6, turn; p 5, turn; k 5, turn; p 4, turn; k 4, turn; p 3, turn; k 3, turn and p to end of row. **Next 2 Rows:** With G, work in st st. **Next 6 Rows:** With H, k or p the first 2 sts of each row tog — 18 sts. Cut yarn, leaving a 24-inch length. **Next 6 Rows:** With G, k or p first 2 sts of each row tog — 12 sts. Cut yarn, leaving a 24-inch length.

3. Finishing: With the tapestry needle, thread the G yarn length through the last 12 sts and gather up to close the opening. Fasten off. With right sides facing, sew the two long edges together from the toe to the cuff, alternating G and H yarn, ending with A. Turn right side out and fold the stocking top down. **Optional:** With G and H yarns held tog, work a 20 st chain with a crochet hook and tack the loop to the inner side of the cuff.

BUYING A CHRISTMAS TREE

Determine where in your home you will display your tree. You should select a tree that is appropriate in size and shape for the chosen space. Cutting off large portions from either end will alter the natural taper of the tree. If you're planning to place your tree in a corner, keep in mind that it doesn't have to be perfectly shaped.

Freshness is the key when selecting a tree. The needles should be resilient, not brittle. Shake or bounce the tree lightly on the ground to see that the needles are firmly attached. If only a few drop off, the tree is fresh and, with proper care, should retain its freshness indoors throughout the holiday season.

The limbs should be strong enough to hold ornaments and strings of electric lights, and the tree should have a strong fragrance and good green color.

Be sure the tree displays the best qualities for that particular species:

Douglas firs are the most popular trees. Dark green to bluish-green in color, they are noted for their graceful upswept branches and excellent needle retention. They also are the most fragrant.

Norway spruces, the second favorite, have stiff, sharp dark green needles with somewhat pendulous branches. They have moderate needle retention.

Scotch pine trees are blue-green or gray-green with needles up to three inches long, and they have excellent retention.

Colorado blue spruces are green to silvery-blue. Rigid, inch-long needles give the tree a compact shape. Good needle retention.

White pine trees are green or bluish-green with flexible branches and excellent needle retention.

CHRISTMAS TREE SAFETY

Be sure the tree stand you use is large enough to support the tree, or else the tree may topple over.

Use only fire-resistant ornaments.

Open flames, such as lighted candles, never should be used on or near the tree. In addition, never leave your home with the Christmas tree lights still on.

To reduce the risk of fire, choose a fresh tree that has no evidence of drying — brown needles that fall off easily.

More fire prevention: Spray the tree with fire retardant before you decorate it; keep it well watered and away from heat sources.

Dispose of the tree when it becomes so dry that large amounts of needles fall off.

Avoid using angel hair; it's made of spun glass, a skin irritant to some people.

CHRISTMAS TREE CARE

If you buy your tree several days before it will be set up and decorated, store it outside. Cut the butt of the tree at a diagonal about one inch above the original cut — this opens the pores and aids in the absorption of water. Store the tree upright with the butt end in a container of water.

When you bring the tree into the house, saw the butt again, squaring off the diagonal. This facilitates placing the tree in a stand, as well as aiding water absorption.

Keep the butt end of the tree in a container of water the entire time the tree is in the house. Check the water level once in the morning and once in the evening; refill the container as needed. To enhance the tree's freshness, replenish the water level with aluminum sulfate or calcium chloride (from hardware or garden-supply stores). Combine 1 pound of either chemical with 1 quart of water. Add a little of the solution each day to the tree stand, along with additional lukewarm water.

Sprinkle water on the branches and needles before you decorate the tree to help retain freshness.

Be sure the base of the tree is well supported and the tree is placed away from fireplaces, radiators, electric heaters, televisions or any other source of heat.

SANTA CLAUS

MERRY CHRISTMAS

JOLLY OLD ST. NICHOLAS

Here comes Santa Claus...plus popcorn garlands and candy canes galore!

DID YOU KNOW . . .

The first recorded mention of a decorated Christmas tree dates back to 1605. The account tells of fir trees set up and hung with paper roses of different colors, apples, flat wafers, gilded candies and sugar.

One of the loveliest Christmas tree tales is that of Martin Luther and the fir tree: It is said that Luther, while walking through a forest one Christmas eve, beheld a tree illuminated by the stars. The beauty of the tree and stars inspired him to take home a small fir tree, to which he attached lighted candles. He felt this to be a recreation of the wonder of the night sky over Bethlehem so long ago.

JOLLY OLD ST. NICHOLAS
(Large Santa: about 9 inches; Small Santa: about 5½ inches—plus tree)

EASY: Achievable by anyone.
MATERIALS: White, pink, green, black and red felt*; scraps of gold soutache braid; fusible interfacing; glue; buckram; red cord; ¼-inch and ³/₁₆-inch paper punches; tracing paper; dressmaker's carbon; tracing wheel.
***Note:** One yard of 72-inch-wide red felt makes about 48 small Santas and 7 large Santas.*

DIRECTIONS:
1. Enlarge the patterns in FIG. II, 5A for the large Santa and FIG. II, 5B *(page 64)* for the small Santa onto tracing paper, following the directions on page 239; reverse the patterns if you wish. Fuse the interfacing to all the felt pieces. For either size Santa, using the dressmaker's carbon and tracing wheel, trace and cut the following patterns onto the interfacing side of

the following felt pieces: From the red felt, cut one Santa, following the broken lines in FIG. II, 5A and FIG. II, 5B. From the white felt, cut a pair of cuffs and one each of the beard/hatband, pompon, and suit trim. From the black felt, cut a pair of boots and a belt. From the pink felt, cut a 1½ x 1-inch face to underlap the white beard/hatband for the large Santa, and a 1¼ x ¼-inch face for the small Santa. From the green felt, cut one tree. From the gold soutache braid, cut one belt buckle. To make an ornament, cut a Santa shape and a tree each from the buckram and from the interfacing.
2. For the hanging ornament, fuse the buckram Santa to the back of the red Santa, and buckram tree to the back of the green tree *(omit the buckram for appliqués)*. Glue the pink face behind the white beard/hatband. Cut two black felt eyes with the ³/₁₆-inch paper punch. Cut a red felt nose with the ¼-inch paper punch. Glue the eyes and nose to the face. Glue the suit

FIG. II, 5A JOLLY OLD ST. NICHOLAS   1 SQ. = 1"

trim, face, cuffs, pompon, belt and boots to the red Santa. Glue the gold braid buckle to the belt. Glue the tree behind one hand.

3. For the hanging ornament, make a small hole at the X. Cut a 6-inch length of red cord, and tie the ends together. Push the loop through the hole and tie a slipknot for a hanger.

ST. NICK STOCKING

AVERAGE: For those with some experience in sewing.
MATERIALS: Forty-four-inch-wide fabric: ½ yard each of gingham and muslin; matching thread; fusible interfacing; adhesive gold craft trim; white glue; small Santa and tree *(directions, page 63, and* FIG. II, 5B*);* paper for patterns.

DIRECTIONS:
1. Enlarge the stocking pattern in FIG. II, 5B onto paper, following the directions on page 239. Cut one pair of gingham stockings and one pair of muslin stockings. Cut a 3 x 17-inch piece of gingham for the cuff, and fuse it to the interfacing.
2. With raw edges even, stack the stockings as follows: muslin, gingham and gingham (right sides together), and muslin. Pin and sew the stockings together except at the top edges; use a ¼-inch seam allowance. Clip the curves, and turn the stocking so the gingham sides are facing out.
3. Make a serrated edge cuff pattern from paper, following the measurements in FIG. II, 5C. Using the paper pattern, draw and cut a serrated edge on the cuff. Using a ½-inch-seam allowance, sew the short ends of the cuff together to make a loop. Stitch the top edge of the cuff to the top edge of the stocking. Cover all the raw edges of the cuff with the gold rickrack.
4. Using FIG. II, 5B as a placement guide, glue the small Santa and tree to the front of the stocking.

FIG. II, 5B ST. NICK STOCKING   1 SQ. = 1"

FIG. II, 5C STOCKING CUFF

ST. NICK TREE SKIRT

AVERAGE: For those with some experience in sewing.
MATERIALS: Forty-five-inch-wide fabric: 1 yard each of gingham and muslin; matching thread; package of adhesive gold craft rickrack; 1 yard of ¼-inch-wide adhesive gold soutache braid; 7 large Santas and trees *(directions, page 63)*; white glue; paper for pattern.

DIRECTIONS
(¼-inch seams allowed):
1. Make a paper pattern for the skirt segment, following the measurements in FIG. II, 6. Using the paper pattern, cut eight skirt segments from the gingham, and seven skirt lining segments from the muslin. Cut ½ yard of 1½-inch-wide bias stripping from the gingham for binding.
2. Sew the gingham segments together, side by side, to make a circle; do not sew the first and last segments together. Sew the muslin pieces the same way. Press all the seams open.
3. With right sides together, stitch the muslin circle to the gingham circle at each end. Fold the extra gingham segment in half vertically; it will be an underlap. Pin the lower edges of the extra segment together, with seams matching, and stitch.
4. Bind the inside edges of the skirt with the gingham binding strip, turning under the raw edges. Turn the skirt right side out.
5. Attach the gold rickrack and gold braid to the outside edges of the skirt. Glue a large Santa and tree to each of the skirt segments.

FIG. II, 6
TREE SKIRT
7½" 2" 1"
CENTER — 16"
15"

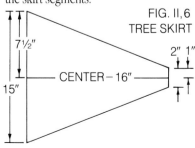

CHRISTMAS TREE LIGHT SAFETY

Remember — tree lights can be fire hazards, too.

Look for the "UL Approved" label on all lights and artificial trees.

Avoid overloading wall outlets — one plug per outlet is the safest.

Never use indoor lights outdoors.

Before plugging in tree lights, make sure there is a working bulb in each light socket.

Never use light strings that have frayed wires or damaged sockets.

Do not use more than 200 midget lights or 50 larger lights per string.

Disconnect the tree lights at bedtime, and whenever you leave your home.

If you have a metal tree, the Consumer Product Safety Commission warns: "The only way to illuminate a metal tree safely is to use colored floodlights, placed where children can't reach them." Do not use ordinary tree lights on a metal tree, because they may cause electric shock.

TREE-TRIMMING GUIDELINES

Tree Height	No. of Miniature Light Bulbs	Garland	Ornaments
2'	35-40	24' × 2"	15
3'	70-80	30' × 2"	24
4'	100-120	48' × 2-3"	36
6'	200-240	72' × 3"	48
7'	240-320	84' × 3-4"	72
8'	320-360	96' × 3-4"	96

NEEDLEWORK ORNAMENTS

Crazy Quilt Ornaments

CRAZY QUILT ORNAMENTS

AVERAGE: For those with some experience in embroidery and sewing.

MATERIALS: Fabric scraps; matching threads; embroidery floss in colors desired; embroidery needle; small beads *(optional)*; lace edging; ½-inch-wide ribbon; synthetic stuffing; thin cardboard.

DIRECTIONS:

1. Patterns: Enlarge the patterns in Fig. II, 7 onto the cardboard, following the directions on page 239. Mark the patch lines on the shapes, and letter each patch as shown in Fig. II, 7. Cut out the cardboard patterns.

2. Cutting: Using the cardboard patterns, cut out a back for each whole shape, adding a ¼-inch seam allowance around each piece. Cut apart the cardboard patterns on the patch lines. Place the patch patterns on the wrong side of the fabric scraps, and cut out the patches adding a ¼-inch seam allowance.

3. Patchwork: Using Fig. II, 7 as a guide, sew the patches together. Press the seams open.

4. Trimming: Using the embroidery needle and floss, embroider over the patch seams in the stitches of your choice, incorporating small beads, if you wish. We used chain, French knot, fly, cross, feather and blanket stitches *(see Embroidery Stitch Guide, page 240)* on the ornaments shown in the photo on page 66. If you wish, add tiny appliqués, or more embroidery, on some of the patches.

5. Edging: With right sides together, sew the lace edging to the edge of each patchwork ornament front. Pin the ornament back to the patchwork front, right sides together and lace edging toward the center. Stitch ¼ inch from the edges, leaving an opening for turning; turn right side out.

6. Finishing: Stuff the ornament, turn in the open edges, and slipstitch the opening closed. Cut a 15- to 18-inch length of the ribbon, and tie it in a bow. Stitch the bow to the ornament *(see photo)*. Fold a 7-inch length of the ribbon in half, and stitch the ends behind the bow for a hanger.

FIG. II, 7 CRAZY QUILT ORNAMENTS

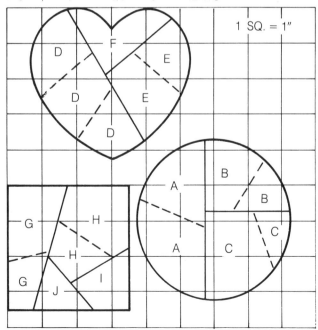

🌿 🌿 🌿 🌿 🌿 🌿

GO CRAZY FOR CHRISTMAS

Victorian crazy quilts were made from lavish, touchable fabrics. Try some of these fabric scraps for your crazy quilt ornaments:

velvet * velour * satin
wide grosgrain ribbon
ultrasuede * moire taffeta
old silk neckties * paisley
old drapery fabric

Beaded Snowflake Ornament

FIG. II, 8 BEADED SNOWFLAKE ORNAMENT

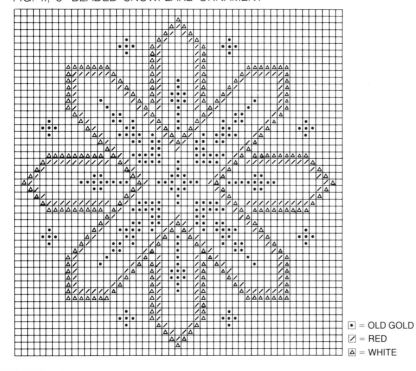

• = OLD GOLD
/ = RED
△ = WHITE

BEADED SNOWFLAKE ORNAMENT

This pretty ornament is both quick and easy to make.

EASY: Achievable by anyone.
MATERIALS: Two 4-inch squares of needlepoint canvas; two 5½-inch squares of emerald green 14-count Aida cloth; matching thread; glass beads: 1 tube each of red, white and old gold; 1½ yards of red middy braid; 1 yard of gold middy braid; glue stick; No.10 crewel or No.11 sharp needle.
Note: *Counted bead embroidery is very similar to counted cross stitch. It is worked with a half cross stitch. Begin the stitch in the lower left corner of the thread intersection, attach the correct color bead, and finish the stitch in the upper right corner of this intersection. All stitches must go in the same direction, or the beads will not align properly. Do not "jump" more than three or four stitches without first securing the thread on the back of the work, or the last bead may be loose.*

DIRECTIONS:

1. Bead the design in FIG. II, 8, centered, on each of the two Aida cloth squares.
2. Baste together the two needlepoint canvas squares. Fringe ½ inch on all four sides of each beaded Aida cloth square. Place a beaded square, design facing out, on each side of the needlepoint canvas squares. Stitch all the pieces together near the edges just inside the fringe.
3. Glue the red middy braid at the inner edge of the fringe. Glue the gold middy braid inside of, and very slightly overlapping, the red braid.
4. Cut a 5-inch length of the red middy braid. Wrap the cut ends with a piece of the gold braid to form a loop. Glue the loop to the corner of the ornament for a hanger.

Loving Bear Ornament

LOVING BEAR ORNAMENT
(2½ inches tall)

AVERAGE: For those with some experience in crocheting.
MATERIALS: Medium-weight thread (250-yard ball): 1 ball of Ecru, or about 25 yards for each bear; size 13 steel crochet hook; stitch markers; darning needle; embroidery needle; embroidery floss: scraps of Red, Brown and Green; synthetic stuffing.

DIRECTIONS:
1. Head: Starting at the tip of the nose, ch 2. **Rnd 1:** 6 sc in 2nd ch from hook. ***Do not join Rnds; mark beg of Rnds.*** **Rnd 2:** (2 sc in next sc, sc in next sc) 3 times — 9 sc. **Rnd 3:** Sc in each sc around. **Rnd 4:** (2 sc in next sc, sc in each of next 2 sc) 3 times —

12 sc. **Rnd 5:** Sc in each sc around. **Rnd 6:** Sc in each of next 2 sc, 2 sc in each of next 8 sc, sc in each of next 2 sc — 20 sc. **Rnd 7:** Sc in each of next 8 sc, 2 sc in each of next 4 sc, sc in each of next 8 sc — 24 sc. **Rnds 8 and 9:** Sc in each sc around. **Rnd 10:** (Sc in each of next 5 sc, 2 sc in next sc) 4 times — 28 sc. **Rnd 11:** Sc in each sc around. **Rnd 12:** (Sk next sc, sc in each of next 6 sc) 4 times — 24 sc. **Rnd 13:** (Sk next sc, sc in each of next 5 sc) 4 times — 20 sc. **Rnd 14:** (Sk next sc, sc in each of next 4 sc) 4 times — 16 sc. Stuff the Head firmly. **Rnd 15:** (Sk next sc, sc in each of next 3 sc) 4 times — 12 sc. **Rnd 16:** (Sk next sc, sc in each of next 2 sc) 4 times — 8 sc. **Rnd 17:** * Draw up a lp in each of next 2 sc, yarn over hook, draw through all 3 lps on hook; rep from * 3 times more. Sl st in next sc. Fasten off.
2. Ear (make 2): Starting at the base of the Ear, ch 5. **Row 1:** Sc in 2nd ch from hook, sc in each of next 3 ch — 4 sc. Ch 1, turn. **Row 2:** Sc in each sc across. Ch 1, turn. **Row 3:** (Sk 1 sc, sc in next sc) 2 times — 2 sc. Ch 1, turn. **Row 4:** Sl st in 2nd sc. Fasten off, leaving a 6-inch-long end for sewing. Sew the Ears' bases to Rnd 9 of the Head, ½ inch apart.
3. Body: Starting at the neck edge, ch 8. Join with sl st to form ring. **Rnd 1:** 12 sc in ring. ***Do not join Rnds; mark beg of Rnds.*** **Rnd 2:** (2 sc in next sc, sc in each of next 2 sc) 4 times — 16 sc. **Rnd 3:** (Sc in each of next 3 sc, 2 sc in next sc) 4 times — 20 sc. **Rnd 4:** Sc in each sc around. **Rnd 5:** (Sc in each of next 4 sc, 2 sc in next sc) 4 times — 24 sc. **Rnds 6 to 9:** Sc in each sc around. **Rnd 10:** Sc in each of next 12 sc (back edge); ***do not*** work rem sts. Ch 1, turn. **Rnd 11:** Sc in each of the 12 sc just worked. Ch 1, turn. **Rnd 12:** Sc in each of the 12 sc just worked, then work sc in each of the 12 sc (front edge) not worked on Rnd 10 — 24 sc. Fasten off. Stuff the Body

firmly. Sew the front and back edges together. Sew the Head to the neck.
4. Leg (make 2): Starting at the center of the footpad, ch 2. **Rnd 1:** 6 sc in 2nd ch from hook. **Rnd 2:** 2 sc in each sc — 12 sc. **Rnds 3 to 10:** Sc in each sc around. Fasten off, leaving a 6-inch-long end for sewing. Stuff firmly. Pinch the top edge of the Leg; using the darning needle and the thread end, sew the opening flat. From the back of the Body, sew the Legs to the Body bottom seam.
5. Arm (make 2): Work the same as the Leg for 7 rnds. Stuff and sew the opening flat as for the Leg. Sew the Arms to the sides of the Body.
6. Facial Features *(see photo):* Using the embroidery needle and three strands of embroidery floss throughout, embroider the nose in Brown satin stitch over Rnd 1 of the Head. Work a Brown straight stitch about ⅛ inch long under the center of the nose; embroider a Brown curved line below for the mouth. Working over Rnd 5 of the Head, embroider the eyes with Green French knots *(see Embroidery Stitch Guide, page 240),* ⅜ inch apart. Work the heart on the left side of the Body in Red satin stitch.
7. To make a loop for a hanger, attach crochet thread to the top of the Head and work a chain 2 inches long. Join with sl st to first ch. Fasten off.

CROCHETED ANGEL
(3¼ inches high)

AVERAGE: For those with some experience in crocheting.

MATERIALS: Medium-weight 100% mercerized cotton thread (175-yard ball): 1 ball of White; size 7 steel crochet hook; stitch markers; 1 cotton ball; wax paper; laundry starch; plastic thread.

DIRECTIONS:

1. Head: Starting at the top of the Head, ch 3. Join with sl st to form ring. **Rnd 1:** Work 6 sc in ring. *Do not join rnds. Mark beg of rnds unless otherwise stated.* **Rnds 2 and 3:** *2 sc in next sc — **inc made;** sc in next sc; rep from * around — 14 sc. **Rnd 4:** Sc around, increasing 4 sc evenly spaced — 18 sc. **Rnd 5:** Sc in each sc around. **Rnd 6:** * Sc in next sc, *draw up a lp in each of next 2 sc, yo and draw through all 3 lps on hook — dec made;* rep from * around — 12 sc. **Rnd 7:** Work in the same way as for last rnd until 7 sc remain. Stuff the Head with the cotton ball. **Rnd 8:** Sc in each sc around — 7 sc. Join with sl st to first sc. *Do not* fasten off.

2. Bodice, Rnd 9: Ch 4, dc in same st as sl st, * (dc, ch 1, dc) in next sc — **V-st made;** rep from * around — 7 V-sts. Join with sl st to 3rd ch of beg ch-4. **Rnd 10:** Sl st in first ch-1 sp, ch 4, dc in same sp, * work a V-st in sp between next 2 dc, V-st in next ch-1 sp; rep from * around — 14 V-sts. Join. **Rnd 11:** Sl st in first ch-1 sp, ch 4, dc in same sp, * dc in sp between next 2 dc, V-st in next V-st; rep from * around — 14 V-sts with single dc between each. Join. *Do not* fasten off.

Crocheted Angel

3. Skirt, Rnd 12: Sl st across first V-st and next single dc, ch 4, dc in same st as last sl st, V-st in next V-st, V-st in next single dc, V-st in next V-st — **4 V-sts made;** sk next 5 single dc and 5 V-sts for one Wing opening, (V-st in next single dc, V-st in next V-st) 2 times — **4 V-sts made;** sk next 5 single dc and 4 V-sts for other Wing opening — **8 V-sts.** Join with sl st to 3rd ch of beg ch-4. **Rnd 13:** Working on the 8 V-sts *only* of Rnd 12, sl st in ch-1 sp of first V-st, ch 3, *holding last lp on hook of each dc, work 3 dc in same sp, yo and draw through all 4 lps on hook — **cluster (cl) made;** ch 3, sk next st, sc in sp between next 2 V-sts, * ch 3, cl in next V-st, ch 3, sc in sp between next 2 V-sts; rep from * around, ending with ch 3, sc in sp between next 2 V-sts —

8 clusters. Join to top of beg ch-3. **Rnd 14:** Sl st across to center ch of ch-3 sp, sc in same sp, * ch 3, sc in next ch-3 sp; rep from * around, ending with ch 3 — 16 ch-3 sps. Join with sl st to beg sc. **Rnd 15:** Sl st across to center ch of ch-3 sp, ch 3, cl in same sp, * ch 3, sc in next ch-3 sp, ch 3, cl in next ch-3 sp; rep from * around, ending with ch 3, sc in next sp, ch 3. Join with sl st to top of beg ch-3. **Rnds 16 to 20:** Rep Rnds 14 and 15 two times more, then rep Rnd 14 once. **Rnd 21:** Sl st across to center ch of ch-3, sc in same sp, * *work 9 dc in next sp* — **shell made;** sc in next sp; rep from * around — 8 shells. Join with sl st to beg sc. Fasten off.

4. First Wing: With the right side facing you, working on the skipped sts of Rnd 12, join thread to first free single dc, sc in same dc, * in next V-st (work 4 dc, ch 3, sl st in top of last dc for picot, 4 dc), sc in next single dc; rep from * around — 5 shells. Join with sl st to beg sc. Fasten off.

5. Second Wing: Work the same as the First Wing.

6. Hanger: Weave a length of plastic thread through the top of the Head. Tie the ends together to make a loop for a hanger.

7. Starching: Mix 3 tablespoons of laundry starch with 6 tablespoons of tap water. Wet the Angel with tap water, and squeeze out the excess water. Dip the Angel in the starch solution. Stuff and shape the Skirt and Body with the wax paper. Suspend the Angel by the hanger loop from a wire hanger; hold the loop in place on the hanger with a clothespin. Smooth and shape the Angel as it dries. When the Angel is hard and dry, in about 8 hours, remove the wax paper.

LACY NOSEGAY

EASY: Achievable by anyone.
MATERIALS: 2½-inch-wide lace; ½- and 1½-inch-wide pastel picot taffeta ribbons; threads to match; clustered pearl stamens; white floral tape; glue; white plastic plate; needle.

DIRECTIONS:

1. Cut 26 inches of the lace. Make running stitches along one edge and gather up the lace into a circle, leaving about a 1-inch-diameter opening at the center. Cut a 3-inch-diameter scalloped circle from the plastic plate, and two short crossed slits at the center. Glue the scalloped circle behind the lace circle, and let dry.
2. Cut three 6-inch lengths from the 1½-inch-wide ribbons. Glue the cut ends of each length together to form a loop. Make a running stitch along one edge of the loop, and pull tightly to make a rosette. Tie off the thread, and insert a cluster of pearl stamens in the center of the flower. Wrap the gathered edge of the ribbon and stamen stems with floral tape. Continue wrapping the floral tape until the flower stem is 3½ inches long.
3. Tie a length of ½-inch-wide ribbon around the three flowers, leaving the ribbon ends free. Insert the flower stems into the center of the lace, through the slits in the plastic circle and tape the stems in place.

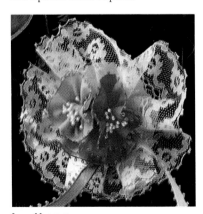

Lacy Nosegay

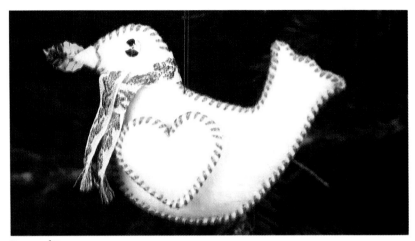

Dove of Peace

DOVE OF PEACE

EASY: Achievable by anyone.
MATERIALS FOR FOUR DOVES: 9 x 12 inches of white felt; tracing paper; vanishing fabric marker; embroidery needle; blue embroidery floss; cotton balls; four ½-inch green leaf sequins; eight 5-mm blue sequins; glue; 28 inches of ⅜-inch-wide woven ribbon; cord.

DIRECTIONS:

1. Enlarge the dove and heart patterns (two patterns) in Fig. II, 9 onto tracing paper, following the directions on page 239. Cut out both patterns.
2. Using the vanishing marker, trace 8 doves and 16 hearts on the felt. Cut out the pieces and set them aside for a few days until the ink marks disappear.
3. Pin together four pairs of dove pieces and eight pairs of heart pieces.
4. To make one dove: Separate the felt layers at the beak. Using two 1⅓-yard-long strands of floss, run the needle through the bottom layer, ⅜ inch from the tip of the beak; leave enough floss free to tie off later. Rejoin the felt layers and work one long overcast stitch at "1" in Fig. II, 9. Continue around the body using ⅛-inch-long overcast stitches spaced ⅛ inch apart. Upon reaching the back of the head, stuff the dove with cotton balls. Continue overcasting, ending with a long stitch at "2" in Fig. II, 9. Cut the floss. Knot the floss ends inside the beak layers and trim the excess.
5. Glue a leaf sequin between the beak layers and a pair of blue sequins for eyes *(see* Fig. II, 9*).* Repeat Steps 4 and 5 to make three more doves.
6. Using two 20-inch-long strands of floss, overcast and stuff eight hearts. Make the first stitch ¼ inch below the center on the back heart piece. Make the last stitch slightly below the first. Knot the floss ends; trim the excess.
7. Using the photo as a guide, glue a heart wing to each side of each dove.
8. Tie a 7-inch length of the woven ribbon around each dove's neck.
9. Run some cord into the back of the neck on each dove. Tie the cord ends to make a hanger loop.

FIG. II, 9 DOVE OF PEACE

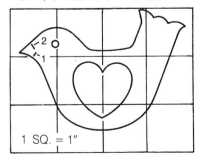

1 SQ. = 1"

CRAFTED
ORNAMENTS

Balsa Wood Orchestra

STORING ORNAMENTS

Wrap strings of tree lights around cardboard paper towel tubes. Tape down the wire ends to keep them from unraveling.

The divided boxes used to ship wine or soda bottles are great for storing fragile ornaments.

Store tiny ornaments in egg cartons to prevent their loss or breakage.

If you store your decorations in one or two big boxes, pack the heavier ornaments on the bottom and lighter ones on top. Place layers of paper toweling or newspaper in between to cushion the ornaments.

BALSA WOOD ORCHESTRA

Use these ornaments on a "musical wreath," as well as on the tree.

AVERAGE: For those with some experience in woodworking and crafts.

MATERIALS: Balsa wood; fine string; brass brads; brass wire; tracing paper; graphite paper; sharp-pointed craft knife; fine sandpaper; dowel; white glue; wire cutters; varnish; white poster paint; purple watercolor; assorted food colorings; watercolor brush; darner needle; ruler; push-pin; transparent tape *(optional)*.

DIRECTIONS:

1. Cutting: Copy the full-size patterns in Figs. II, 10A, 10B and 10C *(pages 74 and 75)*, onto tracing paper. Place the tracing paper over the graphite paper, and transfer each pattern piece separately onto the balsa wood (underlapping portions are indicated with broken lines). Cut out the pieces with the craft knife. Sand them to remove traces of graphite, and to smooth the surfaces. For each small round hole, cut the hole slightly smaller than it is drawn. Then turn a tapered object (such as a pencil) in the hole until the hole is smooth and round. To make the larger hole (sound hole) in the Lute, wrap the dowel with sandpaper, insert it into the balsa wood, and turn it to smooth the hole.

2. Coloring: For white, use the poster paint. For purple, use the watercolor. For other colors, use diluted food colorings. Brush the color on each piece with the watercolor brush *(see photo for color suggestions)*. Allow the pieces to dry before assembling the instruments.

3. Lute and Harp Assembling: Glue the Lute and Harp pieces together, underlying layers first, as shown in Figs. II, 10A and 10C. Nail

brass brads at the black dots around the Lute's sound hole. Glue a small balsa wood patch behind the top of each ornament, and push a 2-inch length of brass wire into the patch. Bend the extending end into a round loop to make a hanger. Varnish the finished instrument.

4. Lute Details: Make a sound box under the sound hole by gluing a 1¼-inch square of balsa wood, painted purple, over two ¼-inch-deep sides so the purple piece sits about ¼ inch behind the Lute. Make small holes with the darner needle at the four black circles on the pegboard (see Fig. II, 10A). On the bridge, cut four evenly spaced slits to hold the strings. Cut four 9-inch lengths of fine string and thread them through the holes. Glue the ends 1 or 2 inches to the back of the Lute along the neck. Glue a scrap of balsa to the back of the Lute behind the holes and over the string ends. To make turning pegs, nail four brads into the balsa scrap *(see photo)*. Stretch the strings down the Lute, over the bridge, and onto the back of the sound box. Glue or tape the strings in place.

5. Harp Details: On the back of the Harp, place the ruler across the two curved pieces, and mark each end of the string positions, parallel and about ¼ inch apart. Push the push-pin through each position to mark the front. Nail a brass brad into each pinmark from the front. Cut about a yard of fine string and wind it up and down the back of the Harp from brad to brad, gluing the first and last ends. Trim away the excess string. If you wish, clip the brads about ¼ inch beyond the Harp back.

6. Viol Assembling and Details: Assemble the Viol pieces in the following order: Cut the two curved slits in the Viol *(see Fig. II, 10B)*, and glue a patch of balsa wood behind them. Make small holes with the

Continued on page 75

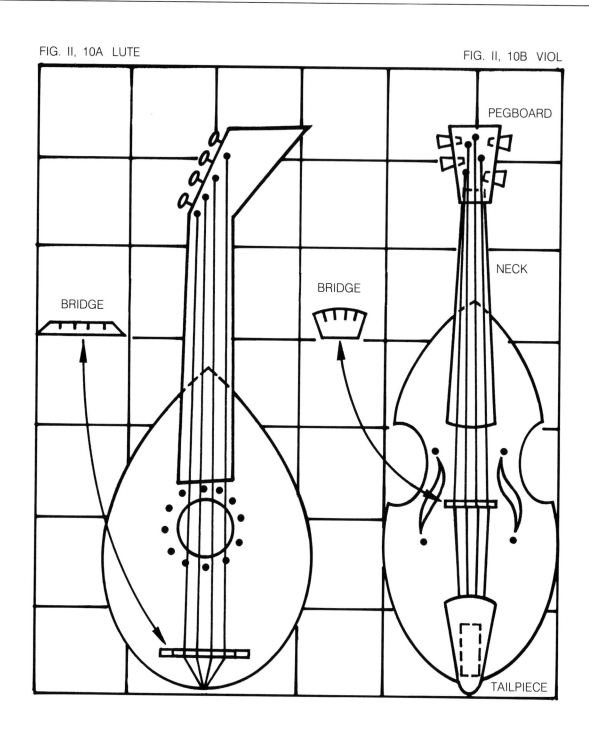

FIG. II, 10A LUTE

FIG. II, 10B VIOL

PEGBOARD

NECK

BRIDGE

BRIDGE

TAILPIECE

FIG. II, 10C HARP

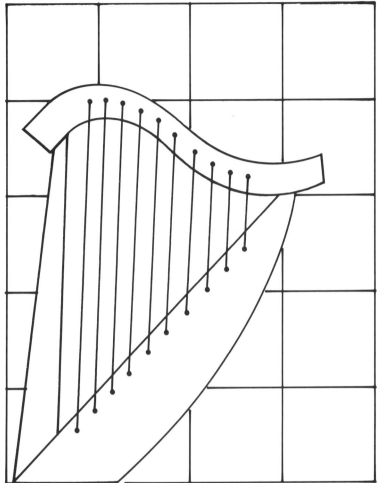

pegboard at the black circles. Glue little triangles of balsa wood (pegs) to the back of the pegboard. Glue the pegboard to the neck. Glue the support *(dotted line in* FIG. II, 10B*)* at the lower end of the Viol. Glue the bridge and neck to the Viol. Cut four 8-inch lengths of fine string. Glue the ends to the back of the tailpiece, and glue the tailpiece over the support. Stretch the strings over the bridge, up the Viol, through the holes and down to the back of the instrument. Glue the strings in place, and cover them with a small scrap of balsa wood. Attach a hanger following the directions in Step 3. Varnish the finished Viol.

5. Harp Details: On the back of the Harp, place the ruler across the two curved pieces, and mark each end of the string positions, parallel and about ¼ inch apart. Push the push-pin through each position to mark the front. Nail a brass brad into each pinmark from the front. Cut about a yard of the fine string and wind it up and down the back of the Harp from brad to brad, gluing the first and last ends. Trim away the excess string. If you wish, clip the brads, about ¼ inch beyond the Harp back.

Mr. & Mrs. Claus

MR. & MRS. CLAUS

EASY: Achievable by anyone.
MATERIALS FOR BOTH: Two 25-mm wooden bead doll heads with rosy cheeks; two 38-mm round red beads for bodies; 3-inch square of white felt; 1-inch square of flesh-colored felt; compass; paper; craft glue; white acrylic paint; paintbrush; 12 inches of cord.
FOR MR. CLAUS: 1½ x 2¼ inches of red felt; one ½-inch red pompon; one ¾-inch white pompon; one 5-mm pearl; 3 red seed beads; tiny holly leaf.
FOR MRS. CLAUS: One 1-inch white pompon; 5 inches of ⅛-inch-wide red ribbon; one 5-mm green sequin; 6½ inches of ¼-inch-wide scalloped lace edging; tiny pieces of green and brown felt; 17 red seed beads.

DIRECTIONS:

1. Using the compass and a piece of paper, draw a 2½-inch-diameter circle. Fold the circle in half and cut the circle exactly in half. Fold one of the halves in half, and cut it in half. You now should have two pieces resembling one quarter of a pie. On one of these pieces, measure ½ inch from the center point along one straight edge, and draw a curved line from there to the intersection where the other straight edge meets the

outside curve of the wedge. Cut along the curved line you just drew. The resulting shape should have two curved edges tapering to a point, and a straight edge measuring ¾ inch. This is the sleeve pattern. Cut out two red felt sleeves for Mr. Claus, and two white felt sleeves for Mrs. Claus.

2. Mr. Claus: Glue a head bead over the hole of a red body bead. When the glue has dried, paint white hair and white eyebrows on the head bead. Cut a 6-inch length of cord, and glue the ends to the top of the head bead to make a hanging loop. Glue the ¾-inch white pompon over the cord ends. On top of the white pompon, glue the red pompon and glue the pearl on top of that. On the front of Mr. Claus' cap, glue the tiny holly leaf and three red seed beads. Glue the red felt sleeves around each side of the body, with the straight edges toward the front and ½ inch apart at the top of the cuffs. Glue flesh-colored felt pieces, about ⅝ x ¼ inch and tapered at one end, under the ends of the sleeves for hands. Cut a 1½ x ⅛-inch strip of white felt. Cut the strip in half crosswise, and glue one piece across the end of each sleeve for a cuff. Cut a piece of white felt about ¾ inch wide and ½ inch deep for a beard, and another piece ⅛ x ½ inch for a moustache. Trim to shape the pieces, and glue the beard and moustache on the face.

3. Mrs. Claus: Glue a head bead over the hole of a red body bead. When the glue has dried, paint on white hair and white eyebrows. Cut a 6-inch length of cord, and glue the ends to the top of the head bead to make a hanging loop. Glue the 1-inch white pompon over the cord ends. Glue the white felt sleeves around the body bead as shown in the photograph, with flesh-colored felt hands glued just under the ends of the sleeves. Between the hands, glue a tiny green felt Christmas tree, ⁵⁄₁₆ inch high, with a trunk of brown felt ¹⁄₁₆ inch wide and ³⁄₁₆ inch long. Glue the scalloped lace edging around her head at the edge of the pompon, and around her neck for a ruffle. Tie a tiny bow of red ribbon for her hair, and glue it over her left eye on the pompon "hair." Cut two ¾-inch lengths of red ribbon, and glue them to the ends of the sleeves for cuffs. Leave a ⅛-inch space and glue a row of eight red seed beads alongside each piece of ribbon. Glue the green sequin under her chin, and glue a red seed bead in the center of the green sequin.

FIG. II, 11   BALSA WOOD ANGEL
HALF PATTERN
FULL SIZE

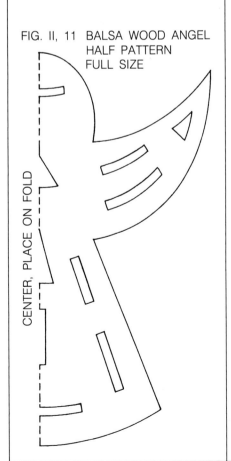

CENTER, PLACE ON FOLD

Balsa Wood Angel

BALSA WOOD ANGEL

EASY: Achievable by anyone.
MATERIALS: 4 x 5 x ¹⁄₃₂ inch of balsa wood; graphite paper; craft knife; fine sandpaper; emery board; hanging cord; tracing paper.

DIRECTIONS:
1. Trace the angel half-pattern, including the inner openings, in FIG. II, 11 onto folded tracing paper. Cut out the shape and inner openings.

Open the tracing paper for the full 4 x 4¼-inch pattern.
2. Using the graphite paper, trace the shape and openings onto the balsa wood. Cut out the shape and openings with the craft knife; first make a light cut, then a second pass, to avoid splintering. Sand all the edges; use the emery board on the edges of the openings. Cut a length of cord and tie the ends together. Push the loop through the opening at the top of the angel, and tie a slipknot for a hanger.

THE LITTLEST REINDEER

This endearing reindeer will enchant your little ones. They even can assemble him themselves, after you cut the pieces to size.

EASY: Achievable by anyone.
MATERIALS: Four flat wooden clothespins; small saw; 2 brown pipe cleaners; white glue; 2 buttons for eyes; 1 red bead for nose; green felt; red felt; 3 tiny gold beads.

DIRECTIONS:

1. Saw the legs off one of the flat wooden clothespins to make the reindeer body. Set aside the clothespin legs.

2. To make the head and ears, cut off the legs of a second clothespin 1 inch away from the separation *(see photo for guide)*, and discard those legs. Bend the pipe cleaners to make the antlers *(see photo)*. Glue the bottom ends of the antlers between the ears. Glue the button eyes and bead nose to the face.

3. Glue a whole clothespin to each side of the body pin. Glue the head to the front top half of a leftover leg. Glue the back bottom half of the leg to the front of one of the whole clothespins. Glue the other leftover leg for the tail to the other whole clothespin.

4. Cut out a harness breast piece from the green felt *(see photo for guide)*. Cut a small diamond shape and a thin band from the red felt. Make a loop with the red band, slip the band over the reindeer's head and glue the ends together. Glue the green harness piece to the red band as shown. Glue the red diamond in the center of the green harness piece. Sew the beads to the red felt strip as shown in the photo.

The Littlest Reindeer

Ribbon Fans

RIBBON FAN

EASY: Achievable by anyone.
MATERIALS: Ten to twelve inches of 2¾-inch-wide or wider craft ribbon; stapler or wire; needle and thread; lace *(optional)*.

DIRECTIONS:

Fold over one short end of the ribbon ½ inch. Continue folding the ribbon into ½-inch accordion pleats, folding first in one direction and then in the other. Fasten the bottom of the folded ribbon in place by stapling it, stitching it, or wrapping a piece of wire around it. If you wish, trim the top of the fan with lace. Attach a thread loop to the top of the fan for a hanger.

QUILT BASKET

EASY: Achievable by anyone.
MATERIALS: 2 scraps of contrasting Christmas print fabric; child's holiday coloring book; graphite paper; dressmaker's carbon; stiff cardboard; white glue; drill; narrow red ribbon.

DIRECTIONS:

1. Using the graphite paper, trace a simple basket motif from the holiday coloring book onto the cardboard. Trace a bow separately. Cut out the cardboard basket and bow.
2. Using the dressmaker's carbon and the cardboard shapes, trace the basket on one of the Christmas print fabrics and trace the bow on the contrasting fabric. Cut out the fabric basket and bow, leaving a ¼-inch allowance.
3. Trace and cut another piece, from the first fabric, the exact size of the cardboard basket shape *(no cutting allowance)*. Trace and cut a piece from the contrasting fabric the exact size of the cardboard bow shape.
4. Spread glue on one side of the cardboard basket shape. Place the wrong side of the larger fabric basket piece on the glued side of the cardboard. Spread the fabric evenly so the ¼-inch allowance extends beyond all the cardboard edges. Clip the overlapping fabric at the curves.
5. Spread more glue on the back of the cardboard basket shape, and press the overlapping fabric onto the glue. Place the smaller fabric basket piece on the back of the basket, on top of the glued overlap.
6. Repeat Steps 4 and 5 with the bow fabric pieces and cardboard shape.
7. Glue the contrasting fabric bow on the front of the basket *(see photo)*. Carefully drill a hole through the "knot" part of the bow. Thread both ends of a length of red ribbon through the hole and tie the ends in a bow leaving a hanger loop.

Quilt Basket

PINE CONE STARS

EASY: Achievable by anyone.
MATERIALS: Assorted pine cones of various sizes and shapes; aluminum foil; hot glue gun or carpenter's wood glue; silver and gold metallic cord; ⅛-inch-wide red and/or green satin ribbon. **Optional decorations:** artificial snow spray; small artificial sprigs of holly; artificial holly berries; tiny painted pine cones.

DIRECTIONS:

1. Cover your work surface with aluminum foil. For each star, place six slender cones in a circle with their bottom ends together, and glue them to form a six-pointed star. Cover the center where they meet with a larger cone standing straight up. Surround that cone with smaller cones or tiny, painted cones. Glue the cones in place. When the glue has dried, turn over the star and repeat to cover the center on the other side. Cut a length of silver or gold cord, and glue the ends of the cord to the back of the star for a hanger.
2. If you wish, decorate the stars with the artificial snow, holly sprigs and berries, and red and green satin ribbons tied into bows; vary the decorations among the stars.

Pine Cone Stars

CHRISTMAS CONES

There's almost no limit to the ways in which you can use pine cones as decorations.

Fill baskets, bowls, brass buckets or terra cotta pots with pine cones of all shapes and sizes. Tie a big, bright bow around the container. If you wish, add miniature glass ball ornaments to catch the light. Garlands of red wooden beads wound around and through the cones add warmth and color.

Spray pine cones with craft glue (available at craft supply stores) and roll them in glitter — gold or silver for an elegant look, multicolored for fun.

Tuck pine cones around a crèche, intersperse them with tall candlesticks on a mantel, glue or tie ribbons to them and hang them in your windows; let your imagination run wild!

COUNTRY DOVE ORNAMENT

A year-round accent for country decor, this dove reminds us of a weathervane figure.

EASY: Achievable by anyone.
MATERIALS: 24-gauge shiny tin; tin snips; hammer or medium-grade sandpaper; awl; acrylic paints: dark red, off-white, brown; various size paintbrushes; antiquing stain (available at craft supply stores; see *Note* below); cotton rag; twine; cardboard; graphite paper; stylus or old ballpoint pen.
Note: *Some antiquing stains are not compatible with acrylic paints. Check with your local craft store before purchasing your supply.*

DIRECTIONS:

1. Enlarge the pattern in FIG. II, 12 onto the cardboard, following the directions on page 239.
2. Using the graphite paper and the stylus or old ballpoint pen, trace the pattern onto the tin. Cut out the pattern with the tin snips. Hammer out or sand down any sharp edges.
3. Paint the dove and heart with several base coats of acrylic paints. Use the off-white paint for the body of the dove and the dark red for the heart. Let the paint dry. Use the brown paint for the eye, beak and contour lines on the dove body at the base of the wings and the tail *(see photo)*. Allow the paint to dry completely.
4. To "antique" the dove, dip a clean paintbrush into the antiquing stain and brush it over the ornament. Wipe lightly with the clean cotton rag, leaving more stain near the edges. Allow the stain to dry completely.
5. Punch the hole in the wing with the awl *(see FIG. II, 12)*. Run a length of twine through the hole, and tie the ends together to make a hanger loop.

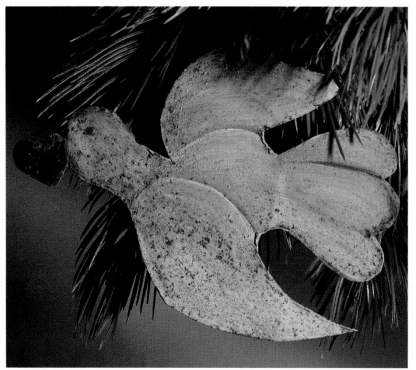

Country Dove Ornament

FIG. II, 12 COUNTRY DOVE ORNAMENT

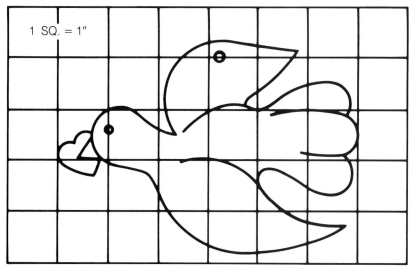

1 SQ. = 1"

ELFIN MAGIC ORNAMENTS

The elves also can be used as table decorations or place markers.

AVERAGE: For those with some experience in crafting.
Makes about 12 elves.

MATERIALS:

1   can (8 ounces) almond paste
2   egg whites
½   teaspoon lemon extract
1   package (1 pound) 10X (confectioners' powdered) sugar, sifted if lumpy
     Assorted food colorings
     Brandy

Plastic wrap; small paintbrush; toothpicks; sewing needle; metallic or nylon thread.

Elfin Magic Ornaments

DIRECTIONS:

1. Break up the almond paste with your fingers in a medium-size bowl. Add one of the egg whites and the lemon extract. Mix the ingredients together with a fork until they are blended. Gradually add enough of the 10X (confectioners' powdered) sugar to form a soft dough.

2. Knead the dough with more of the 10X (confectioners' powdered) sugar in the bowl until a smooth, firm ball forms. Divide the dough into 12 pieces; keep the pieces covered with plastic wrap to prevent the dough from drying out.

3. Refer to the photo to help shape the elves. Each is about 2½ inches tall. Divide each of the 12 dough pieces into smaller pieces for the body, head, arms, legs and other parts of each ornament. To color the dough, knead in a drop of food coloring until the desired shade is reached. Mold the smaller pieces between the palms of your hands into balls, pear shapes, ropes and so on. Shape all the parts of a figure first, then attach the parts

using a little of the remaining egg white as glue at the points of attachment. If the dough is too dry to mold, knead a bit of the egg white into the dough to moisten it.

4. To paint colors on parts such as the candy cane or scarf, dilute the food colorings with the brandy and brush the colors onto the pieces with the small paintbrush. To make the facial features, mark the eyes and smiles on the elves with a toothpick, and paint the indentations with a bit of diluted food coloring.

5. To make a sitting elf, mold the body and place it on the edge of an upside-down cup. Attach the legs so that they hang over the side of the cup.

6. Let the ornaments dry for about 1 hour. Thread the sewing needle with the metallic or nylon thread. Insert the needle and thread twice through the body of each ornament, so that the thread ends meet at the same side. Let the ornaments dry until they are very firm. When firm, place each ornament directly onto a tree branch, and tie it securely with the thread to the branch above or below it.

A-DOUGH-ABLE ORNAMENTS

Be sure to hang these ornaments out of reach of inquisitive pets.

AVERAGE: For those with some experience in crafting.
Bake at 375° for 20 to 40 minutes.
Makes about 3 ornaments.

MATERIALS:
- 1 cup water
- ½ cup (1 stick) butter or margarine
- 1 cup all-purpose flour
- 4 eggs
- Buttercream Frosting (recipe follows)
- Red food coloring
- Cocoa
- Chocolate sprinkles, silver dragées, colored sugar crystals, candy canes, peanuts, green candied cherries

Drinking straw; wax paper; sewing needle; metallic or nylon thread.

DIRECTIONS:
1. Bring the water and the butter or margarine to boiling in a medium-size saucepan. Stir in the flour with a wooden spoon until a ball forms. Remove the saucepan from the heat, and cool the mixture slightly. Grease two large baking sheets. Add the eggs, one at a time, to the flour mixture, beating well after each addition. Be careful to keep the mixture smooth and glossy.

2. Preheat the oven to moderate (375°).

3. Fit a pastry bag with a ¼-inch round tip. Fill the bag with one third of the dough. Pipe the dough onto the baking sheets, spacing the ornaments about 1 inch apart.

4. Christmas Stocking: Use one third of the dough. Pipe the outline of the stocking: about 3¾ inches long, 2½ inches from the heel to the toe. Fill in the stocking shape with the dough to a ¼-inch thickness.

Nutcracker

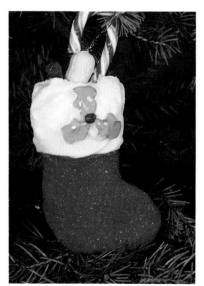

Christmas Stocking

5. Nutcracker: Use one third of the dough. Pipe the hat first, then a ball for the face, then the arms, body and legs.

6. Use the remaining third of the dough to make a second nutcracker or another stocking.

7. Bake in the preheated moderate oven (375°) for 20 to 40 minutes, or until the ornaments are golden brown and firm. Remove the ornaments with a spatula to a wire rack to cool. While

the nutcracker still is warm, make a hole with the drinking straw in the body to hold a peanut.

8. Make the Buttercream Frosting. Spoon about ¾ cup of the frosting into a pastry bag fitted with a small, round tip. Divide the remainder of the frosting among 3 cups, and tint each cup with the food coloring or cocoa. You'll need about ½ cup of red, ½ cup of chocolate brown and a tablespoon of pink frosting. Make wax paper cones, and fill each with a different color frosting. Cut off a tiny opening at the bottom of each cone for a tip, and pipe the frostings to decorate the ornaments using the photos at left for a guide. Sprinkle the frosted ornaments with the candies, or decorate the stocking, as we did, with green cherries cut into leaf shapes. Cut off the top ⅛ inch of the stocking, and insert candies or a miniature candy cane in the stocking opening.

9. When the frosting is dry, thread the needle with the metallic or nylon thread and pierce through each ornament. Tie the ends of the thread together to make a loop for a hanger.

BUTTERCREAM FROSTING
Makes about 2¼ cups.
- ⅓ cup butter or margarine
- 1 teaspoon vanilla
- 1 package (1 pound) 10X (confectioners' powdered) sugar, sifted if lumpy
- 3 to 4 tablespoons milk

Beat together the butter or margarine and the vanilla until creamy in a small bowl with an electric mixer. Beat in the 10X (confectioners' powdered) sugar and 3 tablespoons of the milk until the frosting is smooth and stiff enough to spread, yet stands in soft peaks. Add more milk if the frosting is too stiff. Cover the surface of the frosting with plastic wrap to prevent it from drying out while you work.

FINISHING TOUCHES

Patchwork Tree Skirt

**NDERNEATH THE
CHRISTMAS TREE**

*Before the appearance of all
those beautifully wrapped,
mysterious bundles, the bottom
of your tree can look rather
bare. A colorful tree skirt, such
as our Patchwork Tree Skirt at
left, can add a bright spot of
color and set the stage for the
gifts to come.*

*Try gathering together all the
stuffed animals in the house,
from brand new to worn-with-
love. Group them under the tree
to guard over the presents.*

*If you are lucky enough to have
antique (or just old and well-
loved) toys, dolls, wagons or
rocking horses, place these
under the tree to give an air of
Christmas from days gone by.*

*Miniature villages and train
sets are naturals under the
Christmas tree.*

PATCHWORK TREE SKIRT
This tie quilted tree skirt is a perfect partner for the Raffia and Calico Star Finial (page 93).

AVERAGE: For those with some experience in sewing.
MATERIALS: Forty-five-inch-wide fabric: 1¼ yards of unbleached muslin, and 1½ yards of solid color green or red cotton or polyester/cotton blend; sixty-four 6-inch squares of any assortment of red, green or white solid color or calico print cotton or polyester/cotton fabrics; matching threads; 2½ yards of polyester fleece interlining; embroidery floss or fine yarn; darner or other large needle; pins; yardstick.

DIRECTIONS
(½-inch seams allowed):
1. Assemble and stitch together the 6-inch squares in a pleasing combination as an 8-square by 8-square patchwork. Mark the center of the patchwork with a pin. Using the yardstick as a guide, mark a 40-inch-diameter circle on the patchwork. Cut out the circle. Using the same center point, cut out a 6-inch-diameter circle at the center of the large circle. Discard the small circle. Cut a slit from the outer edge of the patchwork to the center in a straight line *(see photo)*.
2. Using the patchwork top as the pattern, cut two matching pieces of fleece and one of muslin.
3. Cut six 7-inch-wide strips crosswise from the full 45-inch width of the solid color green or red fabric. Sew the short ends of the pieces together to make one long strip. Fold the strip in half widthwise, wrong sides together, and press. Hem the short ends. Sew a gathering stitch near the cut edges,

and gather the strip to fit the outer edge of the patchwork circle.
4. Baste the ruffle to the patchwork circle, right sides together, with the folded edge of the ruffle facing the center of the patchwork, and the cut edges even with the cut edge of the patchwork. Keep the hemmed ends of the ruffle ⅝ inch from the edges of the slit opening.
5. Place the muslin circle on the patchwork circle, right sides together, with the ruffle inside toward the center. Place the two pieces of fleece on top of the muslin. Baste and sew all the layers together ½ inch from the cut edges, being careful not to catch the hemmed ends of the ruffle in a seam. Leave a 5-inch opening along the outer edge of the skirt for turning. Turn the skirt to the right side, and slipstitch the opening closed.
6. Cut six 9 x 4-inch pieces of the same solid color fabric as the ruffle. Fold each piece widthwise. Sew along one short edge and the long raw edge. Turn each piece right side out through the open short end. Turn in the raw edge at the short end and slipstitch the opening closed. Sew the pieces in pairs to the back of the skirt opening for ties *(see photo)*.
7. Using the darner or other large needle, tie quilt the tree skirt with the floss or yarn at the patchwork square intersections. After threading the needle, do not knot the floss. Starting at one intersection, take a short stitch in the intersection through all three layers, leaving about a 2-inch-long tail of floss. Take another stitch on top of the first. Cut the floss about 2 inches from the stitches. Tie the floss into a square knot, and trim the ends to be about ½ inch long.

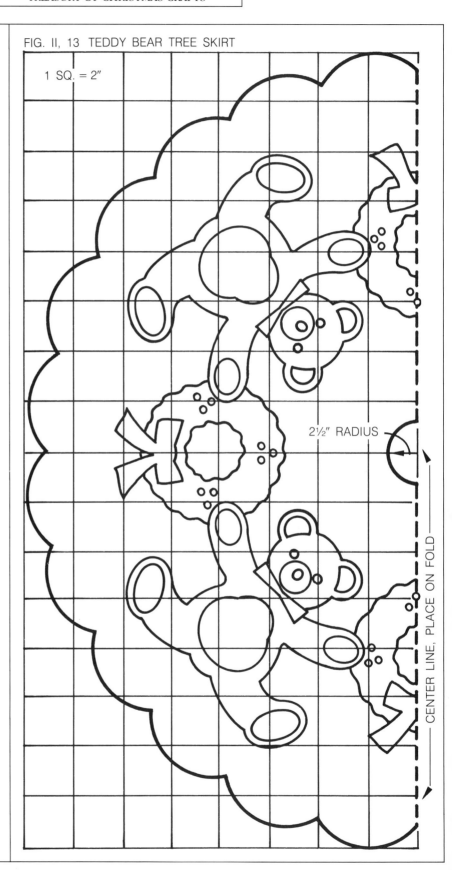

FIG. II, 13 TEDDY BEAR TREE SKIRT

1 SQ. = 2"

2½" RADIUS

CENTER LINE, PLACE ON FOLD

TEDDY BEAR TREE TOPPER

Using the bear pattern from the Teddy Bear Tree Skirt, cut out two extra felt bears and back them with stiff cardboard. Glue on the paw pads, ear linings, facial features and bellies as you did for the tree skirt.

Make two cardboard loops, each about 2 inches in diameter, and attach them to the back of one of the bears with tape or glue. Attach the back of the other bear to the cardboard loops, making sure the bears line up.

Slip the Teddy Bear Tree Topper onto the top branch of your tree through the cardboard loops.

Teddy Bear Tree Skirt

TEDDY BEAR TREE SKIRT

An adorable, easy-to-make project for bear fanciers of all ages.

EASY: Achievable by anyone.
MATERIALS: Felt: 36-inch square of white, four 9 x 12-inch pieces of tan, two 9 x 12-inch pieces of green, and scraps of red, dark brown and light beige or white; 4 small bells; glue stick; paper punch; red thread; sewing needle; yardstick; paper for patterns.

DIRECTIONS:
1. Cut a 36-inch-diameter circle from the white felt. Using the same center point, cut a 5-inch-diameter circle and discard the small circle.
2. Enlarge the patterns in Fig. II, 13 onto paper, following the directions on page 239. Using the photo as a color guide, cut out the shapes from the felt.
3. Glue the muzzles, inner ears, paw pads and bellies to the bear bodies. Glue the eyes and noses to the faces. Let the glue dry completely.
4. Cut scallops along the edge of the tree skirt. Lay out the skirt on a flat surface. Using the photo as a placement guide, place the bears and wreaths on the skirt, with the bear paws slightly overlapping the wreaths. Glue the bears and wreaths to the skirt. Glue the bows on the wreaths, and at the bears' necks.
5. Cut a straight line from the outer edge of the skirt to the inner hole, through the middle of one wreath.
Cut 36 red felt holly berries with the paper punch. Glue the berries to the wreaths; let dry completely.
7. Hand-sew the bells to the centers of the bows on the bears.

Home for the Holidays Tree Skirt

HOME FOR THE HOLIDAYS TREE SKIRT

AVERAGE: For those with some experience in cross stitch and sewing.
MATERIALS: Fifty-two-inch-wide fabric: 1⅜ yards of white burlap, and 1⅜ yards of backing fabric; matching thread; worsted-weight yarn: 95 yards of Scarlet, 60 yards of Emerald Green, 29 yards of Dark Green, 16 yards of Gold, 12 yards of Black, 12 yards of Topaz, and 4 yards of Cinnamon; 5¼ yards of red cording; 4 snap fasteners; sewing thread; tapestry needle; scissors; tailor's chalk.

DIRECTIONS:
1. Cut a 3-inch-wide strip from one selvage of the burlap, and cut the strip in half widthwise. Cut a slit from the center of the burlap to the center of one side edge. Stitch a strip half to each side of the slit. Stay-stitch the edges of the burlap to prevent raveling.

2. Copy the design in FiG. II, 14, onto the burlap with tailor's chalk.

3. Using the tapestry needle and yarn, cross stitch the design *(see Embroidery Stitch Guide, page 240)*, using the photo as a color guide *(see Note, below)*. The crosses are worked over three threads of burlap. Be careful not to miscount threads. Work all the crosses in the same direction, with all the underneath stitches going in one direction, and all the top stitches going in the opposite direction. To begin and end strands, catch the yarn under stitches on the back of the work.

4. When the cross stitching is completed, place the burlap face down and iron it, using a damp pressing cloth. Round the corners of the burlap with scissors.

5. Baste or stitch the cording ½ inch in from the outer edge of the skirt.

6. Prepare the backing fabric the same way you prepared the burlap in Step 1. With right sides together, pin and stitch the backing to the burlap, using a ½-inch seam allowance. Leave the underneath side of the slit open.

7. To form the center opening, cut a 3½-inch square in the center of the burlap. Clip the corners. Turn the skirt right side out. Turn in the edges of the center square between the layers. Topstitch the burlap and backing together along the slit and around the center opening. Sew the snap fasteners along the slit. Press the tree skirt.

Note: *The border and tree trims are worked in Scarlet; the trees are worked in Emerald; the roofs, in Dark Green; the chimneys, in Cinnamon; the windows and doors, in Black; the house fronts, in Gold; the house sides, in Topaz.*

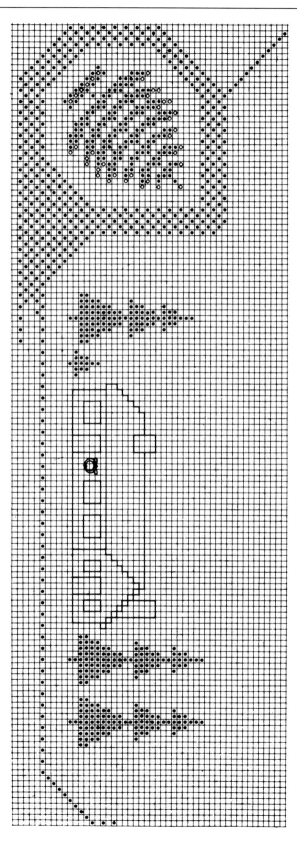

FIG. II, 14
HOME FOR THE
HOLIDAYS
TREE SKIRT

CORNHUSK TREE TOP ANGEL

Crafting this delicate angel takes time and patience, but we think you'll agree the results are exquisite.

CHALLENGING: Requires more experience in craftwork.

MATERIALS: Cornhusks*; fabric dye for dress in color desired; 1 skein of embroidery floss for hair in color desired; narrow lace; baby's breath; miniature dried star flowers; 1-inch-diameter Styrofoam® ball; 14 inches of No. 18 wire; ecru buttontwist thread; 2 cotton balls; cotton swab; cosmetic blusher; white glue; stapler; tissue paper; manila file folder; tracing paper; ⅛-inch-diameter dowel or 2-inch-long nail; 5 or 6-inch-diameter plastic bowl; 2 plastic bags.

__Note:__ Cornhusks are either fine- or coarse-grained; one side is ribbed, the other smooth and "milky." Use the milky side for the head, hands and sleeves, or where the husks are to be turned or bent. We used both dyed and undyed cornhusks.

DIRECTIONS:

1. Coloring: Dye 25 husks in an old pail using a solution of ½ package of the fabric dye to 1 gallon of hot water; keep the husks as flat as possible. For pastel colors, check the husks after 2 minutes; deeper colors need more dye and time. Rinse the husks well in cold water. Squeeze out the excess water, and place the husks in a plastic bag. Soak the undyed corn husks in warm water to soften them, and place them in a plastic bag. Unwrap the husks carefully so they won't break.

2. Head: Roll and "pinch" the Styrofoam® ball into a more oval shape. Place the head at the bottom third of a 6 x 8-inch undyed husk, grain running lengthwise; place the chin toward the short end. Roll the ball in the husk until it is covered, twist the leftover husk at the top, and pull it to

the bottom at the back of the head. Twist the husk at the neck and wrap it with the thread, leaving the tag ends of the husk hanging. Cut a 4-inch length of the wire, and insert it from the bottom into the head.

3. Arms: Using the remaining 10 inches of wire for the arms/shoulder piece, make a tiny loop at each end for the hands. Tear two ¾-inch-wide strips of undyed husk. Put one strip through a loop, cover the end of the hand, and wrap the strip up around the hand to the "elbow." Secure the husk by winding thread around the wrist and up the arm wire. Repeat to make the second hand.

4. Sleeves: Place a 6-inch-wide undyed husk downward from one wrist, milky side facing the wrist. Gather the husk around the wrist and tie it securely with thread. Carefully pull the husk back to the center of the arm, "puff" the sleeve and tie the husk securely in the middle of the wire arm. Place a 6-inch-wide dyed husk at the middle of the first sleeve, turn the husk to the center, puff it and tie it off at the shoulder. Repeat for the second double-puff sleeve.

5. Wrap a ½-inch-wide strip of undyed husk several turns around the neck area of the head. Center the arms/shoulder piece between the head's two husk tag ends. Wind thread around the bottom over the shoulders, and tie it securely.

6. Bodice: Place the two cotton balls in the center of a 6 x 8-inch dyed husk. Turn each husk edge inward about 1 inch, and turn the top half to the bottom. Place this section against the center of the arms/shoulder piece. Tear four 1½-inch-wide and 8-inch-long pieces of dyed husk. With the first piece, cover the bodice from the waist *diagonally* over the shoulder to the back. The second piece of husk goes in the other direction over the shoulder

Continued on page 92

Cornhusk Tree Top Angel

diagonally to the back. Repeat with the remaining two pieces of husk. Gather and pinch all the layers inward at the waistline. Bind around the waistline five times with thread, and tie off the thread tightly.

7. Skirt: Use full-length dyed husks. Bend the arms upward, out of the way. Lay the first skirt husk at the center of the figure, pointing upward from the body and head. Continue lapping the dyed husks around the entire waist. Holding all the husks and the body securely, wrap thread around the waist area many times, and tie it off. Turn the skirt husks downward, and cut them off evenly at the hem. Bend the arms down again. Place crumpled tissue paper under the skirt. Invert the plastic bowl, and stand the angel on top of the inverted bowl; the skirt will conform to the roundness of the bowl. Bend the head, if necessary. Gently position the arms *(see photo, page 91)*. Let the angel dry thoroughly.

8. Wings: Trace the full-size wing pattern in FIG. II, 15 onto tracing paper, and cut it out. Cut four wings from undyed husks and two from the manila folder. Glue a husk wing to each side of the manila wings. Place the wings under a heavy book to dry flat.

9. Hair, Front Curls: When the angel is completely dry, add the hair. Cut the entire skein of floss at the loops at each end. Cut four pieces of floss in half. Dip the dowel or nail into a puddle of glue. Wind a short floss piece around the dowel, and smooth the floss ends with more glue on your finger. Slide the curl off the dowel, and glue it to the front of the angel's head; have a damp washcloth handy to wipe off your fingers. Make and glue six to eight curls to the front of the angel's head *(see photo, page 91, for guide)*.

10. Hair, Long Curls: Use five full-length pieces of floss, and tie each piece in the middle with a strand of floss. Separate each half of the first full-length piece of floss into two groups of

three strands each. Curl one group of three strands on the dowel following the directions in Step 9. Repeat with the remaining groups of strands. Glue the curled piece to the top of the head. The tie in the center of the strands should be at the center "part" of the head. Repeat with the remaining four full-length pieces of floss, placing and gluing them until the whole head is covered. End with a ⅝-inch-diameter doughnut-shaped chignon on top. "Style" the long curls by pushing and gluing them to the shoulder and back areas. The curls will stiffen as they dry.

11. Halo: Wind 6 inches of thread over and under pieces of baby's breath. Form the wound thread into a circle to fit the angel's head, and tie off the thread.

12. Hanging Wreath: Cut a 3-inch-diameter circle from the manila folder, and cut a 1¾-inch-diameter circle in the middle of it. Glue a ½-inch-long thread loop to the center back. Cover the front of the wreath with glue. Place bits and pieces of baby's breath, star flowers and tiny, leaf-shaped pieces of

dyed husk all over the wreath. Let the glue dry. Trim the wreath with a narrow lace bow at the top.

13. Attaching the Wings: Cut a ½ x 3-inch piece of manila. Fold 1 inch of each end toward the center. Glue the wings to the folded piece at the ends. When the glue is dry, glue the center section of the manila piece to the back of the angel.

14. Finishing: Trim the angel with strips of narrow lace on the bodice, and a narrow lace bow at the waist. Add cosmetic blusher to the angel's cheeks with the cotton swab. Glue the baby's breath halo to the head. Make a stand for the angel by cutting a 5¾-inch-radius half-circle from the manila folder. Bend and overlap the half-circle to make a cone, and staple it in place. Cut the top hole slightly larger. Place lots of glue on top of the cone and insert the cone under the skirt. Drop more glue in, if necessary. Let the glue dry. Trim the bottom of the cone, if necessary. Hang the wreath on the angel's hand. The cornhusk angel can top a tree, or stand alone.

FIG. II, 15 CORNHUSK TREE TOP ANGEL WING PATTERN

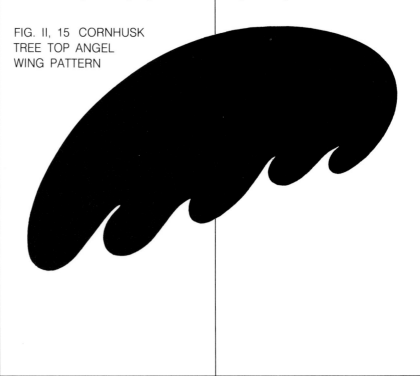

Raffia and Calico Star Finial

RAFFIA AND CALICO STAR FINIAL

AVERAGE: For those with some experience in sewing.

MATERIALS: Twenty 4¼ x 3¼-inch diamond-shaped plastic needlepoint canvas forms; 30 grams of natural-color matte artificial raffia; ¼ yard of red calico fabric with tiny print; sewing thread: red and beige; tapestry needle; large sewing needle.

DIRECTIONS:

1. Using a single strand of raffia and the tapestry needle, overcast all the edges of each diamond shape.

2. Using a double strand of raffia, fill the entire surface of 10 diamond shapes in the following way: Insert the needle in the first row of holes of one of the shapes. Bring the raffia from the underside of the canvas, pass over two holes, and insert the needle in the third hole. Bring the raffia up to the right side of the canvas again, through the fourth hole, and repeat. It will be necessary in some cases to pass over only one hole to stagger the stitches.

Make the stitches parallel to the outer edges of the shape *(see photo)*.

3. For the remaining 10 diamond shapes, use two double strands of raffia and overcast the first plastic line parallel to the outer edge of each shape, to form a second band of raffia *(see photo)*.

4. Cut 10 pieces of fabric the same size as the diamond shapes. Turn under the raw edges of the fabric pieces so the pieces fit exactly within the open plastic areas of the raffia-edged diamond shapes. Using the sewing needle and red thread, sew the fabric pieces as invisibly as possible to the raffia-edged diamond shapes to cover the open plastic areas.

5. Arrange five of the all-raffia diamonds into a star. Using the sewing needle and beige thread, join the diamonds with an overcast stitch done over the adjacent sides. Stop sewing 1¼ inches from the center of the star. Repeat with the remaining five all-raffia diamonds.

6. Sew five of the fabric diamonds to one of the raffia stars, with the diamonds' points placed between those of the star. The edges of the fabric diamonds do not quite touch each other. Repeat with the remaining raffia star and five fabric diamonds.

7. Cut two 3-inch-diameter fabric circles. Gather the circles along the raw edges to form 2-inch-diameter puffs with the raw edges turned under. Sew one puff to the center of each star, over the fabric diamonds.

8. Sew five crossed 2-inch-long pieces of raffia to each puff *(see photo)*.

9. Place the two completed stars wrong sides together, with their points even. Using an overcast stitch, stitch together four pairs of the all-raffia points; leave the fifth pair of all-raffia points unstitched. Stitch together *only* the outer points of the five pairs of fabric diamonds. The unstitched pair of all-raffia points leaves an opening to slip the star over the tip of the tree.

Boxwood Wreath (directions, page 97)

Wreaths of Welcome, Stockings to Stuff

 wo of the happiest sights of the holidays: beautiful wreaths welcoming friends and neighbors to your home, and stuffable stockings hanging by the chimney.

Bringing fresh greenery into the home during the long, dark winter is one of the oldest customs of the season. We offer wreaths made of shiny boxwood, overflowing with nuts and pine cones, decorated with bright carnations—even covered with dried hydrangea blossoms! Make a farmyard of patchwork critters to hang on a grapevine wreath, or adorn an evergreen wreath with graceful origami birds. Hang a wreath in every window, on every door, and say "welcome" to Christmas.

Stockings make wonderful decorations all through the house. From sumptuous creations of brocade and lace to quaint cross-stitch and pretty patchwork, this chapter has the perfect stocking for every member of your family. But remember, what's hidden inside is up to Santa!

WONDERFUL
WREATHS

Winter Woods Wreath

BOXWOOD WREATH

Make a full-size wreath to hang on your door, or decorate your table with a small Boxwood Wreath encircling a chunky red candle.

EASY: Achievable by anyone.
MATERIALS: Boxwood; Styrofoam® or straw wreath form; variegated holly; red pyracantha (firethorn) berries; ice pick or skewer and white glue (for use with Styrofoam® wreath form); floral wire (for use with straw wreath form).

DIRECTIONS:

If using a Styrofoam® wreath form, insert the boxwood into the form following the directions in Winter Woods Wreath *(at right)*. Space the boxwood evenly throughout the wreath form. Fill in the spaces with the variegated holly and pyracantha berries. If using a straw wreath form, wrap short pieces of floral wire around the stems of the boxwood, holly and berry sprigs, and insert the wires into the wreath form.

BASIC WREATHS

Decorate these basic natural and artificial wreaths with satin Poinsettias (page 102), Cranberry Ornaments (page 104), or store-bought decorations and ribbons.

EASY: Achievable by anyone.

EVERGREEN WREATH

MATERIALS: Variety of evergreen branches, each about 12 inches long (branch tips are best); 3- to 4-wire-ring wreath form; floral wire; large ribbon bow *(optional; see Basic Bow and Streamers, page 110)*; wire cutters or heavy scissors.

DIRECTIONS:

1. Small Wreath (less than 17 inches in diameter): Wind the end of the floral wire around one wire of the wreath form. Do not cut the floral wire; the evergreen branches will be bound individually to the wreath form with one continuous length of wire.
2. Position the branches at a slight angle to the wreath form, alternating the direction of each branch; this results in a more natural-looking wreath than if the branches were placed all in a straight line. Bind the branches individually to the wreath form with the floral wire until there are no openings in the wreath.
3. If you wish, attach a large ribbon bow with floral wire to conceal the stem end of the last branch attached. Or tuck the stem end under the tips of the first branches attached.
4. Wrap the floral wire to the underside of the wreath form to fasten it, and cut off the excess wire.
5. Large Wreath: Bind the branches into bunches of three with the floral wire. Follow the directions for the small wreath, treating the bunches of evergreens as individual branches.

ARTIFICIAL WREATH

MATERIALS: Artificial greens; Styrofoam® wreath form; green floral tape; floral wire; wire cutters or heavy scissors.

DIRECTIONS:

1. Wrap the wreath form with the floral tape.
2. Insert the sprays of artificial greens into the wreath form at a slight angle, covering the top and sides. If it is necessary to divide the greens, cut the floral wire into 7-inch lengths, bend the lengths into hairpin shapes, and use them like pins to secure the greenery to the wreath.

WINTER WOODS WREATH

A perfect family project! You can gather the materials for this wreath on a walk through the woods — or even in your backyard.

EASY: Achievable by anyone.
MATERIALS: Styrofoam® wreath form of size desired; pine cones (include enough large cones to fill the body of the wreath); ice pick or skewer; craft glue; any of the following: Brazil nuts, walnuts, almonds, pecans, grasses, horse chestnuts, milkweed pods; floral wire or wooden picks; ribbon for bow *(optional)*; coat hanger-weight heavy-gauge wire; wire cutters.

DIRECTIONS:

Poke holes in the wreath form with the ice pick or skewer where the largest pine cones will go. Dip the stems or pointed ends of the pine cones in glue, and insert them in the wreath form. Begin to form the wreath body with the largest size pine cones and any other large dried pieces. Using floral wire or wooden picks, fill in all the gaps with the nuts, grasses and seed pods, being careful to keep the look of the wreath balanced. If you wish, tie a ribbon into a large bow, insert a piece of floral wire through the bow back, and twist the wire ends around the wreath to secure the bow to the wreath. Form a loop for a hanger with the heavy-gauge wire. Poke holes in the back of the wreath form where you want to place the hanger, dip the ends of the loop in glue, and insert the loop into the holes. Let the glue dry completely.

The Holly & The Ivy

THE HOLLY & THE IVY

EASY: Achievable by anyone.
MATERIALS: Light, medium, dark and darkest green felt; white glue; red berries; green floral tape; tracing paper; cardboard or heavy paper; tie wire; No. 18 wire; No. 21 wire; heavy spool wire; wire cutters; large grapevine wreath.

DIRECTIONS:
1. Enlarge the patterns in Fig. III, 1 onto tracing paper, following the directions on page 239. Cut the three sizes for each leaf from the cardboard or heavy paper.
2. Use double layers of felt for each leaf. Use light green felt for the small ivy leaves, medium green felt for the medium-size leaves and dark green felt for the large ivy leaves. Use medium, dark and darkest green felt for the holly leaves.
3. Cut a piece of heavy spool wire at least 3 inches longer than each leaf. Separate a pair of leaves. Spread glue on one leaf, and place the wire on top for the central "vein." Press the second leaf over that. Wrap floral tape around the extending wire to make a stem.
4. Ivy Vines: Cut two 20-inch lengths of No. 21 wire, and wrap them with floral tape. Beginning with the small leaves, attach the ivy to the vine wires with tie wire, spacing the leaves an inch or two apart. The leaves should stand up about an inch. Cover the tie wire with floral tape.
5. Holly Swags: Wrap the berries with tie wire into clusters of about 2 dozen berries each. Cut 4-, 8- or 10-inch-long No. 18 wire stems, and wrap them with floral tape. For each stem, attach holly leaves with tie wire about ½ inch apart. Add a cluster of berries close to the stem after five or six leaves. Shape the leaves as you like.
6. Wreath: Twist the ivy vines into the grapevine wreath, and arrange the holly swags at the top of the wreath.

FIG. III, 1 THE HOLLY & THE IVY

1 SQ. = ½"

Candy Canes & Carnations Wreath

CANDY CANES & CARNATIONS WREATH

EASY: Achievable by anyone.
MATERIALS: Evergreen Wreath *(page 97)*; twelve 5½-inch candy canes; 18 miniature carnations; baby's breath; floral wire; floral water picks; ¼-inch-wide red and green satin ribbons; ½-inch-wide red satin ribbon; tape.

DIRECTIONS:
1. Arrange the candy canes in four sets of three canes each, and tape each set securely. Tie each set with ½-inch-wide red satin ribbon; make a double bow. Attach the sets to the wreath with floral wire, spacing them evenly and leaving space at the top of the wreath.
2. Arrange three carnations with some baby's breath in each of the floral water picks. Attach five bouquets to the wreath, alternating them with the candy cane sets and leaving space at the top *(see photo)*.
3. Using ¼-inch-wide red and green satin ribbons, make a large bow with 1- to 1½-foot-long streamers *(see Basic Bow and Streamers, page 110)*. Attach bow to top of wreath; attach remaining bouquet to the center of the bow.

CORNHUSK WREATH

Hang this lovely wreath at Thanksgiving time, and leave it up through the New Year.

EASY: Achievable by anyone.
MATERIALS: Cornhusks; 24-inch-diameter Styrofoam® wreath form; fabric dye *(optional)*; 4-inch Styrofoam® square; 7 large dried yarrow heads; 6 wired pine cones; bunch of dark brown dried grasses or wheat; cinnamon sticks; spool of floral wire; craft glue.

DIRECTIONS:

1. Using the spool of floral wire for continuous wiring, wire cornhusk loops three across, with a 2-inch overlap, onto the wreath form. Leave a space at the bottom of the wreath to attach the Styrofoam® square. If you wish, dye some of the cornhusks, following the directions in Step 1 for the Cornhusk Tree Top Angel, page 90, and use the dyed cornhusks to create a design, blending light color to dark color *(see photo)*.
2. Secure the Styrofoam® square at the base of the wreath with craft glue or floral wire.
3. Insert the yarrow heads into the Styrofoam® square. Fill in with the pine cones, the dark brown grasses or wheat, and the cinnamon sticks.

Cornhusk Wreath

POTPOURRI MINI-WREATH

Hang this wreath in a sunny window or near the fireplace. As it warms, the potpourri's fragrance is released.

Materials: 1/3-cup capacity gelatin mold; shortening; 1 tablespoon of white glue; 3 tablespoons of water; 3/4 cup of potpourri; wire rack; ribbon.

Lightly grease the interior of the mold with the shortening, and set aside the mold. Blend together the glue and the water in a small bowl. Add the potpourri, and stir to coat it evenly. Set aside the potpourri mixture for 5 minutes.

Spoon the potpourri mixture into the mold, including all the liquid. Pack the potpourri firmly, and set aside the mold for 30 minutes.

Carefully pour off the excess liquid from the mold by holding it almost vertically. Place the mold, rim up, on the wire rack in a warm, dry room. Let the mold set, undisturbed, for 12 hours, or overnight.

When ready to unmold, rap the bottom and sides of the mold sharply on a counter. Turn over the mold and dislodge the wreath onto the wire rack, flat side down. Dry the wreath in a warm room for 2 days, or until it is quite firm. Decorate the wreath with a ribbon bow.

Hydrangea Wreath

HYDRANGEA WREATH

A stunning wreath to hang outside in warm-weather regions. Hang it indoors in colder climates.

EASY: Achievable by anyone.
MATERIALS: Ten fresh or dried hydrangea heads; 10-inch-diameter Styrofoam® wreath form; 3 dozen 3-inch-long wooden picks; floral wire; floral tape; wire cutters or heavy scissors; 5 yards of ¼-inch-wide gold tinsel ribbon.

DIRECTIONS:

1. Insert the hydrangea heads into the wreath form using wooden picks and short pieces of floral wire covered with floral tape.

2. Make a bow with streamers from the gold tinsel ribbon, following the directions in Basic Bow and Streamers *(page 110).* Attach the bow to the wreath with floral wire. Scatter small gold tinsel bows on wooden picks around the wreath.

Poinsettia Wreath

POINSETTIA WREATH

EASY: Achievable by anyone.
MATERIALS: ½ yard of 45-inch-wide off-white slipper satin; 3½ yards of 3-inch-wide green velvet floral ribbon; clear acrylic spray varnish; ¼- to ⅜-inch-diameter pink, red and green glass beads; paper for patterns; dressmaker's carbon; floral wire; No. 30 brass wire; wire cutters; white glue; 2 small watercolor brushes; Alizarin Crimson watercolor paint (available in art supply stores); green fine-point permanent felt-tip pen; green floral tape; 18 inches of wide dark rose velvet ribbon; large Evergreen Wreath *(directions, page 97).*

DIRECTIONS:

1. Enlarge the patterns in FIG. III, 2 onto paper following the directions on page 239.

2. Sizing: Following manufacturer's directions, lightly spray wrong side of satin with two coats of acrylic varnish. Let coats dry between applications.

3. Cutting for Each Flower: Using the dressmaker's carbon, mark and cut six large and six small petals from the satin. Mark and cut two leaves from the green ribbon. Cut six 6-inch (large) and six 5-inch (small) lengths of floral wire for the petals. Cut two 6½-inch lengths of floral wire for the leaves. Cut eight 3-inch lengths of brass wire for the beads. Cut enough materials to make 14 poinsettias and 28 leaves.

4. Petals and Leaves: Stretch the edges of the petals to make them ripple. Starting ½ inch from the top point of a petal, center one of the pieces of floral wire lengthwise and glue it to the back of the petal. Repeat for the remaining large and small petals, and the leaves.

5. Painting: With right side up, brush half a petal, from base up, with water. Using a different brush, brush on the crimson paint, shading and softening the color as you work up and over one third of the petal *(see photo)*. Lightly color edges of the petal with the green felt-tip pen, then brush edges with water to soften the color. Repeat with remaining petals. For leaves, lightly sketch in veins *(see FIG. III, 2)* with the green pen. Color edges with the green pen, and soften color with water.

6. Flower Centers: Use eight beads per flower in a mixture of red, pink and green. For each bead, thread a 3-inch-long brass wire through the bead, ends even, and twist the ends. Then twist the wire ends of the eight beads together, leaving ½ inch of wire.

7. Assembling: Place six small petals, evenly spaced, around a bead center, twisting the wire ends together. Repeat with six large petals. From the top down, wrap the wire stem with floral tape, adding two leaves as you wrap. Repeat with the remaining bead centers, petals and leaves.

8. Wreath: Using photo as a guide, attach poinsettias to the wreath with floral wire. Tie the dark rose velvet ribbon into a bow; attach the bow at the top of the wreath with floral wire.

FIG. III, 2 POINSETTIA WREATH

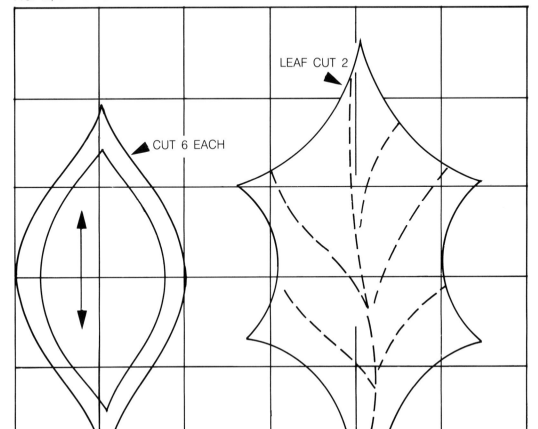

LEAF CUT 2

CUT 6 EACH

1 SQ. = 1"

CRANBERRY ORNAMENTS WREATH

Hang these country critters on your tree as individual ornaments, too.

EASY: Achievable by anyone.
MATERIALS: Scraps of gingham or checked fabric; synthetic stuffing; paper for patterns; grapevine wreath (we used a large one, and suspended a tiny wreath in the center); tie wire; string of red wooden beads.

DIRECTIONS
(¼-inch seams allowed):

1. Stuffed Bow: From the fabric, cut one 5 x 7-inch rectangle and two 2½ x 9½-inch strips.

2. Fold the 5 x 7-inch piece in half, short ends together, and stitch ¼ inch from the three raw edges, leaving 1 inch open on a long seam. Turn the rectangle right side out, and stuff it. Turn in the open edges, and slipstitch the opening closed.

3. Pin the two strips right sides together, and cut a slant at each end. Stitch the edges together, leaving an opening on a long edge. Turn the strip right side out, turn in the open edges, and slipstitch the opening closed. Wrap the strip tightly around the center of the rectangle to form the "bow." Slipstitch the strip in place.

4. Stuffed Ornaments: Enlarge the patterns in FIG. III, 3 onto paper, following the directions on page 239. Using the paper patterns on a double thickness of fabric, cut out the figures.

5. Stitch each pair right sides together, leaving a 1-inch opening for turning.

6. Turn each figure right side out, and stuff it. Turn in the open edges, and slipstitch the opening closed.

7. Using the photo as a placement guide, attach the stuffed figures to the grapevine wreath with tie wire. Thread the string of red wooden beads through the wreath.

FIG. III, 3 CRANBERRY ORNAMENTS WREATH

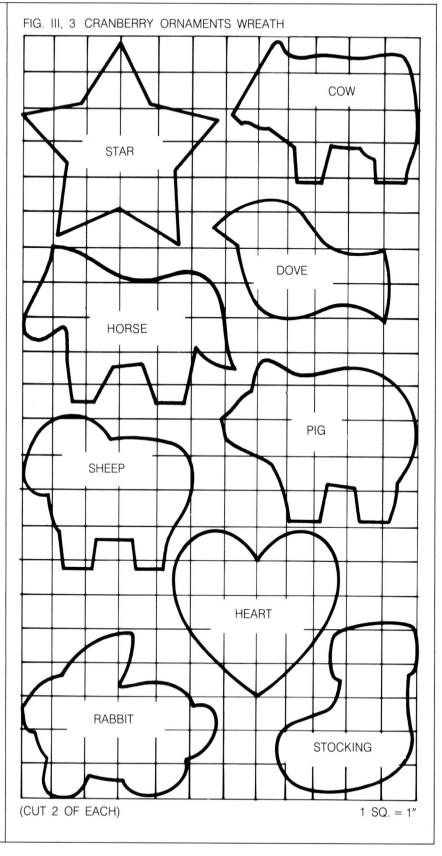

STAR
COW
DOVE
HORSE
SHEEP
PIG
HEART
RABBIT
STOCKING

(CUT 2 OF EACH)   1 SQ. = 1"

Cranberry Ornaments Wreath

Farm Country Wreath

FARM COUNTRY WREATH

Use this paper appliqué technique to make holiday gift tags and cards.

AVERAGE: For those with some experience in crafting.
MATERIALS: 20-inch square of lattice wood; ⅛-inch-thick craft wood; spray paints: white and black; green and red construction paper; drill and ⅛-inch bit; Dremel saw; tracing paper; graphite paper; sandpaper; glue; tie wire; 20- to 22-inch-diameter bleached grapevine wreath.

DIRECTIONS:
1. Enlarge the partial patterns in FIGS. III, 4A and 4B, and the full patterns in FIG. III, 4C, onto tracing paper, following the directions on page 239.
2. Square Motifs: Cut five 4-inch squares from the lattice wood. Spray the squares with the white paint.
3. Paper Appliqués *(glue each design to a white square)*: Cut four pattern A pieces from the green paper, and one ⅝-inch square from the red paper. Using the photo as a placement guide, glue the pieces in place counterclockwise. Fold a piece of tracing paper in half, and trace

partial pattern B on one half of the folded paper. Retrace the pattern on the other half. Open the paper for the full pattern. Cut the background from the red paper and the triangle from the green paper. Glue the pieces in place. Cut four C patterns from the green paper, and one 1-inch square from the red paper. Glue the pieces in place *(see photo)*. For the next motif, cut a 2-inch green paper square and glue it to the center of a white square. Cut four 1-inch squares from the red paper, and cut the squares again on the diagonal. Using the photo as a placement guide, glue the red triangles to the outside of the green square. Cut two ⅝-inch squares from the red paper, cut the squares on the diagonal, and glue the triangles pinwheel-style in the center of the green square. For the last motif, reverse the colors for pattern B.

4. Drill a hole in one corner of each square, add tie wire, and attach the square to the grapevine wreath using the photo as a placement guide.

5. Weathervane Figures: Using the tracing paper patterns and graphite paper, trace the figures in FIG. III, 4C onto the craft wood. Cut them out with the Dremel saw. Round all the edges with the sandpaper, and spray the figures with the black paint. Drill a hole in each figure, and add tie wire. Attach the figures to the wreath, alternating them with the paper appliqué squares.

FIG. III, 4C WEATHERVANE FIGURES 1 SQ. = 1"

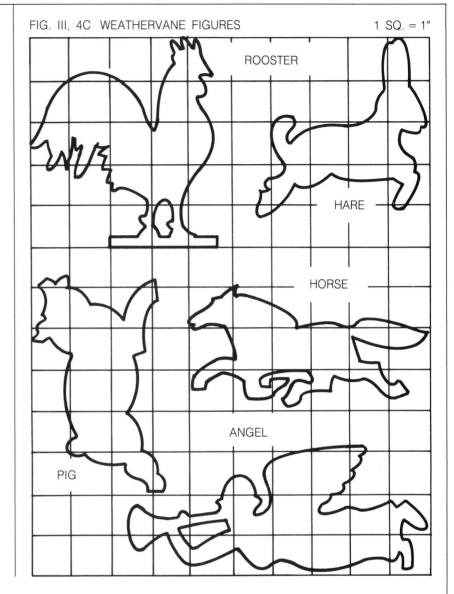

FIG. III, 4A QUILT BLOCK APPLIQUÉ PATTERNS

PEONY

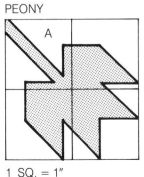

1 SQ. = 1"

GOOSE TRACKS

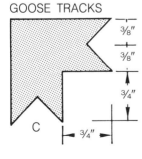

(MAKE FOUR)

FIG. III, 4B CACTUS HALF PATTERN

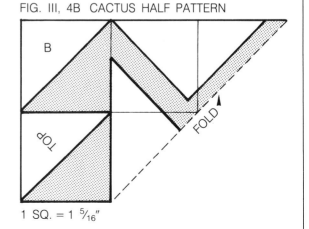

1 SQ. = 1 5/16"

Birds of Gold Wreath

BIRDS OF GOLD WREATH

AVERAGE: For those with some experience in origami.

MATERIALS: Gold foil gift wrap or gold origami paper; 16-inch-diameter Artificial Wreath *(directions, page 97)*; decorative gold sequins (we used stars, snowflakes, paillettes and leaves); glue; 4 feet of floral wire;

wire cutters; transparent tape; 6 yards each of gold novelty ribbon in three different widths.

Note: *The key to producing origami is careful, sharp creasing and perfectly matched edges and corners. Follow the diagrams in FIG. III, 5, A to O exactly.*

Continued on page 110

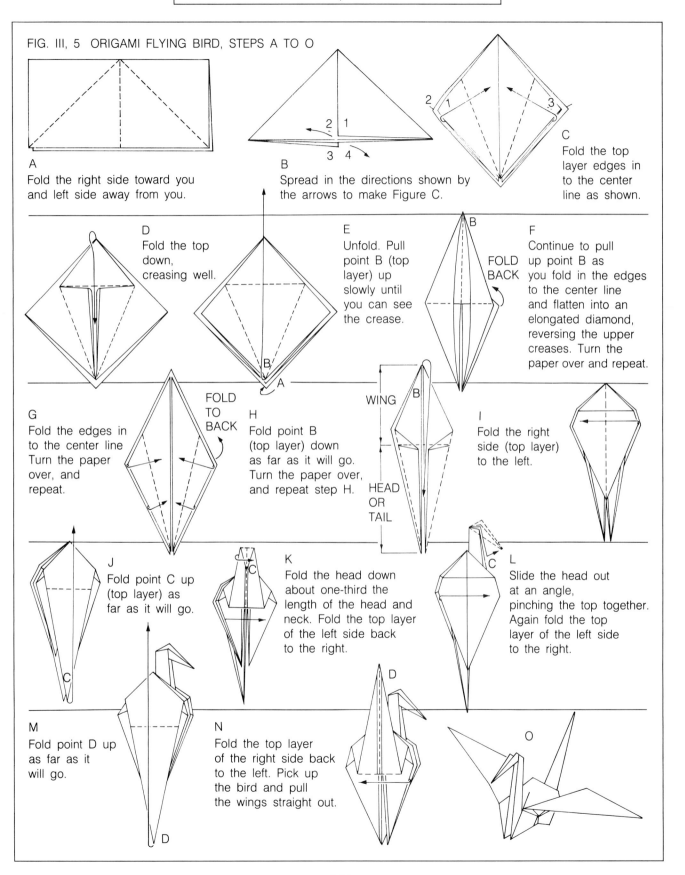

FIG. III, 5 ORIGAMI FLYING BIRD, STEPS A TO O

A
Fold the right side toward you
and left side away from you.

B
Spread in the directions shown by
the arrows to make Figure C.

C
Fold the top
layer edges in
to the center
line as shown.

D
Fold the top
down,
creasing well.

E
Unfold. Pull
point B (top
layer) up
slowly until
you can see
the crease.

F
FOLD
BACK
Continue to pull
up point B as
you fold in the edges
to the center line
and flatten into an
elongated diamond,
reversing the upper
creases. Turn the
paper over and repeat.

G
Fold the edges in
to the center line
Turn the paper
over, and
repeat.

FOLD
TO
BACK

H
Fold point B
(top layer) down
as far as it will go.
Turn the paper over,
and repeat step H.

WING

HEAD
OR
TAIL

I
Fold the right
side (top layer)
to the left.

J
Fold point C up
(top layer) as
far as it will go.

K
Fold the head down
about one-third the
length of the head and
neck. Fold the top layer
of the left side back
to the right.

L
Slide the head out
at an angle,
pinching the top together.
Again fold the top
layer of the left side
to the right.

M
Fold point D up
as far as it
will go.

N
Fold the top layer
of the right side back
to the left. Pick up
the bird and pull
the wings straight out.

O

DIRECTIONS:

1. Glue the gold sequins to the wreath leaves as desired.

2. Cut eight 6-inch squares from the gold foil or origami paper, and use one square for each bird. Fold a square in half to form a rectangle. Fold the rectangle in half again to form another square. Unfold the paper and continue to fold following the directions in FIG. III, 5, A to O *(page 109)*. When the bird is completed, inflate it by blowing gently into the small hole in its stomach. Make eight birds.

3. Cut the floral wire into eight 4-inch lengths, and tape each length to the bottom of a bird. Attach the birds to the wreath with the wires, spacing the birds evenly and leaving space at the top and bottom of the wreath *(see photo, page 108)*.

4. Using 3 yards each of the three different widths of gold ribbon for each bow, make two large bows with long streamers *(see Basic Bow and Streamers, at right)*. Attach the bows to the top and bottom of the wreath.

BASIC BOW AND STREAMERS

EASY: Achievable by anyone.
MATERIALS. Ribbon; floral wire; wire cutters or heavy scissors; transparent tape.

DIRECTIONS:

1. Bow: Cut the ribbon into 18-inch lengths, unless otherwise indicated. Fold the lengths into loops so the ribbons are right side out and the loose ends meet at the back. Wrap together two or three ribbon loops at a time with floral wire, gradually enlarging the loops, until the desired size bow is achieved.

2. Streamers: Cut several lengths of ribbon, and fold the lengths in half. Wrap the lengths together at the folds with floral wire.

3. Assembling: Cut a 5-inch length of floral wire for the bow, and another 5-inch length for the streamers. Bend each of the wires into a hairpin shape. Tape the bow to one bent wire and the streamers to the second. Wrap the bow and streamers together at their bases with the bent wires. Attach the bow and streamers to a wreath by either inserting the wires into the wreath form, or wrapping the wires around the wreath form. Or attach the bow and streamers individually to the wreath with floral wire.

BUTTONS AND BOWS WREATH
(18 inches in diameter)

EASY: Achievable by anyone.
MATERIALS: 16 yards of 2-inch-wide pink print craft ribbon; 12 yards of 1-inch-wide lace ribbon; 5 yards of 1¼-inch-wide pink print craft ribbon; 5 yards of 2-inch-wide white print craft ribbon; assorted mother-of-pearl buttons; 16-inch-diameter flat Styrofoam® wreath form; synthetic batting; pink thread; heavy-duty thread; glue stick; silicone glue; floral wire; wire cutters or heavy scissors.

DIRECTIONS:

1. Pad the entire wreath form with a 1-inch thickness of batting. Wrap with the heavy-duty thread to secure.

2. Wrap the wreath with the 2-inch-wide pink craft ribbon, overlapping the ribbon slightly. Secure the ribbon end with the glue stick.

3. Cut 24 lengths of the lace ribbon, each equal to the girth of the wreath. Wrap the strips around the wreath in groups of three *(see photo)*. Secure the ends with the glue stick.

4. Sew the pink thread through the button holes. Attach the "stitched" buttons to the wreath in groups *(see photo)* using the silicone glue.

5. Make four sets of Basic Bow and Streamers *(directions at left)*, using the 1¼-inch-wide ribbon, the white ribbon, the remaining lace ribbon and the floral wire. Sew a large button in the center of each bow to cover the wire. Trim the ribbon ends as shown. Insert the bows, evenly spaced, into the outer edge of the wreath.

SMALL WREATHS: Use 6- and 3-inch-diameter flat Styrofoam® wreath forms. Follow Steps 1 to 5 above, but omit the batting for the 3-inch wreath. Scale down the Bow and Streamers to match the wreaths, and use only 1 bow per wreath.

Buttons and Bows Wreath

BEAUTIFUL STOCKINGS

Taffeta & Lace Stocking; Victorian Brocade Stocking

TAFFETA & LACE STOCKING

AVERAGE: For those with some experience in sewing.

MATERIALS: ½ yard of gold taffeta or moire; ½ yard of white lace; ½ yard of polyester fleece interlining; ½ yard of white lining fabric; matching threads; medium-size pearl beads (amount varies with lace design); 1½ yards of white and gold lace trim; 1½ yards of 1½-inch-wide green velvet ribbon; ¼ yard of gold cord; paper for pattern.

DIRECTIONS
(½-inch seams allowed):

1. Enlarge the stocking pattern in FIG. III, 6, following the directions on page 239. Make a full-size paper pattern.
2. Using the pattern, cut out two stockings each from the taffeta or moire, lace, fleece and lining. Place one lace piece, right side up, on the right side of a taffeta piece. Place both on a fleece piece. Baste all the pieces together along all the edges. Repeat for the second set.
3. Sew on the pearl beads to accent the lace. Do not sew beads within the seam allowance.
4. Place the two sets of stocking pieces right sides together and all edges even. Sew them together along all but the top edge. Clip the seam at the curves. Turn the stocking right side out.
5. Sew the lining pieces right sides together; do not turn. Insert the lining into the stocking. Sew the top edges of the stocking and lining together.
6. For the ruffle, cut one 28 x 5¾-inch piece of taffeta with the short end parallel to the grain. On one long edge, turn up 1 inch to the right side of the fabric and baste in place near the raw edge.
7. Sew white and gold lace trim over the turned-up raw edge of the ruffle, with the trim's scalloped edge ¼ inch above the ruffle's folded edge. Pleat the ruffle's unhemmed long edge to fit

the top edge of the stocking.
8. Sew the pleated ruffle to the stocking near the raw edges. Turn under one of the ruffle's short ends at the back and sew it, overlapping slightly, to the other short end.
9. Sew the green velvet ribbon to the top edge of the stocking as binding. Sew white and gold lace trim over the ribbon, turning the top white edge under the gold before sewing.
10. Cut streamers from the green ribbon, and sew them to the stocking.
11. Make a bow of separate green ribbon loops sewn over the streamers. Sew a "knot" of green ribbon to the center of the bow.
12. Make a hanger from the gold cord, and sew it to the top of the stocking.

FIG. III, 6 TAFFETA & LACE/ VICTORIAN BROCADE STOCKING

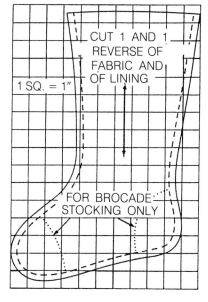

CUT 1 AND 1 REVERSE OF FABRIC AND OF LINING

1 SQ. = 1"

FOR BROCADE STOCKING ONLY

VICTORIAN BROCADE STOCKING

AVERAGE: For those with some experience in sewing.

MATERIALS: ½ yard of red metallic brocade; ½ yard of polyester fleece interlining; ½ yard of white lining fabric; 2 yards of 1-inch-wide white cotton lace; 4½ yards of ⅜-inch-wide green satin ribbon; 3½ yards of ¼-inch-wide gold picot edge braid; 1 yard 1½-inch-wide red velvet ribbon; matching threads; paper for pattern.

DIRECTIONS
(½-inch seams allowed):

1. Enlarge the stocking pattern in FIG. III, 6, following the directions on page 239. Make a full-size paper pattern.
2. Using the pattern, cut out two stockings each from the brocade, fleece and lining. Place one brocade piece, right side up, on a fleece piece. Baste them together along all the edges. Repeat for the second set. Mark the heel and toe on the right side of each brocade piece. Sew a straight edge of lace to each marking, gathering the lace as necessary to allow it to lie flat. Invisibly stitch the scalloped edge of the lace to the stocking. Sew one long edge of green satin ribbon slightly overlapping the straight edge of the lace. Sew the free edge of the green ribbon to the stocking, gathering the edge slightly as necessary. Sew gold picot edge braid over each edge of the green ribbon.
3. Place the two sets of stocking pieces right sides together. Sew them together along all but the top edge. Clip the seam at the curves. Turn the stocking right side out.
4. Sew the lining pieces right sides together; do not turn. Insert the lining into the stocking. Sew the top edges of the lining and stocking together.
5. For the cuff, cut two 18-inch-long pieces of red velvet ribbon and one 18-inch piece of the green satin

ribbon. Sew one long edge of each piece of velvet ribbon to each edge of the satin ribbon. Sew gold braid over each stitching line. Cut a 26-inch-long piece of lace. Gather it to fit one long edge of the velvet ribbon cuff. Sew the lace to the cuff. Sew gold braid over the stitching line. Sew green satin ribbon to the opposite long edge of the velvet ribbon cuff. Pin the cuff to the stocking, with the green ribbon inside the stocking as the binding. Sew the cuff to the stocking on the lining side, stitching along the free edge of green ribbon. Overlap and invisibly sew the short back ends of the cuff.

6. Make a half-rosette bow of 2-inch loops of green satin ribbon. Cut five green satin streamers of varying lengths, and sew them to the back of the bow. Sew the bow to the cuff.

7. Make a flat disc of gold braid, and sew it to the center of the bow. Make a hanger loop of green satin ribbon, and sew it to the inside top of the stocking.

NOËL PATCHWORK STOCKING
Extra large for extra goodies.

AVERAGE: For those with some experience in sewing.
MATERIALS: ⅜ yard each of red broadcloth, white piqué and muslin; ⅛ yard each of red stripe, red calico, green calico, red and green stripe, holly print and candy cane print fabrics; ⅜ yard of synthetic batting; ½ yard of ½-inch-wide cluny lace; ½ yard of 1-inch-wide eyelet beading with ¼-inch slits for ribbon; 1 yard of ¼-inch-wide red satin ribbon; matching threads; paper for pattern.

DIRECTIONS
(½-inch seams allowed):
1. Enlarge the stocking pattern in FIG. III, 7 *(page 116)*, following the directions on page 239. Make a full-size paper pattern.
2. Cutting: Using the pattern, cut one stocking from the red broadcloth for the back, two stockings from the muslin for the lining, and two stockings from the batting. For the cuff, cut a 9 x 16½-inch piece from the piqué and a 4½ x 16½-inch piece from the batting. Cut all the print and striped fabrics into 2 x 4-inch strips, for a total of 85 strips.
3. Patchwork: Using the photo as a guide, stitch the strips together at the short ends to make 17 rows of five strips each. Press open all the seams. Stitch the rows together so that the short seams of one row meet the center of the strips on the next row. The vertical edges of the patchwork piece will not be even. Press open the seams. Using the stocking pattern, cut one stocking from the patchwork for the front.
4. Quilting: Place one muslin stocking, wrong side up, on a flat surface. Place a batting stocking and then the patchwork stocking, right side up, on top. Baste the layers together at

the edges and across the front. Using 8 to 10 stitches per inch, machine quilt on top of all the seams.
5. Stocking Back: Place the remaining muslin stocking, wrong side up, on a flat surface. Place the remaining batting stocking and then the red broadcloth stocking, right side up, on top. Baste the layers together at the edges. Machine quilt the stocking back, if you wish.
6. Cuff: Baste the batting cuff piece to the wrong side of the piqué cuff piece. Stitch the 9-inch edges of the cuff together to form a ring. Press the seam open. Fold the cuff in half, wrong sides together, matching the raw edges, and crease the fold line. Open out the cuff. Baste the cluny lace to the cuff along the crease. Stitch the eyelet beading on top of the basted edge of the cluny lace. Refold the cuff and baste its raw edges together.
7. Finishing: Stitch the two sets of stocking pieces right sides together, leaving the top edge open. Trim and overcast stitch the seam. Turn the stocking right side out, and lightly press the edges flat. Cut a 7-inch length of red satin ribbon, fold it in half and baste the cut edges together, forming a loop for hanging. Position the hanging loop and stitch the cuff, right side out, to the wrong side of the stocking at the top edge, encasing the loop in the seam. Trim and overcast stitch the seam. Turn the cuff to the outside of the stocking. Thread the remaining length of ribbon through the slits in the eyelet beading, starting at the front center of the cuff *(see photo)*. Tie the excess ribbon into a bow at the front center of the cuff.
Note: The photo shows the stocking made without the "patchwork toe" and "patchwork heel" patterns shown on page 116. However, you may incorporate this additional patchwork in your stocking, if you wish.

Noël Patchwork Stocking

FIG. III, 7 NOËL PATCHWORK STOCKING

1 SQ. = 1"

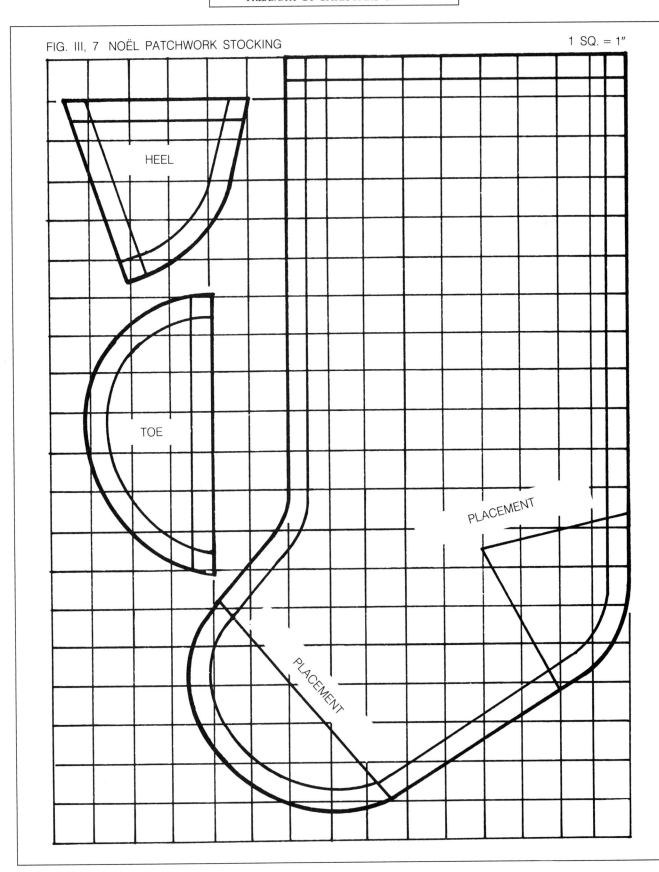

HEEL

TOE

PLACEMENT

PLACEMENT

Snow & Lace Stockings

SNOW & LACE STOCKING

Made from rich fabric, this stocking is a vision of beauty in winter white.

AVERAGE: For those with some experience in sewing.

MATERIALS: ½ yard of white or off-white velvet, brocade, Marseilles spread, silk, old quilt top, or fabric desired; ½ yard of unbleached muslin; 15 inches of lace trim of desired width; matching threads; paper for pattern.

DIRECTIONS
(½-inch seams allowed):

1. Enlarge the stocking pattern in FIG. III, 8 *(page 118)*, following the directions on page 239. Cut out a full-size paper pattern for the stocking.

2. Using the pattern, cut out two stockings each from the fabric and the muslin (turn over the pattern to make a front and a back).

3. Pin the fabric pieces right sides together, and stitch around the sides and bottom, but not across the top.

Trim the seam, clip the curves, turn the stocking right side out and press it. If you are using velvet, press on the wrong side of the fabric before turning the stocking. Then, with a cloth between the iron and the velvet, gently press around the edges of the turned stocking. Repeat with the muslin lining pieces, leaving a 3-inch opening in the toe seam. Trim the seam, clip the curves, but do not turn the muslin lining right side out.

4. Slide the fabric stocking inside the muslin lining so the right sides are together and the seams match. Stitch around the top, placing a fabric or ribbon loop for a hanger between the stocking and the liner so that the loop is attached in the rear seam. Turn the stocking right side out through the opening in the toe seam of the lining. Slipstitch the opening closed.

5. Position the muslin lining inside the stocking and press it. Pin the lace to the right side of the stocking, with the edge over and just inside the stocking, and slipstitch the lace in place.

FIG. III, 8
SNOW & LACE STOCKING

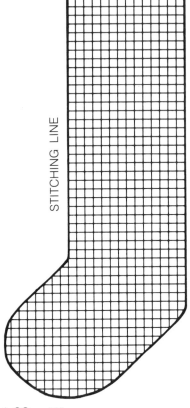

STITCHING LINE

1 SQ. = 1/2"

CHICKEN SCRATCH CHRISTMAS STOCKING

Embroider a bright holiday motif on gingham-checked fabric.

AVERAGE: For those with some experience in embroidery and sewing.

MATERIALS: 1/2 yard each of tan and white 1/8-inch check gingham, and lightweight lining fabric; matching threads; 6-strand embroidery floss: 1 skein each of Coffee, Emerald, Fuschia, Lavender, Light Emerald, Nectarine, Pale Green, Peach, Scarlet, Sky Blue and Tan; embroidery hoop; No. 7 embroidery needle.

Note: *The gingham checks are used as a guide for the embroidery stitches. Each square in Fig. III, 9 (page 121) represents one check on the gingham. All the embroidery is worked with two strands of floss, except the French knots and straight stitches, which use four strands (see Embroidery Stitch Guide, page 240). The gingham has three shades of tan checks — dark, medium and light — plus white.*

DIRECTIONS:

1. Hold the gingham so the lines of dark and medium-color tan run vertically. Cut two 12 x 20-inch pieces for the stocking front and back, with the 20-inch lengths placed vertically.

2. Outline the stocking shape in Fig. III, 9 *(page 121)* with sewing thread on one stocking fabric piece, allowing a 2-inch margin of fabric around the edges. Place the fabric in the embroidery hoop.

Continued on page 120

Chicken Scratch Christmas Stocking

3. Following the design and stitch details in FIG III, 9, and using the embroidery floss and needle, embroider the design starting with the girl and boy. Center the girl and boy on the upper part of the stocking outline 2 inches below the upper edge of the fabric. Start with the Coffee Star stitches, and work the stitches over a *white* check on the gingham. Work all the Star stitches first, following the symbols in the Key for the colors. Follow the Key for the symbols that indicate the French knot and Wheels and Spokes stitches, and the colors of these stitches (some symbols have been used several times to indicate the same stitch but in different colors). When the embroidery is finished, carefully press the fabric on the reverse side, using a pressing cloth.

4. Cut out the stocking shape on the embroidered fabric piece, leaving ½ inch of fabric beyond the stocking outline on the sides and bottom, and 1 inch on the top edge. Using the embroidered stocking piece as a guide, cut out the stocking back piece and two stocking lining pieces.

5. Baste a lining piece to the wrong side of each stocking piece. Pin the stocking pieces right sides together, and sew a ½-inch seam along all but the top edge. Turn down 1 inch on the top edge of the stocking, turn under the raw edge ¼ inch, and hem. Clip the seams at the curves and turn the stocking right side out.

6. Cut a 2 x 6-inch piece of gingham and fold it lengthwise. Fold both long raw edges to the center fold, and sew the folded edges together to secure. Place the two short ends together to form a loop, and sew the loop to the inside top of the stocking for a hanger.

GIRL/BOY
- ⊙ —Emerald Fr. knots
- ⊡ —Scarlet Fr. knots
- ✳ —Coffee Stars
- ⊠ —Emerald Stars
- A —Tan Wheels/Spokes
- ◪ —Fuschia
- J —Pale Green Wheels/Spokes

COOKYLAND
- ✳ —Coffee Stars
- CA —Scarlet Stars
- ON —Sky Blue Stars
- OD —Emerald Stars
- K —Fuschia Stars
- Y —Peach Stars
- L —Lt. Emerald Stars

HEARTS
- ✳ —Coffee Stars
- ⊡ —Coffee Fr. knots
- ⊠ —Sky Blue Stars
- ◪ —Fuschia Stars
- B —Peach Wheels/Spokes
- C —Lt. Emerald Wheels/Spokes
- D —Scarlet Wheels/Spokes
- ⊡ —Coffee Fr. knots
- ◮ —Lavender Stars

HOUSE
- ✳ —Coffee Stars
- ⊙ —Emerald Fr. knots
- ⊠ —Nectarine Stars
- ⊡ —Scarlet Fr. knots
- —Peach Stars, Wheels/Spokes
- ■ —Scarlet Stars
- ◇ —Scarlet Wheels/Spokes
- ⊡ —Lt. Emerald Fr. knots
- ⊗ —Sky Blue Stars
- ◪ —Fuschia Stars
- ◇ —Sky Blue Wheels/Spokes
- ▽ —Lavender Fr. knots
- ◨ —Fuschia Fr. knots
- S —Smoke-mix of Fuschia, Sky Blue, Lavender Fr. knots
- H —Fill with Coffee Wheels/Spokes
- LTE —Lt. Emerald
- E —Emerald
- --- —Coffee Straight stitches

STAR WORKED
ON GINGHAM

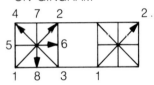

WHEEL WORKED
ON GINGHAM

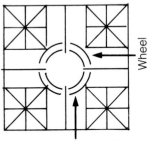

The Wheel is made by drawing the thread under 4 spokes twice.

SPOKES WORKED
ON GINGHAM

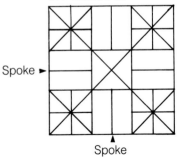

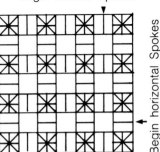

FIG. III, 9 CHICKEN SCRATCH CHRISTMAS STOCKING   1 SQ. = 1 GINGHAM CHECK

COFFEE
FR. KNOT
PATH

Outline of
finished stocking

Christmas Goose Stocking

CHRISTMAS GOOSE STOCKING

Muted colors and a simple country motif make this stocking a favorite.

CHALLENGING: Requires more experience in knitting and some experience in crocheting.

MATERIALS: Worsted weight wool: 1 skein each of Red, Natural and Gray, partial skeins each of Turquoise, Orange and Dark Green; 1 pair size 7 knitting needles, OR ANY SIZE NEEDLES TO OBTAIN GAUGE BELOW; 1 double-pointed needle in any size; stitch holder; size 5 or F crochet hook; tapestry needle.

GAUGE: In Stockinette Stitch (st st), 5 sts = 1 inch.

Notes: When changing colors, pick up the color to be used under the color previously used, twisting the yarns on the wrong side to prevent holes in the work. Carry the unused colors loosely on the wrong side of the work. When possible, use bobbins to eliminate bulk in the knitted work (for geese beaks and feet, hearts, trees).

The chart in FIG. III, 10 is shown upside down because the stocking is worked from the top (the cuff) down to the toe. Each square on the graph represents one stitch.

DIRECTIONS:

1. Cuff and Stocking: With Red yarn, cast on 52 sts. Work in k 1, p 1 ribbing for 1½ inches. Change to Natural. Starting with row 1 and working in st st (k 1 row, p 1 row), follow FIG. III, 10 to row 82. Follow the color key for the yarn color changes.

2. Heel: Take the first 13 sts from the single-pointed needle and put them on the double-pointed needle; the next 26 sts (for instep) are put on the stitch holder. Join Natural and k rem 13 sts. Turn the double-pointed needle around and, with the single-pointed needle, k the 13 sts off the other side of the double pointed needle. This will close the heel. Continue on these 26 sts in st st for 3 inches, ending with a k row.

To shape the heel, p 23, p 2 tog, p 1, turn. *Slip the first st as if to p, k until 3 sts rem, k 2 tog, k 1, turn. Slip the first st as if to p, p until 3 sts rem, p 2 tog, p 1, turn. Repeat from * until 16 sts rem. K last row.

Do not turn work. Pick up and k 10 sts on right side of heel. Turn and p back across heel (26 sts). Pick up and p 10 sts from left side of heel (36 sts). K 1 row. On next row and each k row, k 2 tog at each end 5 times (26 sts). Work the 11 rows from the Instep Hearts chart shown within the stocking chart in FIG. III, 10, beginning and ending with 3 or 4 sts in Natural. P 1 row. Break off Natural, attach Red. Work in st st on 26 sts for 2½ inches.

3. Toe, Row 1: *K 1, k 2 tog, work to last 3 sts, k 2 tog, k 1. **Row 2:** P. Repeat from * until 8 sts remain. Bind off.

4. Top of Foot: Using Natural, pick up the 26 sts from holder and work in st st. When work is same length to beg of Instep Hearts on foot bottom, repeat Instep. Change to Red and shape toe as directed in Step 3.

5. Finishing: Block the stocking lightly. Sew the back seam using matching yarn. Draw Red yarn through the bound-off stitches on the toe to close the opening; secure. Use matching yarns to sew the foot seams. Use Red yarn to sew the top 1½ inches of ribbing; leave the end loose. With the crochet hook, chain 4 inches with Red. Attach to the seam to form a hanging loop. Fasten off.

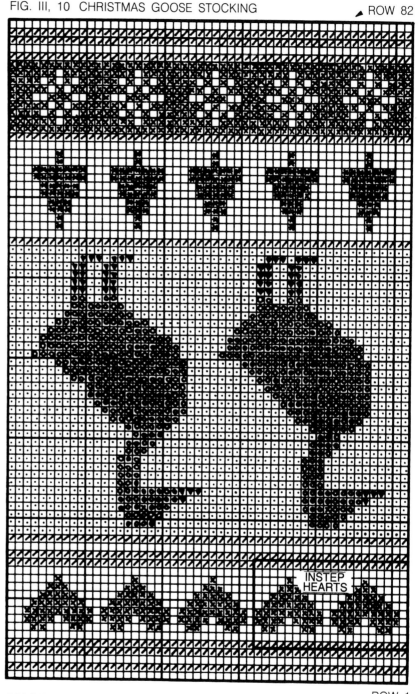

FIG. III, 10 CHRISTMAS GOOSE STOCKING ◢ ROW 82

INSTEP HEARTS

ROW 1

COLOR KEY

☒	= RED	◉	= NATURAL ON GRAY
✖	= DARK GREEN	▼	= ORANGE
◪	= TURQUOISE	⊡	= GRAY
		☐	= NATURAL

❧ ❧ ❧ ❧ ❧ ❧

DID YOU KNOW . . .

Just why, where and how the tradition of the Christmas stocking developed is uncertain.

One legend about the origin of the Christmas stocking is a story about St. Nicholas.

A nobleman had lost everything in an unsuccessful business venture, and thus had no money to provide dowries for his three unmarried daughters. St. Nicholas, hearing of the plight of the dowerless young women, decided to help them. In the dark of the night, he crept silently to their house and threw a bag of gold into the eldest daughter's room. Legend has it that the bag of gold fell into a stocking hung near the fire to dry — and so began the tradition of hanging a stocking on the mantel in hopes of receiving gifts.

SATIN STOCKINGS

Use your scraps of lace and ribbon in any way that suits your fancy. Large or small, no two stockings will be alike.

AVERAGE: For those with some experience in sewing.

MATERIALS FOR ONE STOCKING: ½ yard of 45-inch-wide satin; lace and satin ribbons of varying widths, including 1¼-inch-wide lace or ribbon, and 2½-inch-wide lace; matching threads; pearl stamens; artificial leaves; white floral tape; clear acrylic spray; glue; paper for patterns.

DIRECTIONS
(½-inch seams allowed):
1. Enlarge the patterns in FIG. III, 11, following the directions on page 239. Make a full-size paper pattern for each stocking size you wish to make.
2. Size the satin by spraying it on the wrong side of the fabric with two coats of acrylic spray. Allow the coats to dry completely between applications.
3. Using the patterns, cut out two large or two small stockings from the satin. Using the photo as a guide, pin pieces of lace and ribbon to the right side of one of the stocking pieces (front). Stitch the lace and ribbons in place. With right sides together, sew the plain stocking back to the front except along the top edge.
4. Cut a 5-inch-wide strip of satin 1 inch longer than the top edge of the stocking. Stitch pieces of lace and ribbon across the strip. Sew the short ends of the strip together. Stitch the cuff to the stocking, wrong sides up, along the top edges.
5. Turn the stocking right side out and turn down the cuff. Fasten flowers or lace rosettes to the cuff.

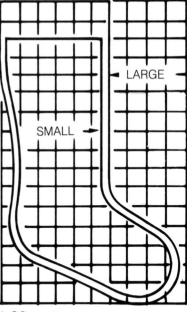

FIG. III, 11 SATIN STOCKINGS

LARGE

SMALL

1 SQ. = 1″

6. Flower: Cut a 6-inch length of 1¼-inch-wide lace or ribbon. Glue the cut ends together. Make a running stitch at the bottom long edge, pull up tightly, and fasten the thread ends. Insert pearl stamens at the center of the flower. Wrap the gathered edge of the ribbon and the stamen stems with floral tape. Add leaves, or colored ribbon bows and streamers.
7. Lace Rosette: Gather one edge of a 12-inch strip of 2½-inch-wide lace. Tack the rosette to the cuff. Tack bows and streamers of colored ribbons to the center of the rosette.
8. Tack a ribbon loop to the inside of the stocking's back seam for a hanger.

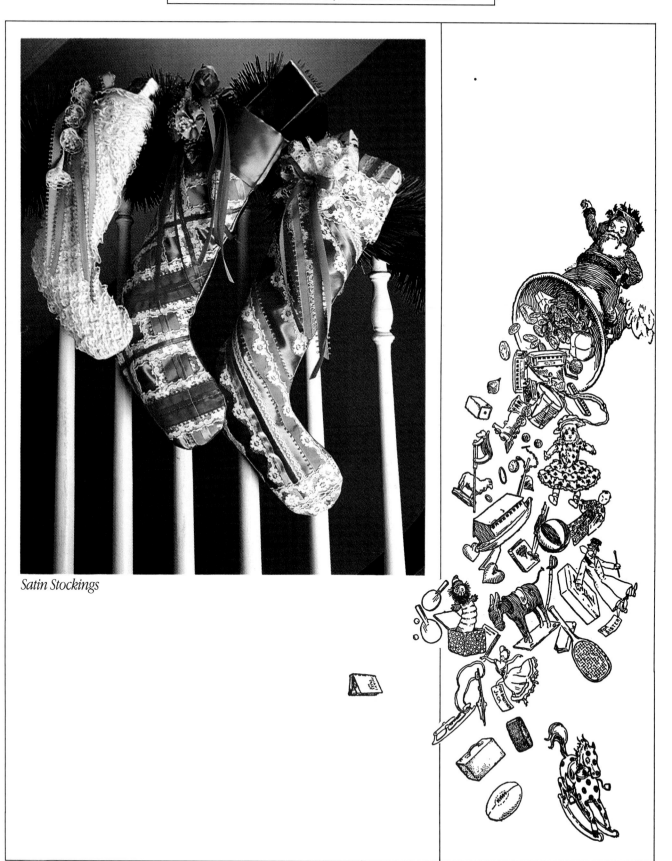

Satin Stockings

Beautiful Bay Window (directions, page 133)

Outdoor Magic

ecember is the time of year that houses look especially beautiful. This year, make your home a vision of beauty that delights your family and welcomes friends. Creating a little outdoor magic with lights and decorations sets the scene for the wonders inside your house, and cheers everyone passing by.

Outdoor decoration can range from elaborate to easy. Keep individual pieces fairly simple in design, and sturdy enough to stand rough weather. Remember to check the wires and plugs on outdoor lights every year before putting them up, and be sure any items attached to the roof or front of the house are secured firmly. Double-check the safety features of any pieces accessible to children or pets (including the type of paint used).

Try to use colors and decorating themes that suit the style of your house. If you have an older house in Victorian style, let the architecture dictate the decor; the same theory applies to a "deco" house or a Western ranch-style house.

The projects in this chapter include something for everyone, at every level of expertise. We provide fresh and lovely ideas for window dressing, a beautiful outdoor crèche for experienced woodworkers to craft, and a simple, sensational walkway studded with lights to welcome all to your holiday home.

Your home is the heart of your Christmas celebration—make it as wonderful outside as it is inside.

WINDOW
WONDERLAND

Snow & Ice

SNOW & ICE

We created this wonderfully wintery look with three different kinds of clear, white lights.

EASY: Achievable by anyone.
MATERIALS: Evergreen garland; three small to medium-sized pine trees; two small potted pine trees; strings of white icicle lights; strings of clear, white miniature lights; strings of clear, white regular-size lights; paper; scissors; aerosol snow; masking tape; paper toweling; glass cleaner.

DIRECTIONS:

1. Outline the top and sides of the window frame with the evergreen garland. String the icicle lights along the garland. String the miniature lights on the three pine trees and set them indoors, in front of the window. String the regular-size lights on the potted trees and place the trees outside, on either side of the window *(see photo)*.
2. Enlarge the stencil quarter patterns in FIGS. IV, 1A and 1B, onto paper squares following the directions on page 239. Fold the paper squares in half, then in half again, and then diagonally from the center point so the stencil lines are on top. Cut out the shapes along the fold lines, following the stencil patterns. Most cutouts are V's or half circles in different sizes and combinations. Do not cut away the edges of the squares, and be careful to leave space between the cutouts; these are stencils, not cutout snowflakes.
3. Tape the stencils to the window with masking tape. Create "snowflakes" by spraying the aerosol snow over the stencils.
4. Carefully peel away the tape, and gently remove the stencils. Wipe the areas around the sprayed snowflakes clean with paper toweling dampened with glass cleaner. Do not spray glass cleaner directly on the window, or the snowflakes may run.

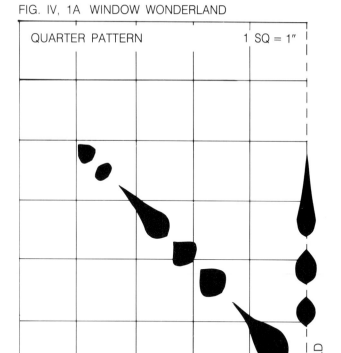

FIG. IV, 1A WINDOW WONDERLAND

QUARTER PATTERN   1 SQ = 1″

FOLD

FOLD

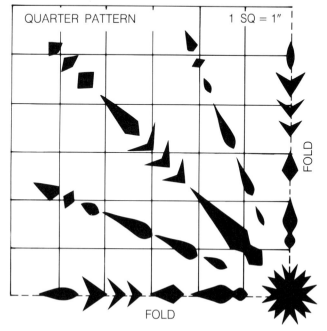

FIG. IV, 1B WINDOW WONDERLAND

QUARTER PATTERN   1 SQ = 1″

FOLD

FOLD

ICICLE MAGIC
Create a magical effect with evergreen boughs and icicle lights.

EASY: Achievable by anyone.
MATERIALS: Evergreen boughs or garlands; strings of white icicle lights.

DIRECTIONS: Using the photo as a guide, outline the window with the evergreen boughs or garlands. String the icicle lights only along the top and bottom of the window frame, to create the look of real icicles hanging from the window.

WONDERFUL YULETIDE WINDOWS

Line up a few potted evergreens on the windowsill, and add some tinsel, white miniature lights and artificial snow.

Use evergreen garlands to tie back drapes, and to decorate windowsills and window panes. Decorate the garlands with miniature lights, ornaments, ribbon bows or pine cones.

Put leftover ribbon to use: Make bows of various sizes, and use them to decorate window panes and sills. Or outline the outside edges of the windows with wider ribbon. Hang ribbon streamers from the tops of window frames and attach ornaments, pine cones, gingerbread men or cookie cutters to the streamers.

Icicle Magic

Twinkling lights shining through the winter darkness are one of the loveliest sights of the season. And outdoor lighting is easy to vary, so you can try a different color or theme each year. Red and green are traditional, all white or gold are strikingly elegant, and multi-colors provide a bright, cheery look. Use the architecture of your house to its full advantage: windows, arches, columns, deep porches. And don't forget trees, shrubs, fences, even bird houses—let the spirit of the season be your guide!

A LIGHT IN THE WINDOW

Real candles can't be left unattended in a window, but the electric "candles" shown in the photo are as pretty as the real thing.

EASY: Achievable by anyone.
MATERIALS: Strings of clear, white miniature lights; strings of amber-colored miniature lights; battery-operated candle lights; artificial doves; tie wire.

DIRECTIONS:

1. Frame each window with the white miniature lights. Place one battery-operated candle light in the center of each light-framed window.
2. Decorate indoor house plants with the amber-colored miniature lights and artificial doves, using tie wire to attach the doves to the plants.

BEAUTIFUL BAY WINDOW

Is your home blessed with a bay window? Now's the time to show it off! Ordinary colored Christmas lights might overwhelm the charm and elegance of the window. Transparent miniature lights emit softer, almost pastel colors that look graceful, not garish. Shown on page 126.

EASY: Achievable by anyone.
MATERIALS: Strings of clear, multi-colored miniature lights.

DIRECTIONS:

Using the photo on page 126 as a guide, outline the trim of the bay window with the miniature lights. Place your decorated Christmas tree in front of the window for a spectacular view from outdoors.

VISIONS OF DE-LIGHT

Icicle lights are a pleasant change from the standard round or "flame" bulbs, but why stop there? There are strings of lights in all sorts of wild and whimsical shapes: carriage lamps, candles, even frogs and jalapeño peppers. Read the manufacturer's directions before hanging light strings. If your novelty light set is not recommended for outdoor use, hang it indoors to frame a window.

For a dramatic look to your outside lighting display, try floodlighting evergreens. Use blue, green, clear, or deluxe white mercury lamps — these colors enhance the colors of evergreens. Avoid using red, yellow, amber or pink lamps, which turn the trees a muddy brown color.

Illuminate deciduous trees as well as evergreens. Flood a tree with a single spotlight to highlight its shape and pattern. Or place shiny ornaments on the tree, and light it from below with several smaller spotlights. If the tree is close enough to the house, use strings of small lights for a festive look.

Get more sparkle and glitter by using transparent bulbs. These, unlike color-coated bulbs, allow the filaments to show through.

Use light bulb colors that are in the same color family. Blue and green are "cool colors." Red, orange, yellow and white are "warm."

Place floodlights and spotlights in strategic positions. Your efforts at holiday time can be left in place and used year-round for beauty and security.

Set up your display while it's still light outside, then check the effect after dark; you can't get an accurate picture in daylight. Note whatever adjustments you want to make, and wait until it's light again to change the display. Be careful when using a ladder outside; have a helper steady the ladder while you work.

Every year, before setting up your illumination display, check the light sets for cracked insulation, frayed wires or damaged sockets. Any one of these can cause a short circuit.

Don't overload string sets. Check the manufacturer's directions on each package to find out how many light sets can be connected together.

Avoid overloading circuits. Most home circuits can take 15 amps, or 1,800 watts. If you're not sure, play it safe and scale down your lighting display.

Cover each outdoor plug and connector joint with plastic wrap to protect it from rain, sleet and snow; seal the wrapped joint with electrical tape.

If you use staples instead of tape to secure lights, be sure they're **insulated** staples.

Make sure your decorations pose no danger to children or pets: Don't leave cords dangling, loose on the floor, or on the stairs.

Note: *If you have questions about using decorative lights outdoors, call the GE Answer Center® information service 24 hours a day: 1-800-626-2000.*

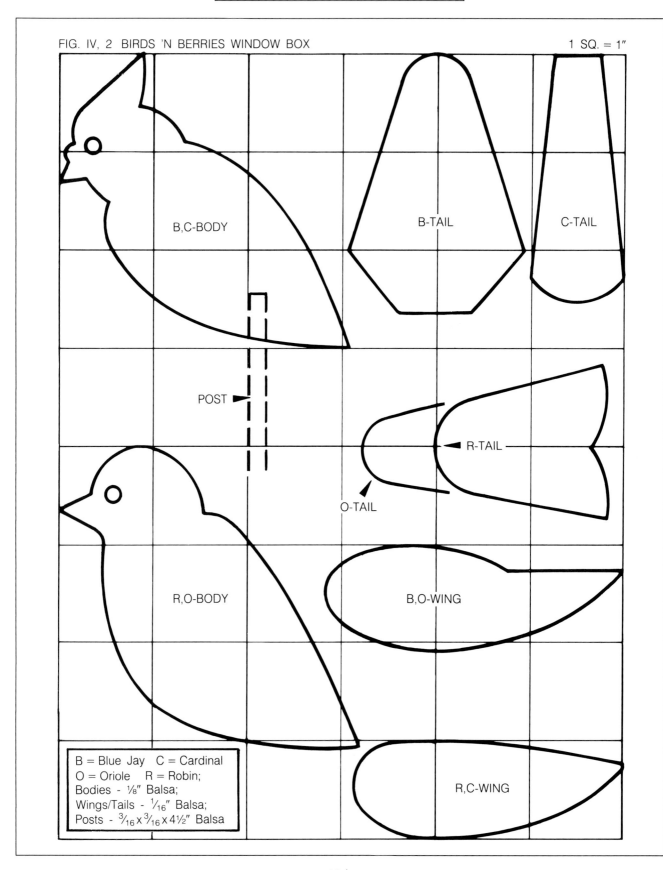

FIG. IV, 2 BIRDS 'N BERRIES WINDOW BOX

1 SQ. = 1"

B,C-BODY

B-TAIL

C-TAIL

POST

R-TAIL

O-TAIL

R,O-BODY

B,O-WING

R,C-WING

B = Blue Jay   C = Cardinal
O = Oriole   R = Robin;
Bodies - ⅛" Balsa;
Wings/Tails - ¹⁄₁₆" Balsa;
Posts - ³⁄₁₆ x ³⁄₁₆ x 4½" Balsa

Birds 'n Berries Window Box

BIRDS 'N BERRIES WINDOW BOX

Make some extra birds and hang them indoors, or outdoors from trees.

AVERAGE: For those with some experience in woodworking.
MATERIALS: ⅛-inch-thick balsa wood; ¹⁄₁₆-inch-thick balsa wood; ³⁄₁₆ x ³⁄₁₆ x 4½-inch balsa wood posts; tracing paper; graphite paper; stylus or old ballpoint pen; saw; sandpaper; flat polyurethane paints: red, black, white, gray, gold and medium blue; paintbrush; tacky glue; floral wire; real or artificial holly berries; gingham ribbon bow.

DIRECTIONS:
1. Enlarge the patterns in Fig. IV, 2 onto tracing paper, following the directions on page 239. Transfer the patterns to the balsa wood using the graphite paper and the stylus or ballpoint pen.
2. Cut out the pattern pieces from the balsa wood, and sand any rough edges.
3. Using the photo as a color guide, paint the bird parts and let them dry. Glue the parts together. Glue each bird to a post (*see* Fig. IV, 2).
4. Wire the holly berries into clumps, and scatter the clumps throughout the window box greenery. Arrange the birds in the box, inserting the posts gently. Attach wire to the bow, and insert the wire ends into the box.

SCENES OF THE SEASON

Stairway to Heaven

STAIRWAY TO HEAVEN

If you like, stencil the terra cotta pots with simple seasonal motifs. Try our snowflake stencils on page 129, or create your own.

EASY: Achievable by anyone.
MATERIALS: Terra cotta pots; tall red candles; hurricane shades; sand; gravel; strings of clear, white miniature lights.

DIRECTIONS:

Fill each terra cotta pot with sand, and insert a candle. Top the sand with gravel, and add a hurricane shade. Complete the scene by entwining the white miniature lights in nearby foliage. After the guests have arrived, bring the candles indoors to use as table or mantel decorations, or extinguish them; do not leave the candles burning outdoors all evening.

DECKING THE HALLS

If you live in a climate where the temperature drops below freezing, make and hang "ice panels" outside your house. For each panel, coil yarn around the bottom of a tin pie pan, leaving an end free to use as a hanger. Pour some water in the bottom of the pan. When the water is almost frozen, place leaves, nuts or grains on top in a pretty arrangement. Let the items freeze in place, pour a little more water on top, and freeze completely. When the panel is frozen solid, gently press it out of the pan; if the panel sticks, briefly dip the bottom of the pan in hot water. Hang ice panels from the branches of trees or from the eaves of your roof.

Make paper snowflakes. Plain, white bond or typing paper works very well for these pretty decorations. Fold the paper in half, then in half again, and finally along the diagonal from the center. Cut out small shapes along the folded edge (geometric shapes work best), then cut along the other side, following the fold cuts. Make sure to leave enough connecting paper on the folded edge and at the center so the snowflake keeps its shape. Carefully open the snowflake. Press it under a heavy book, or very lightly with a dry iron. Affix the snowflakes to windows or glass doors with double sided tape or a glue stick. Like real snowflakes, no two designs will be alike!

Turn your front door into a Christmas present. Cover the door with wrapping paper: Metallics give pizzazz, plain brown paper adds a country touch, pretty florals are Victorian. Run a wide ribbon across the door both vertically and horizontally. Tie a big bow from a piece of the same ribbon, and attach the bow to the ribbon on the door. Add sprigs of holly or dried flowers, if you like. (Ribbon designed for outdoor use can be found in the tree-trimming department of most stores.)

Make homemade lanterns. Fill coffee cans with water to within $1/8$ inch of the rim, and place them in the freezer; the ice will keep the cans from losing their shape while you work on them. Measure the height and circumference of the cans. Using these measurements, draw a square on a piece of paper. Create a stencil design on the paper square, and cut out the square. Tape the paper to a can, and place the can on its side on a folded towel. Using a hammer and nail, make evenly spaced holes along the lines of the pattern, tapping the nail firmly two or three times to make each hole. When the design is complete, remove the paper pattern. Repeat with each can, or create and hammer a different design onto each. Allow the ice to melt, drain the water, dry the cans, and spray them with aluminum paint. Secure a votive candle in each can. Candles can be a fire hazard, so keep the flames below the tops of the lanterns, and keep the lanterns out of children's reach.

FIG. IV, 3 CANDY CANE LANE

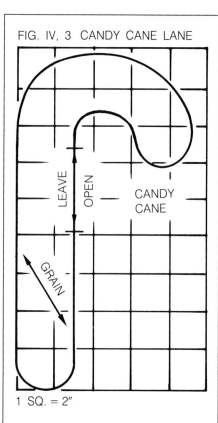

LEAVE OPEN

CANDY CANE

GRAIN

1 SQ. = 2"

CANDY CANE LANE

By weatherproofing these candy canes, you can use them for many Christmases to come.

EASY: Achievable by anyone.
CANDY CANES
(about 15 inches tall)
MATERIALS: Several different types of red or green striped fabric, weatherproofed with a stain-repellent finish; matching threads; 2½-inch-wide ribbons in a variety of red patterns; synthetic stuffing; paper for pattern.

DIRECTIONS
(¼-inch seams allowed):
1. Enlarge the pattern in FIG. IV, 3 onto paper, following the directions on page 239.
2. For each candy cane, cut a pair of candy canes from a piece of fabric, reversing the pattern to make both sides. Follow the grainline indicated in the pattern to be sure the stripes run in the right direction.
3. Stitch the candy cane front to the back, right sides together, leaving an opening between the short lines marked on the pattern.
4. Turn the candy cane right side out, and stuff it firmly. Slipstitch the opening closed.
5. Tie a ribbon bow around each candy cane, or tie two or three candy canes together with a bow.

CANDY CANE BASKET
(about 15 x 20 x 12 inches)
MATERIALS: Red or green striped fabric, weatherproofed with a stain-repellent finish; matching sewing thread; carpet thread; synthetic stuffing; sturdy needle; three 5 x 8½ x 2-inch pieces of Styrofoam®; white glue; 2½-inch-wide patterned red ribbon; artificial greenery *(optional)*; heavy wire; floral wire.

DIRECTIONS:
1. Stack and glue together the Styrofoam® pieces. Draw a curve from the center of one 8½-inch-long edge to each end of the opposite edge. Cut along the curve.
2. Make ten candy canes, following the directions at left. Using the carpet thread and sturdy needle, sew the candy canes together side by side, taking long stitches through the backs 2 inches from the bottom. Repeat near the top curves.
3. Cut a 40-inch length of the red ribbon and weave it through the canes, starting 3 inches from the bottom. Repeat just above the first ribbon *(see photo)*.
4. Fold ten 12-inch lengths of the heavy wire into U shapes. Hold the canes against the foam curve so that they extend 3 inches below the curve. Push a wire U around each cane underneath the ribbon into the foam. Pull the ribbon ends to the back of the foam curve, and fasten them with smaller heavy wire U's.
5. Push a wire U into the top of the foam near the center back edge. Push lengths of the floral wire into the backs of some canes, and tie the floral wires to the central fastener.
6. Wire a ribbon bow to the "basket" *(see photo)*. If you wish, fill the basket with artificial greenery.

Candy Cane Lane

Outdoor Crèche

OUTDOOR CRÈCHE
(26 x 65 x 69 inches)
If you are an experienced woodworker, try using the crèche figure patterns as full-size patterns for a balsa wood tabletop crèche. Scale down the stable accordingly.

CHALLENGING: Requires more experience in woodworking and craftwork.

MATERIALS: AB-EXT grade plywood: four 4-foot x ½-inch sheets, one 48 x 68 x ¼-inch sheet, and one 17 x 68 x ¼-inch sheet; lumber: 6 feet of 1 x 1, 29 feet of 1 x 2, 6 feet of 1 x 4, and 23 feet of 2 x 4; 1-inch and 1½-inch flathead wood screws; 2d and 4d finishing nails; ¾-inch and 1-inch brads; waterproof glue; four 3-inch flat corner braces; two 3-inch T braces; 2 x 7-foot sheet of Mylar® (opaque, thin plastic sheet available at art supply stores); 10 feet of ⅛-inch-diameter copper or aluminum wire or rod; 6 screw-eyes to fit diameter of wire; flat paint: beige and medium green; wood stain *(optional)*; 48-inch-long fluorescent shop light fixture, or regular lightbulbs, or floodlight bulbs; power saw; jig or sabre saw; hammer; drill and screwdrill set; screwdriver; staple gun; portable belt sander; C clamps; sandpaper.

DIRECTIONS:

1. Stable: Refer to FIG. IV, 4A *(page 143)* for the cutting directions. The A1 bottom is cut from one sheet of ½-inch plywood, the B sides from the second sheet, and the E front and F top from the third sheet. The remaining ½-inch plywood is for the figures and palm trees.

2. Stable Bottom: Lay the A bottom rails on the floor on their 1½-inch sides 24 inches apart. Glue, and nail with 4d nails, the A1 bottom to the top edges of the A rails, flush all around *(see FIG. IV, 4A)*.

3. Stable Sides: Place a B side face down on a flat surface. Glue, and nail with 2d nails, a B1 cleat to, and flush with, one long (back) edge of the B side and 4 inches from its bottom edge. Glue and nail a B2 cleat to the opposite long edge 1½ inches from the top edge. Repeat for the opposite B side *(see FIG. IV, 4A)*.

4. Stable Back: Cut a 5-inch-diameter hole 12 inches from each end of the D1 back and 8½ inches from one long edge. Place the D and D1 backs face down on a flat surface, and butt their edges to form a 65 x 68-inch piece. Glue, and nail with 2d nails, the D2 cleat to the D/D1 back, centered over the joint and 1¼ inches from each end of D/D1 *(see FIG. IV, 4A)*.

5. Stable Top: Place the F top face down on a flat surface. Glue and clamp the C top rails, wide side down, to the F top 1 inch from each end, 1 inch from one long edge, and ¾ inch from the other long edge. When the glue has dried, turn over the top and remove the clamps. Using 4d nails, nail through the F top into the C rails.

6. Stable Front: Enlarge the star pattern in FIG. IV, 4B *(page 143)*, following the directions on page 239. Trace the star onto the E front as shown in FIG. IV, 4A. Drill a starter hole, and cut out the star with the jig or sabre saw. Sand the inside edges of the cutout. Place the E front face down on a flat surface. Glue, and nail with 1-inch brads, the E1 diffuser support to the back of the E front, 1¼ inches from each end and 15¼ inches from the top edge *(see FIG. IV, 4A)*. Cut a piece of Mylar® large enough to cover the star cutout on the E front. Staple the Mylar® to the back of E, covering the star.

7. Assembling the Stable: With the aid of a helper, place the B sides on end, butted against the A bottom rails and flush at the side edges. Screw a 1½-inch wood screw through one B side into the center of each A rail. Repeat on the opposite B side. Using 1-inch wood screws, screw the D/D1 back to the B1 cleats on the B sides. Be sure the back is flush with the side edges. Using 1½-inch wood screws, screw the E front to the B2 cleats on the B sides. Be sure the front is flush at the top and sides of B. Place the F top on top of the assembly. The C top rails should fit between the B sides, butted against the front and back inner top sides. Screw the E front to the front C top rail with 1½-inch wood screws. Screw the D/D1 back to the back C top rail with 1-inch wood screws. Paint the inside of the stable beige. Paint the outside of the stable medium green.

8. Light Diffuser: Lay the G and G1 diffuser frame pieces on a flat surface. Attach them to each other with the corner braces at the corners and the T braces at the center. Turn over the diffuser frame, and staple the G2 Mylar® piece to it.

9. Lighting: Depending on what you have and what you are willing to spend, hang a 48-inch-long fluorescent shop light fixture, regular light bulbs or floodlight bulbs from the underside of the stable top, above the diffuser *(see* FIG. IV, 4A*)*.

10. Crèche Figures: Paint the remaining ½-inch plywood medium green, and belt-sand it lightly to give it an antique look. Or, if you wish, stain and wipe the plywood to get a similar effect. Enlarge the patterns in FIGS. IV, 4B to 4G *(pages 143-147)*, and trace them onto the plywood. Cut out the figure pieces with the jig or sabre saw. The figures are assembled like a jigsaw puzzle *(see photo, page 140)*.

11. Shepherd: Glue, and nail with ¾-inch brads, the straight lamb legs to the Shepherd. Using 2d nails, nail the lamb to the legs, and the lamb's ear to its head. Glue, and nail with ¾-inch brads, the Shepherd's head piece, crook, hair piece and arm in place. Glue and nail the hand to the crook, and the headband to the head piece.

12. Holy Family: Glue and nail Joseph's body piece 2 to body piece 1. Glue and nail his head piece, beard and arm in place. Then glue and nail his headband to his head piece. Glue, and nail with ¾-inch brads, Mary's body to Joseph's body piece 1, butted against Joseph's body piece 2 *(see photo)*. Glue and nail Mary's robe, head and hand in place. Glue and nail Joseph's hand to his arm. Glue, and nail with 1-inch brads, the crib straight inner legs to Mary's body, then the crib and outer legs to the inner legs. Glue, and nail with ¾-inch brads, the halo to the Child's head at the back. Then glue, and nail with 1-inch brads, the Child's head to Mary's body, butted against the crib edge.

13. Wise Men: Using the photo on page 140 as a placement guide, assemble the first Wise Man. Glue, and nail with ¾-inch brads, the second Wise Man to the first. Repeat to attach the third Wise Man to the second. In turn, glue and nail in place the second and third Wise Man's beard, moustache, arm, crown, and so on.

14. Palm Trees: Nail, *but do not glue,* the palm tree trunks to the front edges of the stable sides *(see photo)*. Nail two groups of palm leaves to the stable front, with a center leaf nailed to the center of each group.

15. The figure groups are held in place with a screw-eye halfway up the back of each group. A corresponding screw-eye is screwed into the stable back. Make three hooks from the ⅛-inch-diameter wire or rod, and run one hook between each pair of screw-eyes.

16. To take apart the stable, knock off the palm tree trunks and leaves. Unscrew the top, front, sides and back of the stable for storage.

*OVERNIGHT SENSATIONS:
FAST AND EASY
DECORATIONS*

F*ill window boxes with glitter-covered pine cones, and tie a weatherproofed ribbon around each box.*

W*ind greens around the gate post, and tie the post with a red oilcloth bow.*

R*eplace the light bulbs near the front door with colored bulbs for a festive look.*

H*ang a small sled on the front door. Pad the runners so they don't scratch the door.*

S*tuff an extra-large stocking with synthetic stuffing, and place a stuffed animal peeking out of the top to greet guests.*

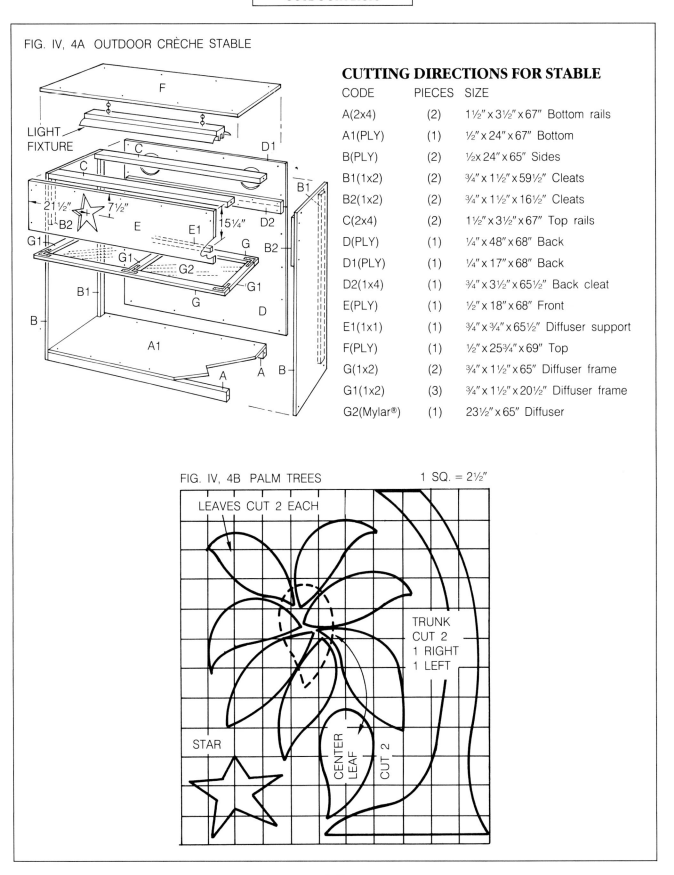

FIG. IV, 4A OUTDOOR CRÈCHE STABLE

LIGHT
FIXTURE

CUTTING DIRECTIONS FOR STABLE

CODE	PIECES	SIZE
A(2x4)	(2)	1½″ x 3½″ x 67″ Bottom rails
A1(PLY)	(1)	½″ x 24″ x 67″ Bottom
B(PLY)	(2)	½x 24″ x 65″ Sides
B1(1x2)	(2)	¾″ x 1½″ x 59½″ Cleats
B2(1x2)	(2)	¾″ x 1½″ x 16½″ Cleats
C(2x4)	(2)	1½″ x 3½″ x 67″ Top rails
D(PLY)	(1)	¼″ x 48″ x 68″ Back
D1(PLY)	(1)	¼″ x 17″ x 68″ Back
D2(1x4)	(1)	¾″ x 3½″ x 65½″ Back cleat
E(PLY)	(1)	½″ x 18″ x 68″ Front
E1(1x1)	(1)	¾″ x ¾″ x 65½″ Diffuser support
F(PLY)	(1)	½″ x 25¾″ x 69″ Top
G(1x2)	(2)	¾″ x 1½″ x 65″ Diffuser frame
G1(1x2)	(3)	¾″ x 1½″ x 20½″ Diffuser frame
G2(Mylar®)	(1)	23½″ x 65″ Diffuser

FIG. IV, 4B PALM TREES   1 SQ. = 2½″

LEAVES CUT 2 EACH

TRUNK
CUT 2
1 RIGHT
1 LEFT

STAR

CENTER
LEAF
CUT 2

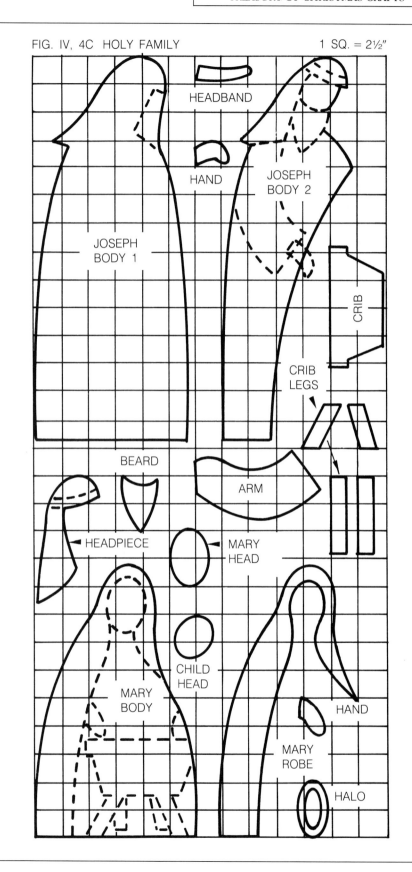

FIG. IV, 4C HOLY FAMILY   1 SQ. = 2½"

HEADBAND

HAND

JOSEPH BODY 2

JOSEPH BODY 1

CRIB

CRIB LEGS

BEARD

ARM

HEADPIECE

MARY HEAD

CHILD HEAD

MARY BODY

HAND

MARY ROBE

HALO

I nfant holy, infant lowly,
For his bed a cattle stall.
Oxen lowing, little knowing
Christ the Babe is Lord of all.
Swift are winging, angels singing,
Nowells ringing, tidings bringing,
Christ the Babe is Lord of all,
Christ the Babe is Lord of all.

— Polish Christmas Carol

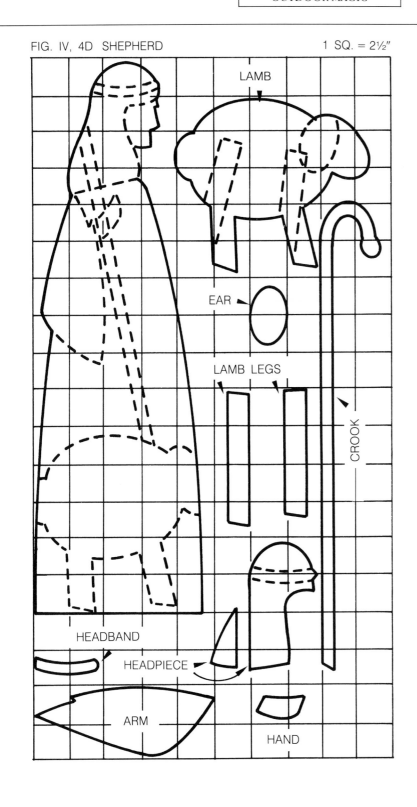

FIG. IV, 4D SHEPHERD   1 SQ. = 2½"

LAMB

EAR

LAMB LEGS

CROOK

HEADBAND

HEADPIECE

ARM

HAND

ALL CREATURES GREAT AND SMALL

Share the spirit of Christmas with the wild birds in your area. The winter is particularly hard on birds — it's difficult to find food. So designate one tree in your yard as the bird's Christmas tree and provide a feast for your feathered friends.

Spread scoops of peanut butter among the scales of pine cones and hang the cones from tree branches with red ribbons.

Slice 1 inch off the top of an orange and scoop out the pulp. Poke four holes around the rim and tie bright ribbons through them for hanging. Fill the orange cup with sunflower seeds or birdseed.

Cover a piece of suet with netting, and tie or tack it to the tree trunk.

Mix raisins and nuts in half of an empty coconut shell; drill holes in the shell near the top rim for hanging.

String garlands of cranberries and popcorn on heavy thread.

FIG. IV, 4G WISE MAN #1   1 SQ. = 2½"

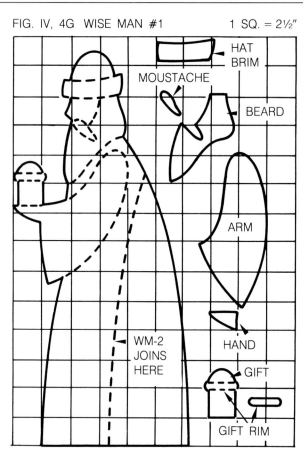

HAT
BRIM

MOUSTACHE

BEARD

ARM

HAND

GIFT

WM-2
JOINS
HERE

GIFT RIM

FIG. IV, 4F WISE MAN #2   1 SQ. = 2½"

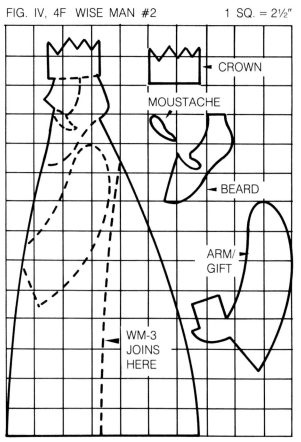

CROWN

MOUSTACHE

BEARD

ARM/
GIFT

WM-3
JOINS
HERE

FIG. IV, 4E WISE MAN #3   1 SQ. = 2½"

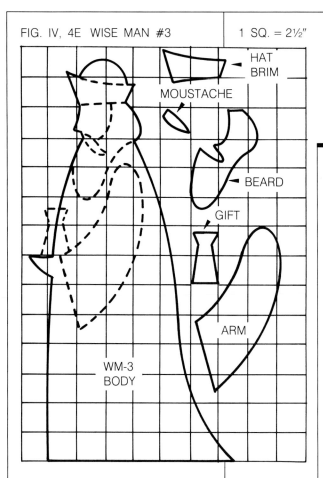

HAT BRIM

MOUSTACHE

BEARD

GIFT

ARM

WM-3 BODY

FOREVER CHRISTMAS TREES

It's always a bit sad to have to throw out your tree after Christmas, so this year why not choose a Christmas tree with roots? The smaller ones come in pots, and the larger ones have rootballs wrapped in burlap. After the holidays, plant your tree outdoors to enjoy for years to come.

Before the ground freezes, dig a hole in your yard 2 feet across and at least 1½ feet deep; you can refill it to the correct depth if you choose a smaller tree. Cover the hole with some sort of insulating material such as straw or leaves.

To prevent the soil dug out of the hole from freezing, place it in a plastic bucket or small trash can as you dig, then store it in the garage or basement.

Choose a tree that isn't more than 4 feet tall and has fresh, not brittle, needles with signs of new growth. Also, be sure you have a pot or sturdy box in which to place the tree in your home.

Keep the tree well watered while in the house — the rootball must be kept moist. And be sure to set the tree in the coolest part of the room, away from radiators, heating vents or the fireplace.

Try not to keep a live tree indoors for more than 4 or 5 days. And never keep it inside for more than 10 days.

Before planting, place the tree in a garage or cold basement for a day or two to accustom it gradually to the cold.

When you plant the tree, adjust the hole you dug so it's twice the size of the rootball and slightly deeper.

Remove the tree from its container and place it in the hole. With a burlaped tree, loosen the ties and plant it as is; the burlap will disintegrate eventually.

Put back enough soil so the top of the rootball will sit just slightly exposed. Hold the tree straight while you fill in the hole, packing soil around the ball. Cover the area with a 3-inch-thick layer of mulch (hay or evergreen boughs).

If you can't plant the tree until spring because the ground is frozen, place it outdoors, surrounded by a 6- to 12-inch layer of mulch. It should be located near the house or in the shelter of other trees. Be sure to plant the tree as soon as the ground thaws.

Under a tree bedecked with cheerful plaid ribbons lie those mysterious bundles just waiting for Christmas morning.

Gifts From the Heart

othing says "I love you" quite the way a hand-crafted gift does. And we provide you with the perfect presents for everyone.

Christmas is a child's wonderland, and these pages are filled with great gifts for the little ones in your life: snuggly sweaters, stuffed toys and dolls, a colonial-style doll house, and more.

For the adults on your gift list, we give you a warming selection of Christmas comforts, including striking quilts, afghans, and chill-chasing pullovers. Sew a matching set of accessory cases in a pretty floral print, make an heirloom of a purchased shelf with a folk art stencil, or stitch a whimsical patchwork pig pillow.

In the holiday rush, you're bound to forget something. So we provide you with some great last-minute gift ideas. Start with store-bought items—sweatshirts, sleeper pajamas, even simple sponges—and turn them into something unique with stencils, stitches and scissors. These quick-fix gifts truly are overnight sensations!

KIDSTUFF!

Child's Norwegian Cardigan & Hat

CHILD'S NORWEGIAN CARDIGAN & HAT

A classic style suitable for girls or boys.

CHALLENGING: Requires more experience in knitting.
Directions are given for Child's Size 2. Changes for Sizes 4 and 6 are in parentheses.

MATERIALS: 100% wool fingering yarn (100-gram skein): 3 (3, 4) skeins of Off White (A), 1 (2, 2) skeins of Blue (B), and 1 (1, 1) skein of Red (C); one pair each Size 2 and Size 5 knitting needles, OR ANY SIZE NEEDLES TO OBTAIN GAUGE BELOW; stitch holders; tapestry needle; five (six, six) ⅜-inch-diameter silver buttons; 4-inch-long piece of cardboard.

GAUGE: On size 5 needles in Stockinette Stitch (st st), 6 sts = 1 inch; 8 rows = 1 inch.

SIZES:	(2)	(4)	(6)
BODY CHEST:			
	21"	23"	25"
FINISHED MEASUREMENTS:			
CHEST:	22"	24"	26"
WIDTH ACROSS EACH FRONT AT UNDERARMS (INCLUDING FRONT BAND):			
	6"	6½"	7"
WIDTH ACROSS BACK AT UNDERARMS:			
	11"	12"	13"
WIDTH ACROSS SLEEVE AT UPPER ARM:			
	10"	11"	12"

Note: When changing colors, pick up the color to be used under the color previously used, twisting the yarns on the wrong side to prevent holes in the work. Carry the unused colors loosely on the wrong side of the work.
Note: The cardigan front, back and top of the sleeve, as well as the hat, are worked with C yarn, as indicated on the charts. The angle of the photograph does not clearly show this.

COLORFUL IDEA

The extra-warm cardigan and hat in the photo at left can be made in a variety of color combinations. Try reversing the red and blue in the pattern as given. Substitute hunter green and lilac for the red and blue. Or reverse the blue and off white in the pattern for a stunning effect.

CARDIGAN DIRECTIONS:

1. Back: Starting at the lower edge with size 2 needles and B, cast on 66 (72, 78) sts. Work in k 1, p 1 ribbing for 1¼ (1½, 1½) inches, decreasing 1 st on the last row worked—65 (71, 77) sts. Change to size 5 needles and st st (k 1 row, p 1 row). Now beg FIG. V, 1A *(page 153)* until completion of Row 10. Change to dot pattern as follows, working in st st throughout: **Row 1 (right side):** With * A k 3, join B and with B k 1; rep from * 15 (16, 18) times more, ending with A k 1 (3, 1). **Rows 2 to 5:** With A only work 4 rows in st st. **Row 6:** With A p 1, with * B p 1, with A p 3; rep from * 15 (16, 18) times more, ending Size 4 only with B p 1, with A p 1. **Rows 7 to 10:** With A only work 4 rows in st st. Rep Rows 1 to 10 for dot pattern until total length is 8 (9, 11) inches from beg, ending with a p row. **Armhole Shaping:** Continuing in dot pattern, bind off 3 sts at beg of next 2 rows—59 (65, 71) sts. Work even in dot pattern until armhole measures 2 (2½, 3) inches, ending with 4 A rows. Now beg FIG. V, 1B *(page 153)* until completion of Row 22. **Neck Shaping, Next Row:** Continuing to follow FIG. V, 1B, work across first 15 (18, 21) sts, place center 29 sts on a stitch holder, join a second ball of yarn and complete the row. Work both sides at once with a separate ball, until completion of Row 24. Bind off 15 (18, 21) sts on each side for shoulders.

2. Right Front: Starting at lower edge with size 2 needles and B, cast on 38 (42, 44) sts. Work in k 1, p 1 ribbing for 1¼ (1½, 1½) inches, decreasing 1 (2, 1) st on last row worked— 37 (40, 43) sts. Place first 7 sts on a stitch holder to be worked for the Front band. Change to size 5 needles and st st. Now beg FIG. V, 1C *(page 153)* until completion of Row 10. Change to dot pattern as follows, working in st st throughout:

Row 1 (right side): With * A k 3, join B and with B k 1; rep from * 6 (7, 8) times more, ending with A k 2 (1, 0). **Rows 2 to 5:** With A only work 4 rows. **Row 6:** With A p 1, with * B p 1, with A p 3; rep from * 6 (7, 8) times more, ending with B p 1 (0, 1), and A p 0 (0, 2). **Rows 7 to 10:** With A only work 4 rows. Rep Rows 1 to 10 for dot pattern until total length is 8 (9, 11) inches from beg, ending with a k row. **Armhole Shaping:** Continuing in dot pattern, bind off 3 sts at beg of next row. Work even in dot pattern until armhole measures 2 (2½, 3) inches, ending with 4 A rows. Now beg Fig. V, 1C at size indicated until completion of Row 14. **Neck Shaping, Row 15:** Continuing to follow Fig. V, 1C, bind off 5 sts at beg of row for Front neck edge. Dec 1 st at neck edge every row 7 times — 15 (18, 21) sts. Work even on rem sts until completion of Row 23. Bind off all sts. **Right Front Band:** Slip the 7 sts from the stitch holder onto size 2 needles and work in k 1, p 1 ribbing the same as the Back until the Front band is long enough to meet the bound-off sts of the neck shaping. Slip sts onto the stitch holder. Mark the position of 5 (6, 6) buttons, with the first button ½ inch from the bottom edge and the last button ½ inch from the top of the Front band. Space the remaining buttons evenly on the band. *Note: When making the cardigan for a girl, mark the position of the buttons on the Left Front band, and make the buttonholes in the Right Front band.* **3. Left Front:** Work to correspond to the Right Front, reversing the shaping. **Left Front Band:** Slip the 7 sts from the stitch holder onto size 2 needles and work in k 1, p 1 ribbing to the first button marker. **Buttonhole Row:** Rib 2, bind off 3 sts, rib 2. On next row rib across, casting on 3 sts over bound-off sts. Continue to work in ribbing, making 5 (6, 6) buttonholes in all opposite markers.

4. Sleeves: Starting at the lower edge with size 2 needles and B, cast on 44 (46, 48) sts. Work in k 1, p 1 ribbing for 1½ inches. **Next Row:** P across, increasing 5 sts evenly spaced — 49 (51, 53) sts. Change to size 5 needles and st st. Now beg Fig. V, 1D until completion of Row 10. Change to dot pattern as for Back, increasing 1 st each end every 6th row 6 (8, 10) times — 61 (67, 73) sts. Work even in dot pattern until total length is 7 (9¼, 10¼) inches from beg, ending with Row 1 or 6 of dot pattern. Now beg Fig. V, 1D until completion of Row 9. Bind off all sts.

5. Finishing: Sew the shoulder seams. Sew the Front bands in place. **Neckband:** With the right side facing, using size 2 needles and B, k 7 sts from the Right Front band stitch holder, pick up 19 sts along the right neck edge, k 29 sts from the Back stitch holder, pick up 19 sts along the left neck edge, and k 7 sts from the Left Front band stitch holder — 81 sts. Work in k 1, p 1 ribbing for 1 inch. Bind off loosely in ribbing. Sew the side and Sleeve seams. Sew in the Sleeves. Sew on the buttons.

HAT DIRECTIONS:

1. With size 2 needles and B, cast on 99 (103, 107) sts. Work in k 1, p1 ribbing for 1¼ inches. Break off B, join A. Change to size 5 needles and st st. Work 2 rows. Beg dot pattern. **2. Row 1 (wrong side):** K 3 A, * k 1 B, k 3 A; rep from * across. **Rows 2 to 5:** With A only work 4 rows. **Row 6:** P 1 A, p 1 B, * p 3 A, p 1 B; rep from *, end p 1 A. **Rows 7 to 10:** With A only work 4 rows. Rep Rows 1 to 10 for pattern. Work to approximately 4 inches above ribbing, end with Row 3, 5, or 9. With A p 1 row, dec 2 (0, 4) sts evenly spaced — 97 (103, 103) sts. Beg Fig. V, 1D as indicated for the cardigan Sleeves. Work to the top of the chart.

Break off A and B. With C only work 7 rows more. **Dec Row:** K 1, * k 2 tog; rep from * across. Break off C, leaving a long strand. Using the tapestry needle, draw the strand through the stitches on the knitting needle. Pull tight, and sew the top of the hat together. Sew the back seam.

3. Pompon: Wind B around the piece of cardboard approximately 50 times. Cut four B strands approximately 27 inches long. Fold the strands in half, and tie them around the middle of the yarn on the cardboard. Cut the cardboard yarn along the top and bottom edges of the cardboard. Trim the pompon's ends neatly, and sew the pompon to the top of the hat.

FIG. V, 1A BACK

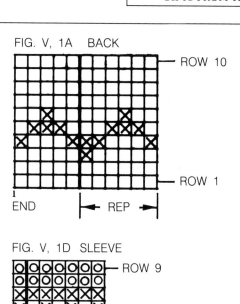

ROW 10

ROW 1

END ← REP →

FIG. V, 1B BACK

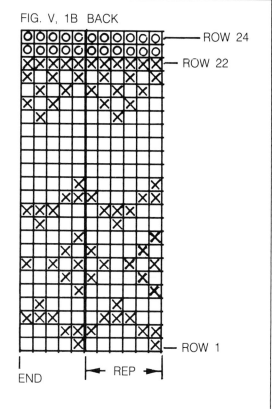

ROW 24

ROW 22

ROW 1

END ← REP →

FIG. V, 1D SLEEVE

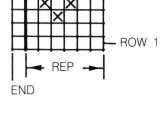

ROW 9

ROW 1

← REP →

END

FIG. V, 1C FRONT

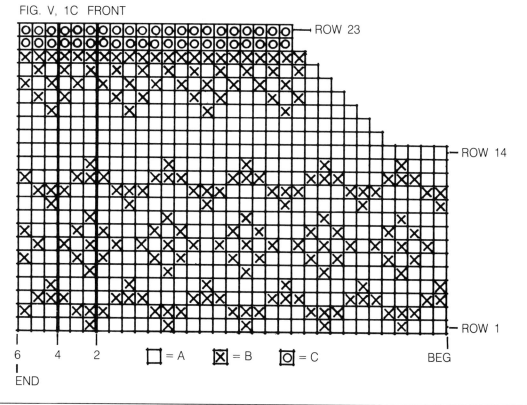

ROW 23

ROW 14

ROW 1

6   4   2   ☐ = A   ☒ = B   ☒ = C   BEG

END

SNOWFLAKE SWEATER SET

A snuggly-warm pullover and cap, perfect for playing in the snow.

CHALLENGING: Requires more experience in knitting.
Directions are given for Child's Size 2. Changes for Sizes 4, 6 and 8 are in parentheses.
MATERIALS: Two-ply sport weight yarn (2-ounce skein): 5 (5, 6, 6) skeins of Red, 1 skein each of White and Green; 1 pair each size 4 and size 5 knitting needles, OR ANY SIZE NEEDLES TO OBTAIN GAUGE BELOW; stitch holders; stich markers; tapestry needle.
GAUGE: On size 5 needles in Stockinette Stitch (st st), 6 sts = 1 inch; 9 rows = 1 inch.

FINISHED MEASUREMENTS:
SIZES: (2) (4) (6) (8)
GARMENT WIDTH AROUND UNDERARM:
              23" 25" 27" 29"

Note: The bottom edging on the body and sleeves, and the center front motif, are worked in duplicate stitch when the sweater is completed.

DIRECTIONS:

1. Back: With size 4 needles and Red, cast on 69 (75, 81, 87) sts. Work in k 1, p 1 ribbing for 1½ inches. Change to size 5 needles and work in st st (k 1 row, p 1 row) until the length is 9¼ (9½, 10, 10½) inches from beg, or the desired length to the underarm.
Armhole Shaping: Bind off 5 (5, 6, 6) sts at beg of next 2 rows — 59 (65, 69, 75) sts. Dec 1 st at each edge every other row 2 (2, 3, 3) times — 55 (61, 63, 69) sts. Work until 5 (5½, 6, 6) inches above beg of armhole shaping.
Shoulder Shaping: Bind off 6 (7, 7, 8) sts at beg of next 4 rows — 31 (33, 35, 37) sts. Sl sts onto a stitch holder for the back of the neck.
2. Front: Work the same as for Back until 3 inches above beg of armhole

shaping. **Neck Shaping:** Work across 15 (17, 17, 20) sts, join another ball of yarn, work next 25 (27, 29, 29) sts and place on a stitch holder for front of neck, work remaining 15 (17, 17, 20) sts. Working both sides at the same time, dec 1 st every right side neck edge row 2 (3, 3, 4) times — 13 (14, 14, 16) sts each side. Work until same length as Back to shoulder.
Shoulder Shaping: Bind off 6 (7, 7, 8) sts at beg of next 2 shoulder edge rows — 7 (7, 7, 8) sts each side. Work 1 row even. Bind off.
3. Sleeves: With size 4 needles and Red, cast on 35 (35, 37, 37) sts. Work in k 1, p 1 ribbing for 1½ inches. Change to size 5 needles and st st, inc 0 (0, 4, 4) sts evenly spaced across first row — 35 (35, 41, 41) sts. Inc 1 st each edge every 1 inch 7 (8, 9, 9) times — 49 (51, 59, 59) sts. Work until 10 (10, 10¼, 10¾) inches from beg, or the desired length to the underarm. **Cap Shaping:** Bind off 5 (5, 6, 6) sts at beg of next 2 rows — 39 (41, 47, 47) sts. Dec 1 st each edge every other row 9 (10, 11, 11) times — 21 (21, 25, 25) sts. Bind off.
4. Finishing: Sew one shoulder seam. **Neckband, Row 1:** Right side facing, with size 4 needles and Red, pick up and k 14 (15, 16, 16) sts along the side of the Front neck, pick up 25 (27, 29, 29) sts from the Front neck holder, 14 (15, 16, 16) sts along the side of the Front neck, 31 (33, 35, 37) sts from the Back neck holder — 84 (90, 96, 98) sts. **Row 2:** With Red, p and dec 0 (0, 2, 4) sts evenly spaced across — 84 (90, 94, 94) sts. **Row 3:** With White, k. **Row 4:** With Green, p. **Rows 5 to 10:** With Red, work in k 1, p 1 ribbing. Bind off loosely in ribbing. Sew the remaining shoulder seam and neckband.
5. Embroidery: Following Diagram A in FIG. V, 2 *(page 156)*, work duplicate stitches around the bottom of the sweater (Front and Back), with the bottom edge of the embroidery

Snowflake Sweater Set

½ inch up from top of the ribbing. In the same way, work duplicate stitches around the bottom of the Sleeves. Following Diagram B in FIG. V, 2 *(page 156)*, work the duplicate stitch motif at the center Front of the sweater. Sew the Sleeves in place, easing them to fit. Sew the underarm and side seams.

6. Hat: Beg at the bottom edge, with size 4 needles and Red, cast on 119 sts. **Row 1 (right side):** Work in k 1, p 1 ribbing. **Row 2:** With Green, p. **Row 3:** With White, k. **Row 4:** With Red, p. Continuing in Red, work in k 1, p 1 ribbing until 2¼ inches from beg, end on right side. **Next Row:** Change to size 5 needles and k. ***Note:** With turn in hat cuff, this k row now is the right side.* **Next Row:** Purl. Continue in st st until 5 inches from beg of the cuff, end on the wrong side. Mark center st on last row, and leave marker in place for duplicate stitch to be worked later. Continue in st st for 18 rows more, dec 1 st at beg of last row — 118 sts.

Crown Shaping, Row 1 (right side): K 4, (k 2 tog, k 10) 9 times, k 2 tog, k 4 — 108 sts. **Row 2:** Purl. **Row 3:** K 4, (k 2 tog, k 9) 9 times, k 2 tog, k 3 — 98 sts. **Row 4:** Purl. **Row 5:** K 3, (k 2 tog, k 8) 9 times, k 2 tog, k 3 — 88 sts. **Row 6:** Purl. Continue working as established, decreasing 10 sts every right side row until 28 sts remain. **Next Row:** *K 2 tog; rep from * across — 14 sts. **Next Row:** P 14. Cut yarn, leaving a 20-inch length.

7. Hat Finishing: Draw the 20-inch length through the remaining sts. Draw the sts together tightly, and secure them. Use the remaining yarn to sew the back seam.

8. Embroidery: Following Diagram C in FIG. V, 2 *(page 156)*, and with the bottom center of the snowflake matched to the marked stitch at the center of the hat, work duplicate stitches. Skip 13 sts at each side of the center snowflake; work a snowflake at each side of the center motif.

FIG. V, 2 SNOWFLAKE SWEATER SET

DIAGRAM A

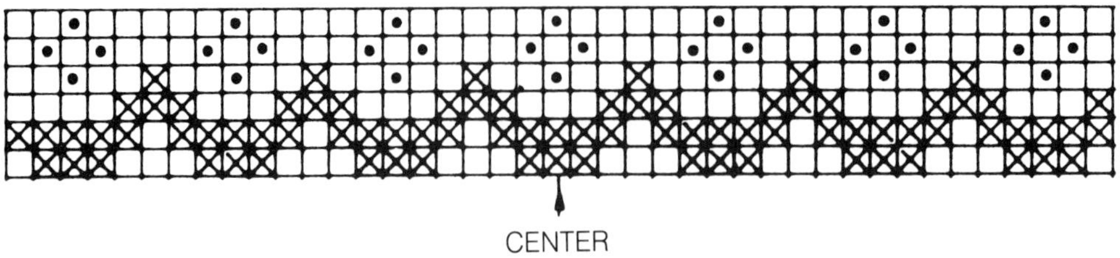

CENTER

DIAGRAM B

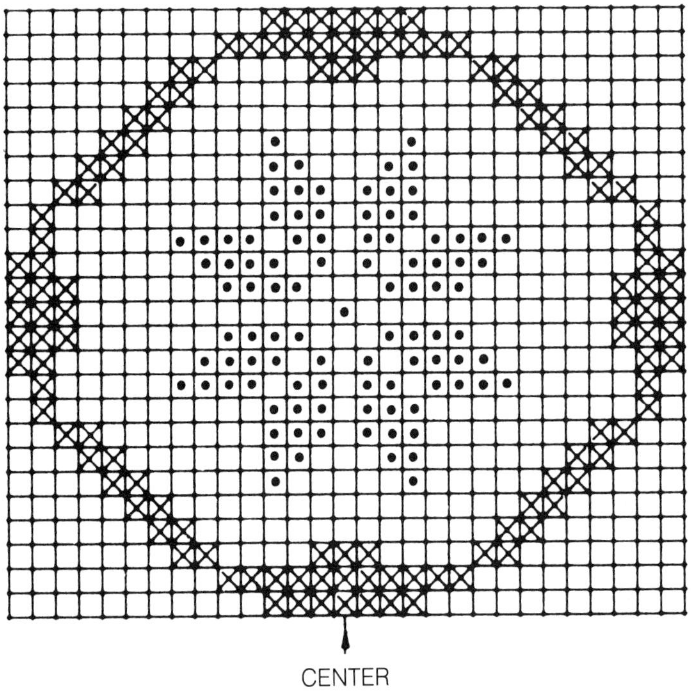

CENTER

FINDING YOUR GAUGE . . .

Make sure your knitted projects turn out perfectly every time by checking the gauge before you begin. Work a 4-inch square swatch using the recommended needles and yarn. Measure the stitches and rows. If the results do not match the gauge given in the pattern, knit another sample on smaller or larger needles, depending on the desired result. If you wish to substitute a yarn, first try out the yarn by making a sample swatch as recommended above.

DIAGRAM C

CENTER

⊠ = GREEN   ⊡ = WHITE

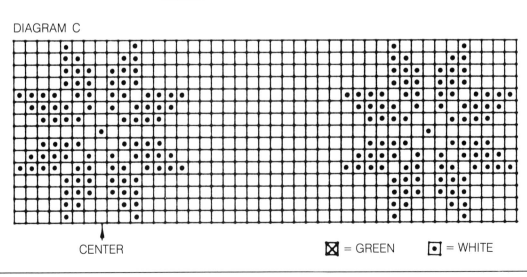

Eddie the Elf Puppet

EDDIE THE ELF PUPPET

*What a Christmas morning surprise —
finding Eddie, Santa's favorite helper,
under the tree!*

CHALLENGING: Requires more
experience in sewing.

MATERIALS: 12 x 3 inches of strong
muslin for body and finger pockets;
10 x 24 inches of red cotton fabric for
legs and foot soles; 20 x 24 inches of
flesh-colored fabric for head, nose,
ears, arms and lining; 18 x 24 inches of
red and white cotton print for shirt;
24 x 33 inches of green felt for cap,
pants and shoes; red, white, green and
brown threads; embroidery floss:
small amounts of Red, Brown,
Charcoal Gray and White; 10 yards or
more of Brown knitting yarn; synthetic
stuffing; rouge; three 1-inch red
pompons; heavy cardboard; fabric
marking pencil; paper for patterns;
pins; scissors.

DIRECTIONS
(¼-inch seams allowed):

1. Enlarge all the pattern pieces in FIG.
V, 3 *(page 159)* onto paper, following
the directions on page 239. Pin the
paper patterns to the fabrics, and cut
the number of pieces indicated. Mark
and keep a paper pattern piece pinned
to a fabric piece until the piece is used.
Cut a Hair Card from heavy cardboard.

2. Nose and Ears: Place the Nose
pieces right sides together and sew
around them, leaving the straight edge
open. Turn the Nose right side out,
stuff it, and blind stitch the opening
closed *(see Embroidery Stitch Guide,
page 240).* Make two Ears following
the directions for making the Nose.
Leave a 1½-inch opening on the long
side of each Ear for stuffing. Set aside
the finished Nose and Ears.

**3. Finger Pocket for Puppet's
Head:** Fold over the edge of one long
side ¼ inch, and stitch it down. Fold
the Finger Pocket piece in half, wrong
side out, matching the C's. Stitch along
the raw edges, forming the pocket.
Turn the Finger Pocket right side out,
press it, and set it aside.

4. Hair: Using the Hair Card, wind the
yarn around the Card, one strand next
to the other. Stitch back and forth
through the slit to fasten the strands
together. Cut the top and bottom of
the yarn, and remove the Hair through
the slit. Set aside the Hair.

5. Muslin Body: Sew the Body Front
pieces together from A to B. Sew the
Body Back pieces together from A to B.
Put the Front and Back wrong sides
together and stitch all around, leaving
an opening from C to A to C. Stuff the
Body firmly, and blind stitch it closed.
Set aside the Body.

6. Lower Body Back Lining: Sew
together the Lower Body Back Lining
pieces from I to B. Make the darts.
Turn the long straight edge down
¼ inch, and stitch it down. Cut the
darts open, press the Lower Body Back
Lining, and set it aside.

7. Arms: Stitch the dart in the Inner
Arm pieces. Lay out all the Arm pieces,
Outer Arm underneath, Inner Arm on
top, right sides together. Put a muslin
Arm Finger Pocket on top of one set,

matching D's and E's. Stitch the curved edge of the Finger Pocket piece along the curved edge of the Inner Arm. Fold the Finger Pocket on the line indicated, and put F and G over D and E. Stitch the Inner Arm to the Outer Arm from E around the hand to D, catching the edges of the Finger Pocket insert in the side seams. Turn the Arm right side out, and stuff the lower arm and hand. Push the Pocket into the upper arm. Baste F and G on the Finger Pocket to F and G on the Outer Arm piece. Repeat to make the other Arm. Set aside the Arms.

8. Flesh-Colored Lining: Place the Body Front Lining pieces right sides together, and stitch from A to B. Fold under ¼ inch on the bottom edge of the Upper Body Back Lining, and stitch. Stitch F and G of the right Outer Arm to the right side of the Upper Body Back Lining, and F and G of the left Outer Arm to the left side of the Upper Body Back Lining. The thumbs should point upward. Stitch D and E of the Inner Arms to D and E of the Body Front Lining. Stitch the Lower Body Back Lining to the Body Front Lining from B center back around the curve, matching G to E.

9. Head: On the right side of one of the Head pieces, lightly trace the face with the fabric marking pencil. Use an outline stitch and Red floss to embroider a mouth. Outline the eyes with Brown floss. Make Charcoal Gray pupils, Brown irises, and put a sparkle in his eyes with a touch of White floss in the iris. Make eyebrows and eyelashes with Charcoal Gray embroidery or a pencil. Tint the cheeks with rouge. Stitch the yarn Hair in place along the top seam from H to H. Fasten the Nose in place with blind stitches. Place the second Head piece on the first, right sides together, and sew around the top of the Head from C to C. Turn the Head right side out, and stuff it. Fasten the Ears in place with blind stitches. Push the Head

Finger Pocket up into the Head, matching C's, and sew around the bottom hem of the Finger Pocket to fasten it to the bottom of the face and back of the Head between C's, leaving the Pocket open. Stitch C and D of the Body Front Lining to C and F of the Upper Body Back Lining. Stitch the face to the Body Front Lining, matching CAC, and the back of the Head to the Upper Body Back Lining, also matching CAC. You now should have a stuffed Head and stuffed Arms, with Pockets inside, attached to a flesh-colored Body Lining. Insert the muslin Body into the Lining, and tack at the C's on the Lining shoulders and front.

10. Legs: Sew the darts in the Leg pieces. Stitch each pair of Leg pieces together, matching M's and J's. Stitch the other side of the Legs, matching K's and L's. Stitch the Foot Soles to the Legs, matching L's and J's. Turn the Legs right side out, stuff, and shape them so the darts are on the sides of the Legs. Close the openings, and fasten the Legs securely to the Body Lining, matching B's on the Lining.

11. Pants: Stitch the two Pants Front pieces together, matching 8's and 9's. Stitch the two Pants Back pieces together, matching 8's and 9's. Stitch the Pants Front and Back together, matching 11's and 9's on the inseam and 12's and 13's on the sides. Pull the Pants over the puppet's Legs, and handstitch the top of the Pants Back to the top of the Lower Body Back Lining. Gather the bottom of the Pants legs to fit the puppet's Legs. Tack the Pants to the Legs and to the puppet Body, through the Body Lining, at the waistline front and sides.

12. Shoes: Stitch each pair of Shoe pieces together, matching 1's and 2's and 3's and 4's. Stitch each Shoe to a Shoe Sole, matching 2's and 4's. Turn the Shoes right side out, tack down each front flap, and put the Shoes on the puppet's feet. Tack the Shoes to the feet to secure them.

13. Cap: Stitch together the Cap Front and Back, matching 1's and 2's. Stitch together the Cap Front Cuff and Back Cuff, matching 1's and 3's. Stitch the Cuff to the bottom of the Cap, matching 1's. Turn the Cuff over twice, and slipstitch the Cuff to the Cap from inside. Stuff the Cap loosely, place the Cap on the puppet's Head, and fasten the Cap around with blind stitches.

14. Shirt: Gather the neckline of the Shirt Front from 5 to 5 until it measures 2 inches. Gather the neckline of the Shirt Back pieces from 5 to the edge until they measure 1 inch each. Stitch the Shirt Back Facing pieces to the Shirt Front Facing, right sides together, matching 1's. Stitch the Shirt Front to the Shirt Back pieces, matching 1's and 2's. Stitch two Shirt Collar pieces right sides together, leaving the shorter inside curve open. Turn and press. Repeat with the other two Shirt Collar pieces. Baste them to the right side of the Shirt neckline, matching 6's and 7's. Pin the right sides of the Facings to the Shirt Back and to the neckline over the Collar, matching 6's and 1's. Stitch through all thicknesses. Turn and press. Make a ¼-inch hem in the Shirt Sleeves from 4 to 4. Stitch the Sleeves to the Shirt, matching 3's. Stitch the Shirt together on the sides and down the underside of the Sleeves, matching 5's, 3's and 4's. Sew the three pompons down the center front. Put the Shirt on the puppet, and stitch the Shirt back seam together by hand. Tack the Shirt securely to the puppet.

FIG. V, 3 EDDIE THE ELF PUPPET

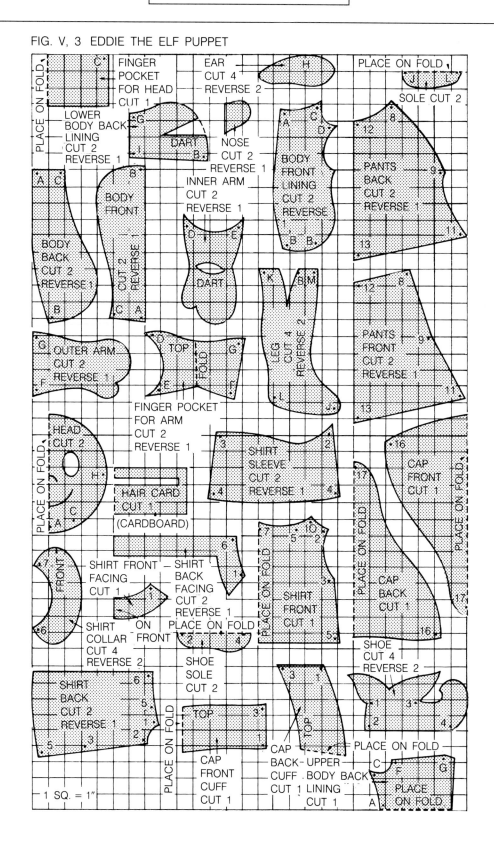

Li'l Critter Earmuffs

LI'L CRITTER EARMUFFS

These critters will keep little ones entertained and warm all winter.

AVERAGE: For those with some experience in crocheting.

MATERIALS: Four-ply worsted weight yarn: 1½ ounces of Gold, Gray or Tan for each pair, 1 ounce of Dark Brown for Lion's mane, small amount of Dark Brown for Dog's ears, small amount of Pink for Mouse's ears, and small amount of Black for facial features; size F and size G crochet hooks, OR ANY SIZE HOOK TO OBTAIN GAUGE BELOW; stitch markers; 9 ounces of synthetic stuffing; 1 yard of ½-inch-wide orange ribbon each for Dog and Mouse; tapestry needle.

GAUGE: With size G hook, 4 hdc = 1 inch; 4 rows = 1 inch.

Note: *Do not join rounds, but use a marker to indicate the end of each round. Use size G hook unless otherwise stated.*

GENERAL DIRECTIONS:

1. Muffs (make 4): With size G hook, ch 3. Join with sl st to form ring. Ch 1. **Rnd 1:** Work 6 hdc in ring. **Rnd 2:** Work 2 hdc in each st around—12 sts. **Rnd 3:** *Work 1 hdc in next st,

2 hdc in next st; rep from * around—18 sts. **Rnd 4:** * Work 1 hdc in each of next 2 sts, 2 hdc in next st; rep from * around—24 sts. **Rnd 5:** * Work 1 hdc in each of next 3 sts, 2 hdc in next st; rep from * around—30 sts. **Rnds 6 to 8:** Continue to increase 6 sts evenly spaced around—48 sts. **Rnd 9:** Work sc around. Join with sl st to first sc. Fasten off, leaving about 10 inches of yarn to sew with. Sew two muff pieces together, stuffing them lightly. Repeat with the second pair of muff pieces.

2. Headband (make 1): Ch 8. **Row 1:** Hdc in 3rd ch from hook and in each ch across—6 sts. Ch 2, turn. **Rows 2 to 42:** Work 6 hdc across. Ch 2, turn. If you wish, work fewer or more rows as necessary to adjust the fit. Fasten off, leaving about 6 inches of yarn to sew with. Sew each end to the top of a muff.

3. Ties (make 2): Ch 77. Hdc in 3rd ch from hook and in each ch across. Fasten off, leaving about 4 inches of yarn to sew with. Sew each tie to the bottom of a muff.

4. Eyes and Nose (make 6): With size F hook and Black, ch 2. Work 4 sc in 2nd ch from hook. Join with sl st to first sc. Fasten off, leaving about 10 inches of yarn to sew with. Sew on two eyes at Rnd 2 of each muff, ¾ inch apart. If you wish, embroider a Black outline stitch around each eye. Sew on a nose at Rnd 2 of each muzzle *(see specific directions for the Lion, Mouse or Dog)*.

5. Facial Features: With Black and an outline stitch, embroider a smile under the nose, and connect the smile to the nose with a straight line of outline stitches.

LION

1. With Gold, follow the General Directions to make the muffs, headband, ties, eyes and nose. Work the facial features following the General Directions.

2. Muzzle (make 2): With Gold, ch 3. Join with sl st to form ring. Ch 1. **Rnd 1:** Work 6 hdc in ring. **Rnd 2:** Work 2 hdc in each st around—12 sts. **Rnd 3:** * Work 1 hdc in each of next 2 sts, 2 hdc in next st; rep from * around—16 sts. **Rnd 4:** Work sc around. Join with sl st to first sc. Fasten off, leaving about 8 inches of yarn to sew with. Stuff and sew each muzzle to a muff, starting at Rnd 1.

3. Mane: Cut about two hundred 4-inch-long pieces of Dark Brown yarn. Tie two strands in each st of Rnd 8. Tie three strands at the end of each earmuff tie. Comb out the mane and tie tufts, and trim them to about 1 inch in length.

DOG

1. With Tan, follow the General Directions to make the muffs, headband, ties, eyes and nose. Work the facial features following the General Directions. Make two bows from the orange ribbon, and add one to each muff *(see photo)*.

2. Muzzle (make 2): With Tan, ch 3. Join with sl st to form ring. Ch 1. **Rnd 1:** Work 8 hdc in ring. **Rnd 2:** * Work 1 hdc in next st, 2 hdc in next st; rep from * around—12 sts. **Rnd 3:** * Work 1 hdc in each of next 2 sts, 2 hdc in next st; rep from * around—16 sts. **Rnd 4:** Work sc around. Join with sl st to first sc. Fasten off, leaving about 8 inches of yarn to sew with. Stuff and sew each muzzle to a muff, starting at Rnd 1.

3. Ears (make 4): With Dark Brown, ch 12. **Row 1:** Hdc in 3rd ch from hook and in each of next 8 chs, 3 hdc in last ch. Work 9 hdc on other side of ch. Ch 2, turn. **Row 2:** Work 1 hdc in each of next 9 sts, 2 hdc in next st, 1 hdc in next st, 2 hdc in next st, 1 hdc in each of next 9 sts. Fasten off, leaving 6 inches of yarn to sew with. Sew on two ears at Rnd 7 of each muff.

MOUSE

1. With Gray, follow the General Directions to make the muffs, headband, ties, eyes and nose. With Gray, make the muzzle following the directions for the Dog's muzzle. Work the facial features following the General Directions. Make two bows from the orange ribbon, and add one to each muff *(see photo)*.

2. Ears (make 4): With Pink, ch 3. Join with sl st to form ring. Ch 1. **Rnd 1:** Work 6 hdc in ring. **Rnd 2:** Work 2 hdc in each st around—12 sts. **Next Rnd:** Work sc around. Join with sl st to first sc. Fasten off. With Gray, rep Rnds 1 and 2. ***Do not*** fasten off. Hold the Gray and Pink pieces together, back to back. With Gray, work 2 hdc in each st around, working through both thicknesses—24 sts. **Last Rnd:** Work sc around. Join with sl st. Fasten off, leaving about 6 inches of yarn to sew with. Sew on two ears at Rnd 7 of each muff.

HEARTS 'N FLOWERS ROCKING CHAIR

A special gift for a child — beautiful enough for any room in the house.

EASY: Achievable by anyone.
MATERIALS: Child's rocking chair, painted or unfinished; acrylic stencil paints: red, green, white and blue; 4 stencil brushes; acetate sheets; utility knife; sheet of cardboard, glass or plexiglass; masking tape; clean cotton rags or paper toweling; rubbing alcohol; polyurethane spray *(optional)*.

DIRECTIONS:

1. Make sure the finish on the chair is clean and smooth. Have the alcohol and rags or paper toweling ready to clean the stencils as they are used.
2. Make one acetate stencil for each color in each design. Trace the full-size designs in Fig. V, 4 onto the acetate sheets, and lightly sketch the grid onto each sheet. Layer the sheets so each design lines up properly; use the grid to help you line up the layers.

On each color's stencil, cut out the details (not the grid) *for that color only,* using the utility knife and working on the sheet of cardboard, glass or plexiglass. Remember the utility knife will scratch the surface below the acetate.
3. Starting with the darkest paint color, tape the stencil for that color in place. Dip a stencil brush in the paint, and rub the brush on the rags or paper toweling in a circular motion until the brush is almost dry. Apply a thin coat of the paint to the stencil, starting at the edges of the cutout and working toward the center. Allow the paint to

dry, and apply more coats until the desired color depth is achieved. Repeat the process until all the colors are used, using a different stencil brush for each color, and allowing adequate drying time between coats.
4. If you wish, apply a coat or two of polyurethane spray to protect the stenciled design.
5. Clean the stencils with the cotton rags or paper toweling soaked in rubbing alcohol. Clean the brushes with soap and water until the rinse water runs clear.
6. Store the cleaned stencils between layers of cardboard for future use.

FIG. V, 4 HEARTS 'N FLOWERS CHAIR STENCIL PATTERN

COLOR ORDER:

VINE IN GREEN

HEART AND FLOWERS IN RED

SWIRLS IN WHITE

BERRIES IN BLUE

BOTTOM BACK AND SEAT

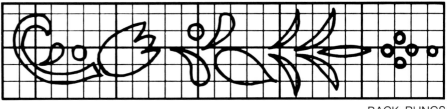

BACK RUNGS

TOP BACK

Hearts 'n Flowers Rocking Chair

Baby Booties

BABY BOOTIES

These extra-tall foot warmers can be crocheted in an evening.

AVERAGE: For those with some experience in crocheting.
Directions are given for Sizes Infant to about 6 Months.
MATERIALS: Bulky weight leftover yarn (or 2 strands of thinner-weight yarn held together to obtain the same gauge): 1½ ounces in 8 or 9 colors; size G crochet hook, OR ANY SIZE HOOK TO OBTAIN GAUGE BELOW; stitch markers; tapestry needle.
GAUGE: 3 sc = 1 inch; 3 rows = 1 inch.

DIRECTIONS:
1. Booties (make 2): Starting at the sole of the Bootie with A, ch 31. **Row 1 (right side):** Sc in each ch across — 30 sc. Ch 1, turn. *Mark center st for center front of Bootie.* **Rows 2 to 5:** Sc in each sc across — 30 sc. Ch 1, turn. **Row 6 (dec row):** Sc in each sc across, decreasing 3 sts on each side of center st — 24 sc. At the end of this row, change to B as follows: Work last sc of row until there are 2 lps on hook. With new color, yo and draw through 2 lps on hook. Fasten off old color. *Hereafter change colors in this way.* **Row 7:** With B, ch 2, turn, skip first sc, * 2 hdc in next sc, skip next sc;

rep from * across, ending with 2 hdc in last sc — 24 hdc. Ch 1, turn. **Row 8:** Sc in front lp *only* of each hdc across — 24 sc. Change to C. **Row 9 (dec row):** With C, ch 1, turn, sc in each sc across, decreasing 2 sts on each side of center st — 20 sc. Change to D, *but do not* fasten off C. **Row 10:** With D, ch 1, turn, work * 1 sc with D, 1 sc with C; rep from * across — 20 sc. Fasten off D *only*. **Row 11:** With C, ch 1, turn, skip first sc, * 2 sc in next sc, skip next sc; rep from * across, ending with 2 sc in last sc — 20 sc. Change to E. **Row 12:** With E, ch 1, turn, sc in front lp *only* of each sc across to within last sc, *2 sc in last sc — inc made* — 21 sc. Change to F. **Row 13:** With F, ch 1, turn, sc in each sc across — 21 sc. Change to E. **Row 14:** With E, ch 1, turn, sc in *both* lps of each sc across to within last sc, inc 1 sc — 22 sc. Change to G. **Row 15:** With G, rep Row 7 — 22 hdc. Change to H. **Row 16:** With H, ch 1, turn, * sc bet next 2 hdc groups, ch 1; rep from * across, ending with sc bet next 2 hdc groups — 22 sts. Ch 1, turn. **Row 17:** Sc in each st across — 22 sc. Change to I, or C if you wish. **Row 18:** With I, ch 1, turn, sc in each sc across. Fasten off.
2. Finishing: For each Bootie, sew the ends of the rows together for the center back. Sew the foundation chain row together for the sole bottom.
3. Drawstrings: With I, work two 18-inch-long chains for drawstrings. Weave a drawstring through the sps of Row 9 on each Bootie, and tie the drawstring into a bow at the center front. With B and the tapestry needle, work a running st through the sps of Row 17 on each Bootie.

"Baby Love" Biscuit Comforter; Patchwork Pals Pillows and Nine-Patch Pillow (directions, page 166)

"BABY LOVE" BISCUIT COMFORTER

(39 x 46 inches)
This pretty, puffy coverlet is the ideal gift for baby's first Christmas.

AVERAGE: For those with some experience in patchwork.

MATERIALS: Forty-four- or forty-five-inch-wide fabric: ⅝ yard each of dark rose and white, ⅝ yard of blue, 1⅝ yards of rose and ¾ yard of unbleached muslin; matching threads; synthetic batting; synthetic stuffing; iron-on patching fabric *(optional).*

DIRECTIONS
(½-inch seams allowed):

1. Cut 18 dark rose and 17 white 6-inch square patches. Cut 35 muslin 5-inch square patches. Cut four 5½-inch-wide blue borders, two 26 inches and two 45 inches long. Cut a rose quilt back 43 x 53 inches. Cut four 7-inch-wide strips of batting, two 45 inches and two 35 inches long.

2. "Biscuits": Pin each 6-inch patch to a muslin patch, wrong sides together, and corners matching. Fold the extra colored fabric into a tuck at the center of each edge. Topstitch around all four sides, ½ inch from the cut edge, through all the layers.

3. Sew seven horizontal rows of five patches each, starting four of the rows with the dark rose fabric, and alternating the colors. Sew one row beneath the other, alternating the colors. To each short edge of the patchwork, sew a short blue border. Sew the long borders to the long patchwork edges.

4. Into the muslin back only of each biscuit patch pocket, cut a short (less than 1 inch) slash. Stuff each pocket through the slash to "raise the biscuit." Close the slash with a few stitches, or a scrap of iron-on patching fabric.

5. Place the quilt top in the center of the quilt back, wrong sides together.

The rose fabric will extend 4 inches on each side for use in binding. First pin, then topstitch along the inside border seams through both layers.

6. Place the batting strips under the borders (the batting will extend 2 inches beyond each border). Pin the outside border edges to the quilt back through the batting, and topstitch ½ inch from all the cut edges of the blue borders.

7. Turn under the rose fabric ½ inch at each short edge of the quilt back. Fold each short edge over to the right side, pin the turned-under edge to the previous topstitching, and edgestitch. Repeat the turning process on the two long edges.

NINE-PATCH PILLOW
(39 x 46 inches)

AVERAGE: For those with some experience in sewing.
MATERIALS: Forty-four- or forty-five-inch-wide fabric: ½ yard of blue and ¾ yard of muslin; matching thread; synthetic stuffing; synthetic batting; compass; ruler; hard pencil.

DIRECTIONS
(¼-inch seams allowed):
1. From the blue fabric, cut one 12½-inch square, twenty 2½-inch squares and four 2½ x 12½-inch strips. From the muslin, cut eight 2½-inch squares and one 24½-inch square.
2. Nine-Patch Block: Sew one small muslin square between two small blue squares; repeat. Sew one small blue square between two small muslin squares. Sew the three rows one below the other, with a small blue square in the center. Make three more patch blocks in the same way, one for each corner.
3. Sew a blue strip between two muslin strips. Repeat the strip blocks three times to make four strip blocks.
4. Sew a strip block to two opposite sides of the large blue square.

5. Sew a nine-patch block at each end of the two remaining strip blocks, and sew them to the large blue square and previously attached strip blocks to complete the pillow top.
6. Baste the batting to the back of the pillow top. Using the compass and hard pencil, lightly draw overlapping 5-inch circles in the center of the large blue square *(see photo, page 165)*. Lightly rule diagonal lines across the border strip blocks. Sew running stitches along the drawn lines to quilt.
7. Pin the pillow top to the 24½-inch muslin square, right sides together. Sew around three sides and four corners of the pillow. Turn the pillow right side out, stuff it firmly, turn under the open edges, and slipstitch the opening closed.

PATCHWORK PALS PILLOWS

AVERAGE: For those with some experience in sewing.
MATERIALS: ⅜ yard of 45-inch-wide muslin for each pillow; scraps of pastel print fabrics; matching threads; synthetic stuffing; synthetic batting; fusible interfacing; scrap of black iron-on fabric; paper for patterns; iron; hard pencil; paper punch.

DIRECTIONS:
1. Enlarge the patterns in FIG. V, 5 onto paper, following the directions on page 239. Fold the muslin in half, bringing the selvage edges together. Trace the paper patterns onto the muslin. Cut out the pattern pieces through both layers of muslin, cutting ¼ inch beyond the traced lines. Place the pastel print fabric scraps on top of the fusible interfacing, and cut 2-inch square patches from both fabrics.
2. Lightly mark the grainline (a gridline up and down the body) on each animal pillow front. Pin pastel print patches along the grainline of the muslin, with a fusible interfacing patch

between each fabric patch and the muslin. Alternate the patches to the right and left of the grainline. Following the same line-up, pin the rest of the patches in place. Press the patches with the iron to fuse them in place. Edgestitch or zigzag stitch the raw edges of the patches to secure them to the muslin. Fuse the yellow beak to the hen pillow muslin, and the pink collar to the cat pillow muslin the same way as the patches.
3. Using the hard pencil, lightly draw lines that connect the opposite corners of the patches. Repeat the lines in the opposite direction, making lines that are at right angles to each other to form squares. Baste the batting to the wrong side of each pillow front. Topstitch along the drawn lines to quilt the pillows.
4. With right sides together, and using a ¼-inch seam allowance, sew each pillow front to its pillow back, leaving a 3-inch opening at the bottom edge. Turn each pillow right side out and stuff it firmly. Turn under the open edges on each pillow, and slipstitch the opening closed.
5. Using the paper punch, cut three "eyes" from the iron-on fabric. Fuse one eye to each pillow as indicated on the pattern. For the cat, cut an ear from a pastel print fabric scrap and a corresponding piece of fusible interfacing. Fuse the cat's ear to the pillow front as indicated on the pattern. Slipstitch each eye and the edges of the cat's ear to secure them to the pillows.

FIG. V, 5 PATCHWORK PALS PILLOWS   1 SQ. = 2″

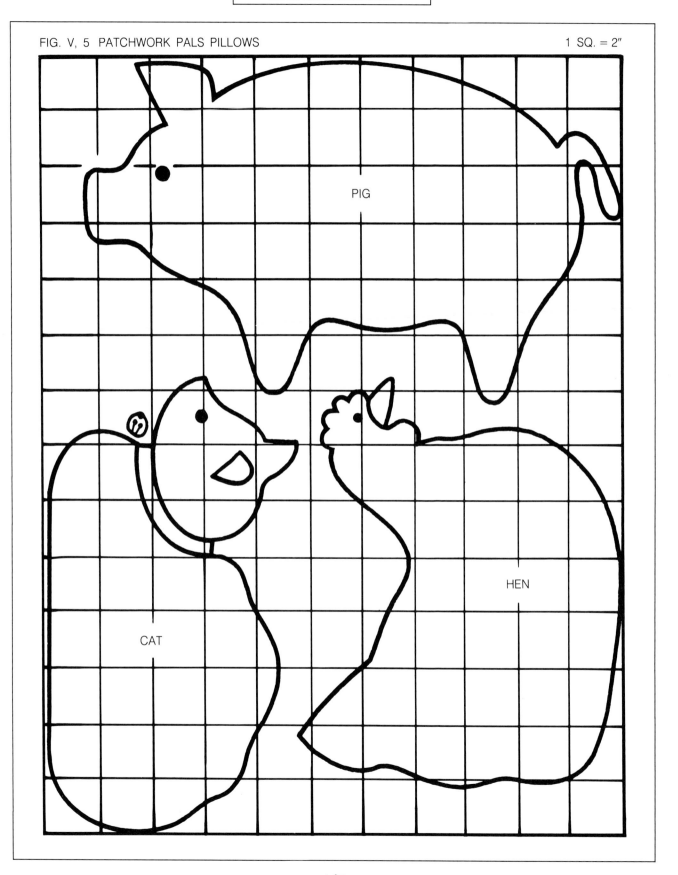

PIG

CAT

HEN

Little Boy Blue and Little Bo Peep

LITTLE BOY BLUE AND LITTLE BO PEEP

A sweet storybook pair for doll collectors of all ages.

CHALLENGING: Requires more experience in sewing and doll making.

DOLLS

MATERIALS: ¾ yard of pale pink percale or chintz; matching thread; rug yarn: 1 skein of dark brown; thread to match rug yarn; embroidery floss: scraps of Blue and Red; synthetic stuffing; paper for patterns.

DIRECTIONS:

1. Enlarge the doll pattern pieces in FIG. V, 6 *(page 170)* onto paper, following the directions on page 239. Cut out the fabric pieces according to the directions on the pattern. All the seams are sewn with right sides together unless otherwise noted.

2. Sew all the darts. Place the Body Back pieces together and sew the back seam, leaving an opening for stuffing as indicated. Attach the Body Back to the Body Front, sewing along all but the bottom edge. Turn the Body right side out. Sew the Leg pieces together in pairs. Sew along the side seams, but leave the top and bottom edges open. Sew a Foot Sole piece into each Leg bottom opening, and turn the Leg right side out. Repeat the procedure with the Arms, but leave only the tops open.

3. Stuff the Legs firmly, keeping in mind that the seams are at the center front and back. Stitch across the top of each Leg at the line indicated on the pattern. Turn up and baste the seam allowance on the Body bottom opening. Insert the seam allowances of the Leg tops into this opening and sew the opening closed; be sure the stitching is very durable. Stuff the Body firmly, and slipstitch the back opening closed. Stuff the Arms firmly up to the line indicated on the pattern. Sew across the Arms at this line; the space above the line is not stuffed. Turn under the seam allowance at the tops of the Arms and sew it closed. Sew the Arms to the Body at the places indicated on the pattern, with half the Arm width on either side of the side Body seam.

4. To finish the doll, cut the yarn to the length desired for the hair. Cut enough yarn hair to cover the head. Drape the yarn across the head, and sew the hair to the head by running the matching thread *through* the yarn and into the fabric of the head. The thread does not show because it does not cross over the yarn. Make the stitches at 1-inch to 1½-inch intervals. Arrange the hair as desired.

5. Draw a face on the doll, making half circles for the eyes and a curve for the mouth. Embroider the eyes with Blue floss using a satin stitch, and the mouth with Red floss using an outline stitch.

LITTLE BO PEEP'S OUTFIT

MATERIALS: ½ yard of white percale (also will make Little Boy Blue's underpants); 2½ yards of 1-inch-wide white lace; ¼ yard of print cotton fabric; ¼ yard of striped cotton fabric; ¼ yard of solid cotton fabric; ¼ yard of second color solid fabric; scrap of brown felt or suede cloth; matching threads; 2½ yards of ⅜-inch-wide lace; ½ yard of ½-inch-wide red satin ribbon; ½ yard of 1½-inch-wide red satin ribbon; 2 brown chenille stems; 1 pair Child's size 6 - 9 white knee socks; four ¾-inch-diameter snap fasteners; ¼ yard of fusible interfacing (also will make Little Boy Blue's hat interfacing); paper for patterns.

DIRECTIONS:

1. Enlarge the pattern pieces for Little Bo Peep's outfit in Fɪɢ. V, 6 *(page 170)* onto paper, following the directions on page 239. Using the pattern as a guide, cut out the Stockings from the pair of child's socks, leaving the ribbed

cuff area for Little Boy Blue's Socks. Sew the back seam and hem the top edge of each Stocking. Cut out one pair each of Shoe and Shoe Sole pieces from the brown felt or suede cloth. Sew the back seam of each Shoe piece, and whipstitch a Shoe Sole to each Shoe piece.

2. Cut out a pair of Pantaloon pieces from the white percale, following the directions on the pattern. Sew the center front seam and center back as indicated. Make a narrow rolled hem at the back opening, and hem the leg bottoms. For each Pantaloon leg, cut a piece of the 1-inch-wide lace twice the width of the leg, and gather it to fit the leg width. Sew two rows of the 1-inch-wide lace to each leg, one extending below the hem edge and the other overlapping the first row. Sew the Pantaloon leg seams. Pleat the top to fit the Body.

3. For the petticoat, cut a 36 x 4¾-inch strip from the white percale. Turn up ¾ inch on one long edge to make a hem. Sew a piece of the 1-inch-wide lace over the hem, with ¼ inch of the lace width extending below the edge of the hem. Sew the short ends together to form the center back seam. This piece is the flounce of the petticoat. Now cut a 13½ x 2¾-inch strip from the white percale. Gather the unhemmed edge of the flounce, and sew it to one long edge of the second piece. Hem the back opening for a placket. Gather the top edge of the petticoat to fit the top edge of the Pantaloons, pinning the wrong side of the petticoat to the right side of the Pantaloons. Cut a waistband 1½ inches wide from the white percale. Sew the waistband to the top of the petticoat/Pantaloons, and sew a snap fastener to the back opening.

4. For the dress and hat, cut the Skirt from the striped fabric, the Overskirt and Hat Brim from the first solid color fabric, the Bodice, Sleeves and Hat Crown from the print fabric, the apron

(5¾ x 6¾ inches) and Hat Brim lining from the second solid color fabric. Sew the Bodice shoulder seams. Gather the top of each Sleeve and sew it to the Bodice. Cut out 1-inch-wide strips for Sleeve bands from the print fabric to fit the doll's arms loosely. Gather the lower edge of one Sleeve, and bind it with one of the bands. Repeat for the second Sleeve. Sew the underarm seams. Turn under the back edges of the Bodice. Cut a 1-inch-wide bias strip from the print fabric and bind the neck edge with it. Sew a piece of gathered ⅜-inch-wide lace to the neck and to the Sleeve edges. Hem two long and one short edge of the apron, and sew ⅜-inch-wide lace around the three hemmed sides. Gather the unhemmed edge of the apron to measure 2½ inches. Sew the apron, centered, to the front of the Bodice. Gather the top edges of the Overskirt pieces, turning under the side seam allowances. Sew the top of the Overskirt pieces to the Bodice bottom, placing the splits at the center front and the center back. Sew the Skirt seams, leaving approximately a 4-inch opening in the back seam at the top of the Skirt; hem the back opening. Hem the Skirt, gather the top edge, and sew the Skirt top to the Bodice bottom. Turn under the seam allowance on the Overskirt, and gather the Overskirt to fit over the Skirt; the bottom edges will turn under to form a puff. Sew a snap fastener to the Skirt waistband, another at the neck line of the Bodice, and the last one midway between the other two.

5. Cut out the Hat Brim interfacing and fuse it to the Brim. Place the Brim and the Brim lining together, and sew along the outer curved edge. Sew the back seam, and turn the Brim right side out. Finger press the edge of the Brim. Sew a piece of gathered ⅜-inch-wide lace around the edge. Gather the edge of the Hat Crown piece, and sew the Crown edge to the inner edge of

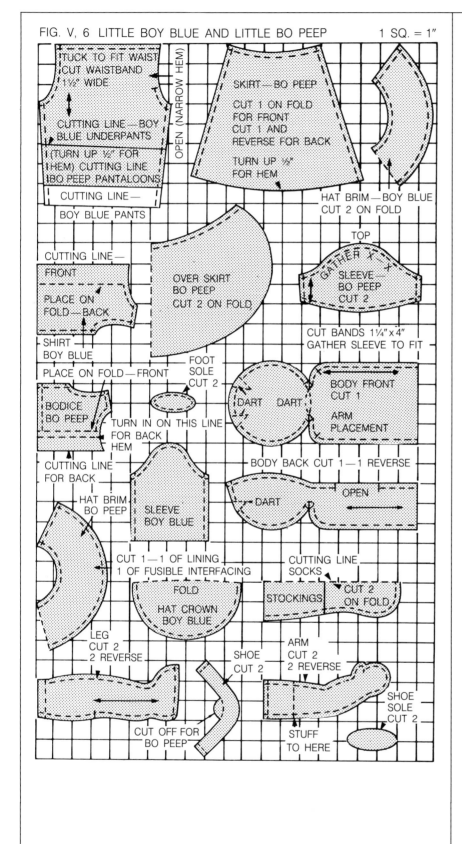

FIG. V, 6 LITTLE BOY BLUE AND LITTLE BO PEEP   1 SQ. = 1"

the Brim. Make a bow with the 1½-inch-wide ribbon, and sew it to the center front of the Hat Brim.

6. Make a shepherd's crook by twisting the 2 chenille stems together. Make a bow with the ½-inch-wide ribbon, and sew the bow to the shaped crook.

LITTLE BOY BLUE'S OUTFIT

MATERIALS: ¼ yard of blue percale; ¼ yard of blue and white gingham; scrap of white fabric; scrap of brown felt or suede cloth; matching threads; 2 small buttons; ½ yard of 1-inch-wide gold grosgrain ribbon; ¼ yard of ½-inch-wide red satin ribbon; ½ yard of 1½-inch-wide red satin ribbon; three ¾-inch-diameter snap fasteners; paper for patterns.

DIRECTIONS:

1. Enlarge the pattern pieces for Little Boy Blue's outfit in FIG. V, 6 onto paper, following the directions on page 239.

2. Use the ribbed cuffs of the child's socks for Little Boy Blue's Socks. Make the Socks following the directions for Little Bo Peep's Stockings, but do not hem the tops. Make Little Boy Blue's Shoes from the brown felt or suede cloth, following the directions for Little Bo Peep's Shoes.

3. Make the Underpants from the white percale, following the directions for Little Bo Peep's Pantaloons, but omitting the lace. Attach the Underpants directly to the waistband.

4. Make the Shirt and Sleeves from the blue and white gingham, following the directions for Little Bo Peep's Bodice, but placing the opening in the front. For the cuffs, cut two 4¼ x 2½-inch pieces from the white fabric. With raw edges even, fold each 2½-inch length in half, wrong sides together. Sew a cuff band to the wrong side of each Sleeve edge, with raw edges even, then turn the cuff to the right side, using the seam as the fold line. Cut a 1¾ x 7-inch bias strip from the white fabric for the collar. Bind the neck with the collar band. Sew the snap fasteners to the front opening. Make a bow with the 1½-inch-wide red satin ribbon, and sew the bow to the front of the collar.

5. Cut out the Pants from the blue percale. Make the Pants following the directions for Little Bo Peep's Pantaloons, adding a cuff to each leg end. Cut each cuff 2¾ x 6½ inches. Fold each cuff in half lengthwise, wrong sides together, and press. Fold the cuff widthwise and stitch the short ends together. Place the cuff on the wrong side of a Pant leg, with all raw edges even, and the short seam facing out on the Pant leg back. Sew the cuff to the Pants. Turn the Pants right side out, and fold the cuff up over the Pant leg. Blindstitch the top of each cuff to the Pant leg. Cut a waistband 1¼ inches wide, and sew the waistband to the Pants. Attach two pieces of the gold grosgrain ribbon, crossing the ribbon on the back, for suspender straps. Sew a small button to the front of each strap.

6. Cut out the Hat Brim, Crown and Brim lining from the blue percale. Cut out the interfacing for the Brim, and fuse the interfacing to the Brim. Sew the Brim and Brim lining together along the outer curved edge. Sew the back seam. Turn the Brim right side out, and press. Leaving the Crown folded, baste the curved edges together. Place the curved edges over the raw edge of the Brim, overlapping the seam allowances. Stitch the Brim to the Crown, overlapping and stitching the Crown's folded edges at the back. Sew ½-inch-wide red satin ribbon to cover the raw edges where the Crown joins the Brim.

Travelin' Toys

TRAVELIN' TOYS

(truck: 3½ x 5½ x 12½ inches; ferryboat: 7¼ x 7¾ x 17 inches; engine: 3¾ x 3½ x 12 inches)
This sturdy trio lets little ones get down to business.

CHALLENGING: Requires more experience in woodworking.
GENERAL MATERIALS: Scraps of plywood, pine and lattice *(see* FIGS. V, 7A to C, *page 172, for the amount of wood needed for each toy)*; jig or sabre saw; drill; hammer; nails; sandpaper; paper for patterns; wood glue; non-toxic paints. **FOR TRUCK:** Four 1½-inch-diameter wheels; 4 wooden pin axles. **FOR FERRYBOAT:** One 1-inch-diameter dowel; scraps of ¾-inch pine; 2 brass hinges.

FOR ENGINE: Four 1½-inch-diameter wheels; 4 wooden pin axles; one 1⅜-inch-diameter dowel; 1½-inch end of Shaker peg; ⅛-inch-wide tape for trim.

DIRECTIONS:
1. Using the jig or sabre saw, cut out the parts of the toys following FIGS. V, 7A to C *(page 172)*.
2. For the vehicles on the Ferryboat, enlarge the patterns in FIG. V, 7D *(page 172)* onto paper, following the directions on page 239. Using the jig or sabre saw, cut out the shapes from the ¾-inch pine.
3. Sand the toy parts smooth. Using the photo as a color guide, paint all the parts. Glue and nail all the parts together, as shown in the diagrams.

FIG. V, 7A FERRYBOAT
(7¼" W. x 7¾" H. x 17" L.)

A (1 x 8)   (1)   ¾" x 7¼" x 15" HULL
B (PLY)   (2)   ½" x 4" x 10" SIDES
C (PLY)   (1)   ½" x 3½" x 6" ROOF
D (DOWEL)   (1)   1"-DIA. x 2¾" STACK
E (1 x 8)   (1)   ¾" x 2" x 7¼" RAMP
F (SCRAP)   (3)   (SEE FIG. V, 7D)

FIG. V, 7B ENGINE (3¾" W. x 3½" H. x 12" L.)

A (LAT)   (1)   ½" x 2½" x 12" BOTTOM
B (DOW)   (1)   1⅜"-DIA. x 4" BOILER
C (LAT)   (1)   1" x 2½" x 2¼" CAB
C1 (LAT)   (2)   ½" x 1⅜" x 1½" CAB SIDES
C2 (LAT)   (1)   ¼" x 2½" x 2⅝" CAB TOP
D (LAT)   (2)   ¼" x 1⅝" x 4¼" TENDER
D1 (LAT)   (1)   ¼" x 1⅝" x 2½" TENDER
D2 (LAT)   (1)   ¼" x ¾" x 2" TENDER
E   (4)   1½"-DIA. WHEELS
F   (4)   WOODEN PIN AXLES
G   1½" END OF SHAKER PIN — STACK

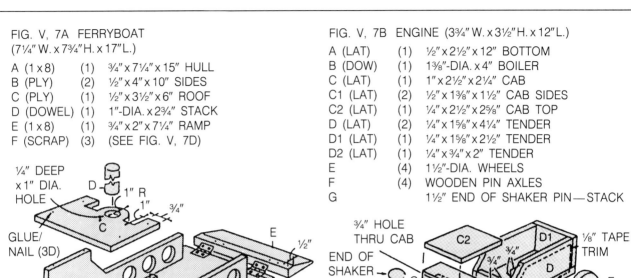

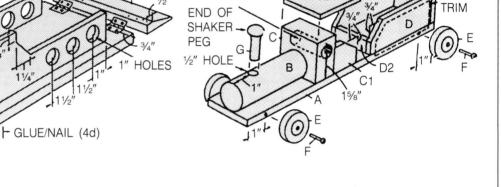

FIG. V, 7D   1 SQ. = ½"

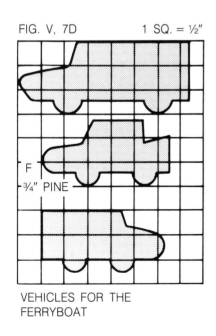

VEHICLES FOR THE
FERRYBOAT

FIG. V, 7C TRUCK
(3½" W. x 5½" H. x 12" L.)

A (LAT)   (1)   ½" x 3½" x 12" BOTTOM
B (2 x 4)   (1)   1½" x 3½" x 3½" CAB
C (LAT)   (2)   ½" x 1" x 10½" BODY
C1 (LAT)   (1)   ½" x 1" x 2⅝" TAILGATE
D (LAT)   (4)   ½" x 1" x 1¼" CHASSIS
D1   (4)   1½"-DIA. WHEELS
D2   (4)   WOODEN PIN AXLES
E (LAT)   (1)   ½" x 1⅜" x 3½" BUMPER
F (LAT)   (1)   ¼" x 1⅛" x 3½" BUMPER

Colonial Doll House

COLONIAL DOLL HOUSE

(about 2 feet high and 34 inches wide)
An easy-access doll house in early
American style.

CHALLENGING: Requires more
experience in crafting and
woodworking.

MATERIALS: AA INT grade plywood
or particle board: ½-inch x 4-foot x 8-
foot sheet, and ¼-inch x 2-foot x 3-foot
piece *(see Cutting Directions, at right,
for dimensions of wood pieces)*; 15 feet
of ½-inch-wide cove molding; 13 feet
of ¾-inch-wide corner guard molding;
7 feet of ½-inch-wide lattice; 6 feet of
1-inch-wide lattice; balsa wood strips:
$\frac{1}{16}$ x ½-inch, ⅛ x ⅛-inch and

⅛ x ½-inch; ½-inch and 1-inch nails;
wood glue; paints: blue and yellow
gold; doll house front door, and doll
house roof shingles *(see photo;
available in doll house and craft
supply stores)*; wallpaper and carpet
remnants; miniature furniture
*(available in doll house and hobby
stores)*; sabre saw; sandpaper.

CUTTING DIRECTIONS:

Code	Pieces	Size
A	1	½" x 15" x 33½" First floor
B	2	½" x 10" x 15" First floor inside walls
C	1	½" x 15" x 33½" Second floor
D	2	½" x 10" x 15" Second floor inside walls
E	2	½" x 15" x 21" Sides
F	1	½" x 21" x 34½" Front
G	1	½" x 16¼" x 35½" Attic floor
H	2	½" x 11¼" x 16" Attic sides
J	1	¼" x 11½" x 36" Roof front
K	1	¼" x 3" x 36" Roof back

DIRECTIONS:

1. Lay out the doll house parts on the
plywood or particle board for the most
economical use of the wood. Cut the
parts to size. Cut the window and door

Continued on page 175

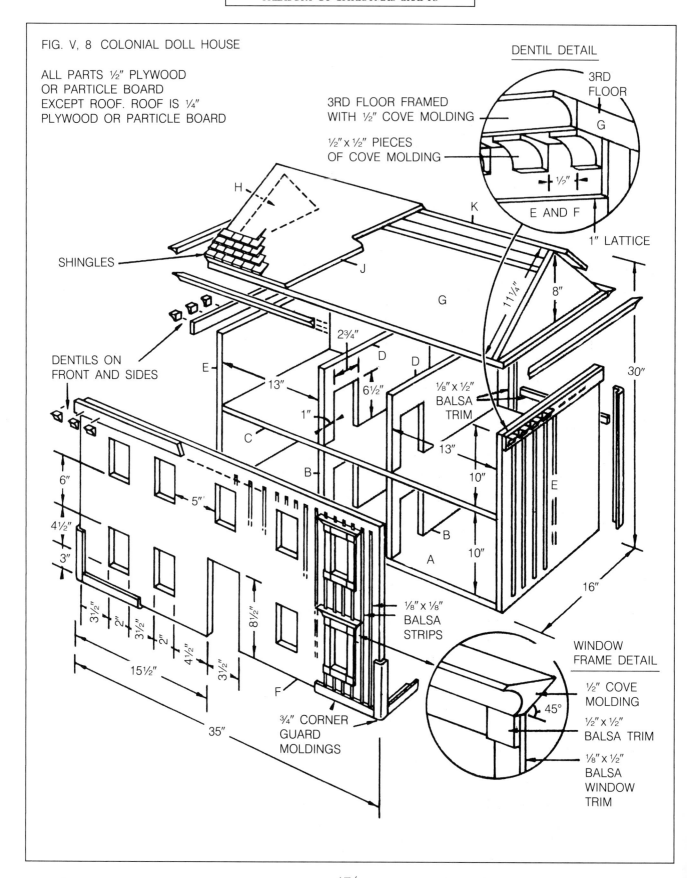

FIG. V, 8 COLONIAL DOLL HOUSE

ALL PARTS ½" PLYWOOD
OR PARTICLE BOARD
EXCEPT ROOF. ROOF IS ¼"
PLYWOOD OR PARTICLE BOARD

DENTIL DETAIL

3RD FLOOR FRAMED
WITH ½" COVE MOLDING

½" x ½" PIECES
OF COVE MOLDING

3RD FLOOR

G

½"

E AND F

1" LATTICE

H

K

SHINGLES

J

G

11¼"

8"

30"

DENTILS ON
FRONT AND SIDES

2¾"

D

D

E

13"

6½"

⅛" x ½"
BALSA
TRIM

13"

1"

10"

C

6"

E

B

5"

B

10"

A

4½"

3"

3½"

2"

3½"

2"

4½"

3½"

8½"

16"

15½"

⅛" x ⅛"
BALSA
STRIPS

WINDOW
FRAME DETAIL

½" COVE
MOLDING

45°

½" x ½"
BALSA TRIM

F

¾" CORNER
GUARD
MOLDINGS

⅛" x ½"
BALSA
WINDOW
TRIM

35"

Doll House Interior

openings with the sabre saw *(see* FIG.V, 8, *page 174, for measurements)*. Sand the parts smooth.

2. Glue, and nail, with 1-inch nails, the A First floor to the B First floor inside walls *(see* FIG. V, 8 *for placement)*. Nail through the underside of A into B. Repeat for the Second floor CD. Carefully toe-nail and glue CD to AB, aligning the First and Second floor inside walls B and D *(see* FIG. V, 8*)*.

3. Glue and nail the E Sides to the First and Second floors A and C. Glue and nail the F Front to the floors and walls.

4. Glue and nail the H Attic sides to the G Attic floor, through G into H, ½ inch in from each end *(see* FIG. V, 8*)*. Glue and nail the Attic floor to the doll house assembly flush at the back, and overlapping the sides ½ inch and the front ¾ inch. Glue and nail the J Roof front and K Roof back to the Attic sides. This completes the basic doll house structure.

5. Paint the outside of the house blue. Paint the ½-inch cove and ¾-inch corner guard moldings, and the 1-inch lattice yellow gold.

6. Miter, then glue and nail, using ½-inch wire nails, the molding trim to the front and sides of the house *(see details,* FIG. V, 8*)*. The dentils are ½-inch cove molding, ½ inch wide with ½-inch spacing.

7. Glue and nail the ¾-inch corner guard molding to the four outside corners, and around the bottom edges of the house.

8. Cut ⅛ x ½-inch balsa wood strips to fit around the windows, and glue them in place to form casings. Cut ½-inch cove molding at a 45° angle, and glue it across the top of each window.

9. See FIG. V, 8, for the window and batten details. Paint the battens blue after gluing them to the house.

10. Affix the front door and roof shingles, using the photos as placement guides.

11. Decorate the interior with wallpaper and carpet remnants. Furnish the doll house with miniature furniture *(see photo above for decorating ideas)*.

TWIG DOLL FURNITURE

AVERAGE: For those with some experience in woodworking.

FURNITURE:

MATERIALS: Twigs: 1-inch-diameter, ¾-inch-diameter, and ⅜- to ½-inch-diameter (*see* FIGS. V, 9A to C, *page 178, for quantities)*; ½ x 12 x 18 inches of common pine, rough on one side; block of scrap wood; wood stain or polyurethane; wood glue; 4d finishing nails; sandpaper; drill with ¼-, ⅜- and ½-inch drill bits; razor blade or knife; rasp or rough file; hammer; saw.

DIRECTIONS:

1. Three drill bit sizes are needed — ¼-, ⅜- and ½-inch — because various size twigs are used.

2. The block of scrap wood is your test block. Drill ¼-, ⅜- and ½-inch holes in the block. With the razor blade or knife, trim ¼ inch of bark from the end of a twig, and fit the trimmed end into the appropriate hole in the block; the end should fit snugly. If the end is too large, trim it with the rasp or rough file. Use that size drill for the support hole.

3. Cut an 11¼-inch square table top and a 6½-inch square chair seat from the common pine. Sand the rough edges to prevent splinters. Stain or polyurethane the pine, and let it dry.

4. Using the appropriate size drill bit, make support holes in the pine and larger twigs for the bed, table and chair, following FIGS. V, 9A to C *(page 178)*. Note that the chair seat has quarter-circle notches for the legs. Put glue on the trimmed ends of the appropriate size smaller twigs, and in the holes. Fit the trimmed twigs into their holes snugly. Drive a nail through each joint from the opposite side to secure it.

5. When the furniture has been pieced together, trim the ends of the legs with the knife or saw until they are even.

BEDDING AND CUSHION

MATERIALS: ½ yard of mattress ticking; 1 yard of 45-inch-wide floral print cotton or chintz; 20 x 24 inches of coordinating fabric; matching threads; embroidery floss in a coordinating color; synthetic batting; synthetic stuffing; darner needle.

DIRECTIONS
(¼-inch seams allowed):

1. Mattress: Cut two 14 x 22-inch pieces of ticking and one of batting. Place the ticking pieces right sides together, and the batting on the wrong side of one piece of ticking. Stitch around three sides and four corners. Turn the mattress right side out, turn in the open edges, and slipstitch the opening closed. Using the darner needle and embroidery floss, tie quilt the mattress in eight places.

2. Quilt: Cut one 20 x 24-inch piece of floral print fabric, one of coordinating fabric and two of batting. Make the quilt following the directions in Step 1.

3. Pillow: Sew two 11 x 14-inch pieces of floral print fabric, right sides together, around three sides and four corners. Turn the pillow right side out and press. Topstitch 1¼ inches from the stitched sides. Stuff the pillow. Turn in the edges, slipstitch the opening closed, and topstitch 1¼ inches from the edge.

4. Chair Cushion: Cut two 8-inch squares and one 2¼ x 16-inch strip from the floral print. Fold the strip in half, and press. Fold the raw edges into the fold, and edgestitch the open side. Cut the strip in half, and knot both ends of each half. Place one square right side up, and pin a folded strip to each of two adjacent corners of the square, with the knotted ends pointed toward the center. Pin the second square, right side down, over the ties, and stitch around three sides and four corners. Turn the pillow right side out, and stuff it. Turn in the open edges, and slipstitch the opening closed.

Note: To make a support for the mattress, use a ⅛-inch size drill bit, and drill 11 holes, at 2-inch intervals, along each ¾ x 24-inch twig (the bed sides), starting one inch from the bottom. Thread a piece of twine through the 22 holes, weaving the twine back and forth to create a ladder effect.

TOYING AROUND

The key to selecting the best gift for a child is knowing his or her interests, abilities and limitations. Avoid buying toys to please yourself, toys that don't involve the child, or toys that may be too sophisticated for his or her interest.

Set a good example for the proper use and maintenance of toys. Get involved in playing, and encourage your youngster to be creative through play — a lesson learned while having fun generally is better retained. And bear in mind that playing is a child's job; those who are creative at play as children are more likely to be creative at work as adults.

Twig Doll Furniture, Bedding and Cushion

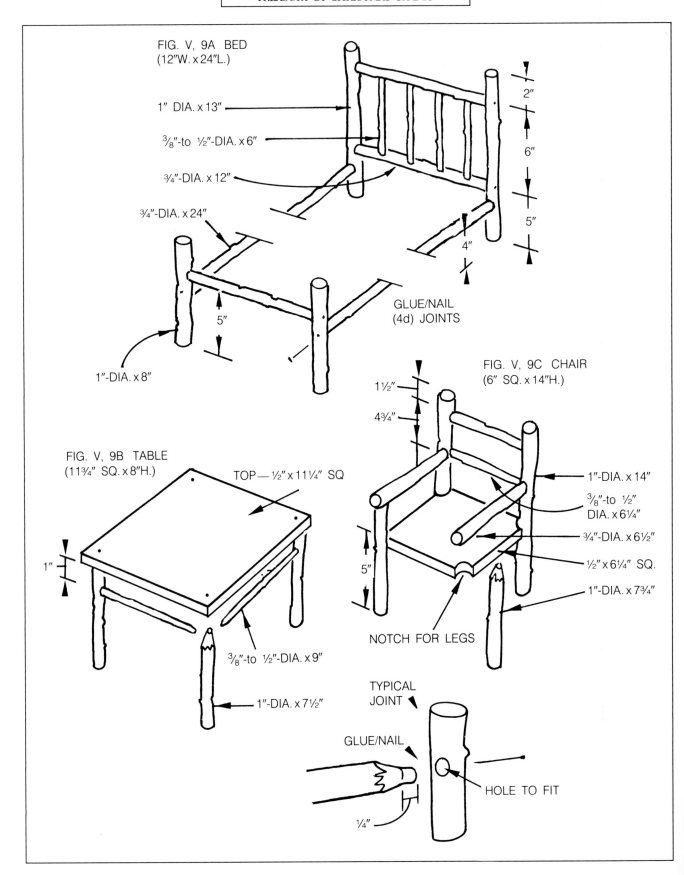

FIG. V, 9A BED
(12"W. x 24"L.)

1" DIA. x 13"

3/8"-to 1/2"-DIA. x 6"

3/4"-DIA. x 12"

3/4"-DIA. x 24"

2"

6"

5"

4"

GLUE/NAIL
(4d) JOINTS

5"

1"-DIA. x 8"

FIG. V, 9C CHAIR
(6" SQ. x 14"H.)

1 1/2"

4 3/4"

1"-DIA. x 14"

3/8"-to 1/2"
DIA. x 6 1/4"

3/4"-DIA. x 6 1/2"

1/2" x 6 1/4" SQ.

1"-DIA. x 7 3/4"

5"

NOTCH FOR LEGS

FIG. V, 9B TABLE
(11 3/4" SQ. x 8"H.)

TOP — 1/2" x 11 1/4" SQ

1"

3/8"-to 1/2"-DIA. x 9"

1"-DIA. x 7 1/2"

TYPICAL
JOINT

GLUE/NAIL

HOLE TO FIT

1/4"

Farm Friends Pull Toys

FARM FRIENDS PULL TOYS
(about 6 x 10 inches)

AVERAGE: For those with some experience in woodworking.

MATERIALS FOR ONE TOY:
⁵⁄₄ x 10 inches of pine; four 2-inch-diameter wooden wheels; 6-inch-long ¼-inch-diameter dowel; 4 wooden beads, or thumbtacks; non-toxic paints *(see* FIG. V, 10*)*; screw eye; pull string; tracing paper; graphite paper; stylus or old ballpoint pen; sabre saw; drill.

DIRECTIONS:
1. Enlarge one of the patterns in FIG. V, 10 onto tracing paper, following the directions on page 239. Using the graphite paper and stylus or old pen, transfer the pattern to the pine. Cut out the shape with the sabre saw.
2. Drill ¼-inch-diameter holes for the wheel axles. Cut the dowel in half, and insert one half through each axle hole. Use the beads or thumbtacks to secure the wheels. Paint the toy. When the paint is dry, insert the screw eye as indicated in FIG. V, 10. Tie the string to the screw eye, and use it as a pull.

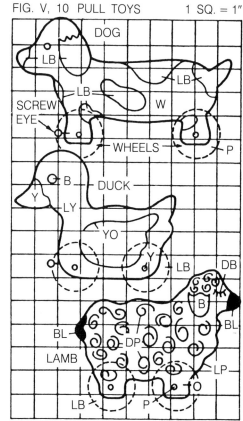

FIG. V, 10 PULL TOYS   1 SQ. = 1"

W = WHITE   LB = LT. BLUE   P = PINK
B = BLUE   LY = LT. YELLOW
LP = LT. PINK   YO = YELLOW OUTLINE
DP = DK. PINK   DB = DK. BLUE
Y = YELLOW   BL = BLACK

CHRISTMAS
COMFORTS

Christmas Lily Quilt

CHRISTMAS LILY QUILT

(wall hanging: about 55 x 65 inches; full-size quilt: about 76 x 86 inches)

CHALLENGING: Requires more experience in quilting.
Note 1: Measurements are given first for the wall hanging; the full-size quilt measurements are in parentheses.
Note 2: All seams are pressed open. All seams are ¼ inch. Due to shrinkage, add ¼ inch to all seams of the flower pieces A through J.
MATERIALS: 8 yards of small cream print (11 yards); 1½ yards of small bright red print (2½ yards); 1½ yards of small dark red print (2½ yards); 3 yards of small green print (6 yards); ½ yard of small yellow print (1 yard); matching sewing threads; quilting thread; embroidery floss: 1 skein of Black and 2 skeins of Gold (1 Black, 3 Gold); three 4-ounce balls of Cream yarn (6); tapestry needle; embroidery needle; darner needle; between needle; firm template material; full-size synthetic batting; 53-inch-long dowel for wall hanging; freezer paper; glue stick; seam ripper; 3 water-soluble fabric marking pens (5); ruler; masking tape.

DIRECTIONS:

1. Wash all the fabrics to shrink them. Iron the fabrics. Enlarge the solid line patterns for the pieced square in FIG. V, 11A *(page 183)*, following the directions on page 239 (the dotted lines will be quilted later). Make templates of pieces A to J. **From the cream print,** cut out: E - 10 (21), F - 20 (42), I - 60 (126), and J - 30 (63). **From the yellow print,** cut out: B - 10 (21) and D - 20 (42). **From the bright and dark red prints,** cut out: H - 80 (168). **From the green print,** cut out: A - 10 (21), C - 20 (42), G - 30 (63) and 130 inches (275 inches) of ⅝-inch-wide bias strips for stems.
2. To piece each square, follow FIG. V, 11A for the position of each pattern

piece. Sew four H's together, alternating shades of red, at the side seams so the points meet in the center; press. Sew a J to the top of the two center H's, and two I's to the side H's; press. Sew a G across the bottom of the four H's; press. Repeat to make two more buds. To form the center, sew D to C, press, sew D/C to the left side of E; press. Repeat for the right side. Press the edges under on the bias strip and appliqué it in place for the stems, using a slipstitch. Leave an opening at the top of the center stem, at the X's on the pattern. Fold the opening back against the sewn stem, and pin it in place. This will keep the stem free for sewing the center bud in place later. Sew A to B; press. Sew the long edge of B to the completed stem section. This completes the center section.
3. To complete the square, sew an F to the right side of the left bud, and press. Sew the left side of the center bud to the other long side of F, leaving an opening below the O on the pattern so the stem can be slipped in later. Press and set aside. Sew an F to the left side of the right bud. Press. Attach the right bud section to the right side of the center section. Press. Sew the two-buds section all the way across the left side of the center section and the left side of the right bud section, leaving an opening between the T and the O. Press. Slip the unsewn portion of the center stem under the tip of the center bud, and slipstitch the stem in place. Press. The pieced square should measure 10 inches. Repeat to make 10 (21) pieced squares.
4. Cut 10 (21) 10-inch squares from the cream print fabric. Sew them to the sides of the pieced squares to make rows of alternating squares, with the flowers on the diagonal; press.
5. From the cream print, cut two border strips 10 x 58 inches (11 x 79 inches). Center and sew them to the top and bottom of the quilt center. Leave an opening ¼ inch from each

edge. Cut two side borders 10 x 67½ inches (11 x 88½ inches). Center and sew them to the quilt sides, ending the seams at the corners. Miter all four corners, sew, and press.
6. For the border design, enlarge the pattern pieces (half patterns are indicated by long broken lines; make full-size patterns) in FIG. V, 11B *(page 183)*, following the directions on page 239. Cut out the following pieces: 1 (dark red) - 20 (26) swags and 4 (4) bows; 2 (bright red) - 14 (22) hearts and 4 (4) bow undersides; 3 (green) - 20 (26) swags and 14 (22) teardrops. Appliqué the pieces to the quilt using the freezer paper method *(see Tip, page 182)*. Wash the quilt top, remove the paper, dry, and press.
7. Using three strands of Gold floss and the embroidery needle, chain stitch around the outside of the red hearts, and between the green and red swags *(see Embroidery Stitch Guide, page 240)*. Embroider the bows in Black and Gold, following the solid lines on the pattern in FIG. V, 11B.
8. Enlarge the four quilting designs in FIGS. V, 11C to F *(page 183)*, and the quilting design in FIG. V, 11A and 11B (dotted lines), following the directions on page 239. Half patterns are indicated by long broken lines. Make a full pattern for Design II *(FIG. V, 11D)*, and the quilting pattern in FIG. V, 11A and 11B. Complete Design III *(FIG. V, 11E)* by continuing the smaller flower along the arrows. Quilting lines in all designs are the short broken lines. Using the fabric marking pens (and a light box if you have one), transfer Designs I through IV to the nonappliquéd squares, repeating as necessary; Design II should be placed on the diagonal. Transfer the quilting design in FIG. V, 11A to the pieced squares, and the quilting design in FIG. V, 11B to the border squares.
9. Fill in the background of the quilted designs by quilting diagonal lines ⅛ inch apart. This will make the

FREEZER PAPER METHOD OF APPLIQUÉ

Place freezer paper dull side up. Trace full patterns (no seam allowance) onto the paper. Make as many patterns as appliqués needed for the finished project. Cut out the patterns and place them, shiny side down, on the wrong side of the fabric. Iron the paper patterns; the wax causes the patterns to stick to the fabric until washed out. Add a ⅛-inch seam allowance and cut out each shape. Run a glue stick over the seam allowance, and roll the edges over the paper to perfect the shape. Glue the appliqués to the main fabric; when dry, stitch around each shape using a single thread.

Soak the finished project in cold water for 10 to 15 minutes to dissolve the glue and release the wax. Blot with a towel to dry slightly. On the back of the project, first make a slit underneath each appliquéd piece, then cut the underside fabric to within ¼ inch to ⅛ inch of the seam line; this makes it easier to quilt. Use a seam ripper to pull out the freezer paper. When all the paper is removed, soak the project in cold water again to remove any remaining glue. When the project is almost dry, press it. Trim all excess fabric, including the seams; this allows for tighter quilting stitches, and fewer layers to quilt through. Don't trim too close to the appliqué seams, and handle the pieces gently to prevent the seams from pulling out.

background very flat, and raise the design. Repeat for the border, running the background lines perpendicular to the border *(see photo)*.

10. For the quilt back, cut two 45 x 70-inch (45 x 91-inch) pieces from the cream print, and sew them together along the long edge; press. For the wall hanging, trim one long side to a 60-inch width; save the extra fabric to make the casing.

11. Cut the batting to fit the quilt back. Place the quilt back on a flat surface, wrong side up, and tape down the corners. Place the batting on top of the quilt back, and the quilt top, right side up, on the batting. Using the darner needles, baste the three layers together from the center outward to each corner, and straight to the edges. Baste additional lines 8 inches apart.

12. Starting in the center of the quilt, and using the between needle and quilting thread, quilt along the transferred design lines. Also quilt ¼ inch in from the seams on each pieced square, and ¼ inch *outside* the seam of each appliquéd piece.

13. The final process is called stuff work. Using the tapestry needle and doubled Cream yarn, run the needle between the quilt top and batting *only*. Begin each area to be stuffed by running the needle down at one edge and through to the other side, just within the quilting lines. Pull the yarn carefully just until it slips inside between the quilt top and the batting. Clip the other end of the yarn right next to the fabric. If necessary, poke the needle down through the quilt top and push or pull the yarn to adjust it. Continue the process until the leaf or berry in the quilting design is fat and full. Holes made by the tapestry needle can be pushed back together easily with the needle, once an area is finished. With a final washing, the fibers will settle back into place.

14. To finish the quilt, cut 2½ x 270 inches (340 inches) of bias binding from the green print. Cut the quilt back and batting to the edges of the quilt top. Sew on the binding, using a ½-inch seam. Miter the corners. Turn the binding over the edges of the quilt, and slipstitch the binding to the quilt back. For the wall hanging, before finishing the top edge of the quilt, sew a 3-inch-wide casing into the seam line along the whole length at the top back side of the quilt. Turn the bottom of the casing under ½ inch. Slipstitch the casing to the quilt back only, allowing room for the dowel rod to hang the quilt. To remove the marked quilting design lines, wash the entire quilt, following the fabric marking pen manufacturer's directions.

FIG. V, 11A PIECED SQUARE

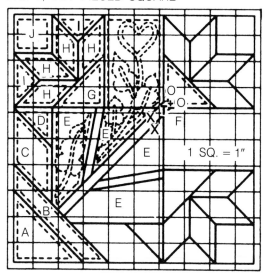

1 SQ. = 1"

FIG. V, 11D
QUILTING DESIGN II

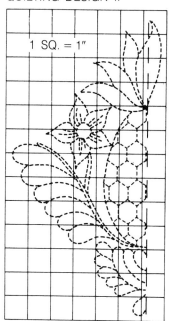

1 SQ. = 1"

FIG. V, 11E QUILTING DESIGN III

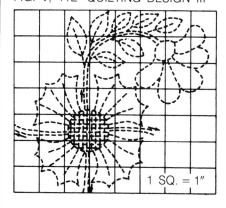

1 SQ. = 1"

FIG. V, 11C QUILTING DESIGN I

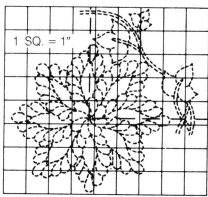

1 SQ. = 1"

1 = DARK RED PRINT
2 = BRIGHT RED PRINT
3 = GREEN PRINT

FIG. V, 11B BORDER

1 SQ. = 1"

BORDER
CORNER

SWAG
MOTIF

FIG. V, 11F QUILTING DESIGN IV

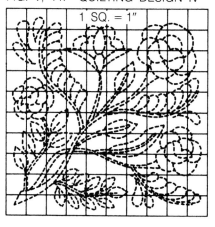

1 SQ. = 1"

THE CRAFT OF QUILTING

Always wash cotton and cotton-blend fabrics to preshrink them, and to test them for color fastness. And always press fabric before marking it for cutting.

Precision is a must when cutting the patches to make a quilt block. Invest in high-quality, steel blade fabric scissors. And never cut anything but fabric with these special shears — using them on paper or hair will dull them.

The purpose of quilting, beyond the decoration it provides, is to fasten the backing, batting and top layers together, and to keep the batting from developing holes or lumps after long use. Hand-quilting a running stitch about 1/4 inch from the patchwork seams is the most secure method. If you use synthetic batting, the quilting rows can be as much as 3 to 4 inches apart.

ROSE GARDEN QUILT

(about 85 x 93 inches)
You'll have to start early to have this queen-size quilt ready for Christmas.

AVERAGE: For those with some experience in quilting.
MATERIALS: Forty-four- to forty-five-inch-wide cotton broadcloth: 12½ yards of white for patches and quilt back, and 1¼ yards of pink for border patches; solid color pastel fabrics: about ¼ yard each of 6 colors, including yellow for rosette centers; print fabrics: ⅜ yard each of 7 prints and ½ yard each of 2 prints; matching sewing threads; 12 yards of pink wide bias binding; 90 x 108 inches of synthetic batting; darner needle; between needle; quilting thread; quilting frame or hoop; thin cardboard; glue or transparent tape; masking tape; tracing paper *(optional)*.
Note: *The patches are sewn into rosettes and diamonds. The rosettes and diamonds are joined to make two alternating rows (see* FIG. V, *12E, page 187). The rows are repeated, and sewn together side by side. A border is added at the left and the right to finish the quilt top. Then the quilt top, batting and quilt back are quilted together, and the edges are bound.*

DIRECTIONS
(¼-inch seams allowed):
1. Cutting Pattern: Carefully trace or cut out the hexagon patch pattern in FIG. V, 12A *(page 186)*. Using glue or transparent tape, fasten the hexagon smoothly to the thin cardboard, and cut it out on the solid lines. The broken lines are the sewing lines. When sewing the patches together, sew only *on the broken lines;* do not sew all the way to the edges.
2. Cutting: ***From the white broadcloth,*** cut two 98-inch lengths measuring the full width of the fabric. Sew them together at the long edges to make an approximately 98 x 88-inch

quilt back. Cut 1,041 white hexagons, tracing them carefully with a sharp pencil, and laying them out with common edges in intersecting rows (like the quilt) to save fabric and time. ***From the pink broadcloth,*** cut 166 hexagons for the border. ***From the solid yellow fabric,*** cut 39 hexagons for the rosette centers. ***From the remaining solid color pastel fabrics,*** cut 39 sets of six same-color patches. ***From the print fabrics,*** cut 39 sets of 12 same-print patches.
3. Block A (white rosette): With right sides up, lay a ring of six white patches around a central white patch. Turn one patch over the center *(see* FIG. V, *12B, page 186)*, pin on the sewing line *(see Note, at left)*, and stitch. Repeat with the remaining five patches *(see* FIG. V, *12C, page 186)*. With right sides together, bring two outer patches together and stitch *(see* FIG. V, *12D, page 186)*. Repeat with the other remaining five adjoining sides to complete the ring. Press, but do not open the seams. Make 71 A Blocks.
4. Block B (colored rosette): Using a yellow center patch and a ring of solid color patches, make an A Block following the directions in Step 3. Around it lay a ring of 12 print patches, and stitch every other one to the outside edge of a solid color patch *(see X's in* FIG. V, *12C)*. Stitch the intervening patches at two sides each. Stitch their side edges to complete the ring. Make 39 B Blocks, varying the color combinations *(see photo)*.
5. Block C (white diamond): Make an A Block with white patches. Add one white patch at an inside corner, stitching the two edges. Add another white patch opposite the first to finish the diamond. Make 10 C Blocks.
6. Block C-1 (white and pink diamond): Make an A Block with five white patches, and two adjoining pink

Continued on page 186

Rose Garden Quilt

patches in the ring. Add a white patch between them and another opposite, to make a diamond. Make 10 C-1 Blocks.

7. Row 1: Following the diagram in FIG. V, 12E *(page 187)*, join six A Blocks, four B Blocks, and fifteen white filler patches. Add pink and white patches at each end. Make six of Row 1.

8. Row 2: Following the diagram in FIG. V, 12E, join seven A Blocks, three B Blocks, two C-1 Blocks, and four white filler patches. Make five of Row 2.

9. Quilt Top: Alternating Row 1 with Row 2 *(see* FIG. V, 12E*)*, stitch the rows together. Add five white patches to the outside of each B Block. Add pink patches, C Blocks, and white patches to complete the borders *(see* FIG. V, 12E*)*.

10. Basting: Place the quilt back on the floor, wrong side up, and tape down the corners. Place the batting on top of the quilt back, and the quilt top, right side up, on the batting. Using the darner needle, baste the three layers together with long stitches from the center outward to each corner, and straight to the edges. Add more basting rows 6 or 8 inches apart.

11. Quilting: Place the quilt in the quilting frame or hoop (work from the center outward if you use a hoop). Using the between needle and quilting thread, quilt in the ditch of all the seams. When you are finished quilting, baste through the three layers from corner to corner around the outside edges, following the broken lines in FIG. V, 12E, to make the top edge straight and the three other edges scalloped. Trim off the quilt just outside the basting.

12. Finishing: With right sides together and raw edges even, stitch the bias binding, along a fold, to the quilt. Turn the tape over to the back of the quilt, and slipstitch to the quilt back.

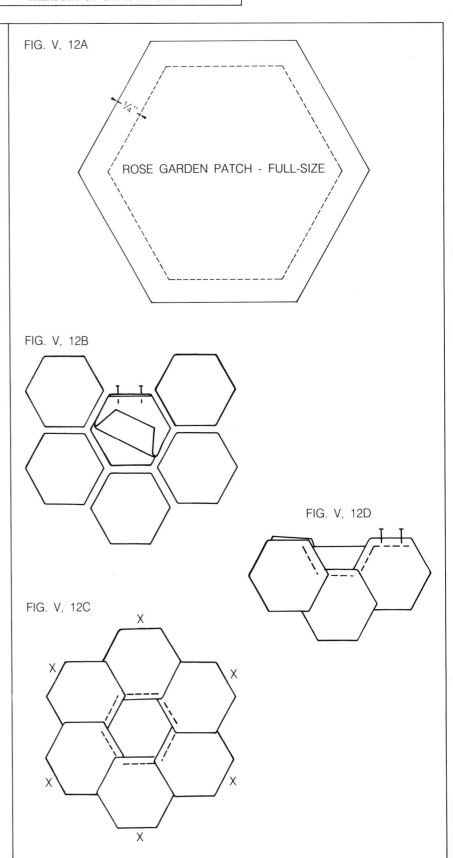

FIG. V, 12A

¼"

ROSE GARDEN PATCH - FULL-SIZE

FIG. V, 12B

FIG. V, 12D

FIG. V, 12C

X
X   X
X   X
X

FIG. V, 12E JOINING DIAGRAM

LEFT BORDER   ROW 1

RIGHT BORDER

ROWS 1 AND 2   4 TIMES

ROW 1

LEFT BORDER   ROW 2

RIGHT BORDER

I am in the habit of looking not so much to the nature of a gift as to the spirit in which it is offered.
—*Robert Louis Stevenson*

Patchwork Wall Hanging

PATCHWORK WALL HANGING

(48¹/₂ x 53 inches)

This eye-catching patchwork piece can be made in holiday colors or, as shown here, in shades that suit any season of the year.

AVERAGE: For those with some experience in quilting.

MATERIALS: One yard of fabric for borders and bias binding; 2 yards of fabric for quilt back in a color to harmonize with those on the front (or pick up one of the minor colors that is used on the front); ¼ yard each of all other fabrics *(see Note, below)*; matching sewing threads; quilting thread; synthetic batting; dowel or rod; paper; pencil; ruler; colored pencils or crayons; darner needle; between needle; masking tape.

Note: The quilt is of one color primarily, with small amounts of other colors introduced in parts of the design. Within your chosen color family, you will need fabrics in tones ranging from dark, through medium dark and medium light, to light. "A" on the pattern (FIG. V, 13) represents the darkest value of the basic color. White or off-white, and black or off-black, can be used for accents. Cotton or cotton-blend fabrics, all solid-color fabrics, all print fabrics, or a mixture of solids and prints can be used. It will be helpful to make a paper pattern and plan color placement before cutting the fabrics. The pattern in FIG. V, 13 illustrates one quarter of the quilt. The four blocks sewn together form the center medallion design.

DIRECTIONS:

1. Wash all the fabrics to shrink them, remove the sizing and assure color fastness. Iron the fabrics.
2. Enlarge the pattern in FIG. V, 13, following the directions on page 239. The patch patterns are represented by the solid lines; the dotted lines may be

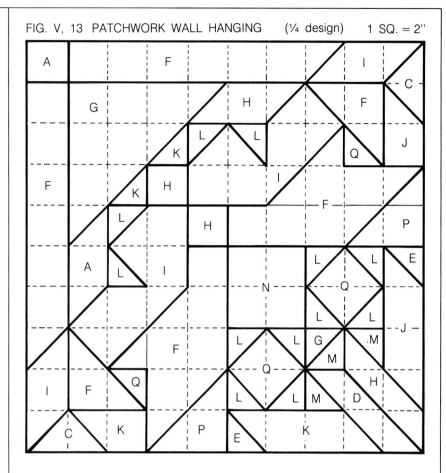

FIG. V, 13 PATCHWORK WALL HANGING   (¼ design)   1 SQ. = 2"

used as quilting lines, if you wish.
3. Mark and cut the fabrics carefully. The drawn lines are the sewing lines. Allow ¼ inch beyond the sewing lines for seams. Stitch the pieces together to make four identical 19- to 20-inch square blocks. Sew the blocks together to form the central design. Add borders, if you wish; we added three border strips to the sides and five to the top and bottom *(see photo)*.
4. Lay the finished top, right side down, on a large flat surface and tape it in place. Cover it with the batting and the quilt back, right side up. Using the darner needle, baste the three layers together in a grid pattern, and quilt or tie the layers together; we used a diamond-pattern quilting design on the outer border *(see photo for additional quilting design ideas)*.

5. Make bias strips by folding a square of fabric in half diagonally. Measure and carefully cut 1⅝-inch strips, and sew the strips together at the short ends. Place the joined bias binding along the edge on the front side of the quilt, right sides together, and stitch ⅛ inch from the edge.
6. Turn the binding to the back, turn it under ⅛ inch, and hand-sew the binding to the back.
7. To hang the quilt, sew a 1-inch-wide fabric strip to the top back to make a casing for the dowel or rod.

✿ ✿ ✿ ✿ ✿ ✿

SWEET DREAMS — IN COLOR

The simple block design used in our Hearts & Checkers Quilt is perfect for a child's or teenager's bedroom. And, the design works beautifully in a variety of color combinations:

French blue and marigold
Pink and violet
Turquoise and plum
Mint and evergreen
Peach and slate blue
Red and golden yellow

Use a matching calico or pin-dot fabric, with a white background, as the background fabric for the quilt.

HEARTS & CHECKERS QUILT
(about 46 x 64 inches)

AVERAGE: For those with some experience in quilting.

MATERIALS: Forty-five-inch-wide small print fabric: 5½ yards of white, 1¼ yards of red and ½ yard of green; white and red sewing threads; white quilting thread; darner needle; between needle; synthetic batting; quilting frame or hoop; brown paper; masking tape; hard pencil.

Note: The quilt is assembled from eight patchwork Blocks A and seven appliquéd heart Blocks B (see FIGS. V, 14A, B and C, pages 190 and 192). Borders are added, with a sawtooth edging (of folded squares) enclosed in the outside seam. The seams are machine sewn, the heart appliqués and quilting are hand sewn.

DIRECTIONS
(¼-inch seams allowed):

1. Pattern: Following the directions on page 239, enlarge the small and large heart patterns in FIG. V, 14A onto folded brown paper, placing the broken line on the fold. Unfold for the full patterns; the large heart (solid line) is the quilting design, the small heart (dotted line) is the appliqué.

2. Cutting: *From the white fabric,* cut two 36 x 52-inch pieces for the quilt back, two 9 x 52-inch borders, one 7 x 49-inch border, one 9 x 49-inch border, seven 10½ x 6½-inch rectangles, fourteen 2½ x 6½-inch rectangles, thirty-two 2½-inch squares for quilt blocks A, and one hundred sixty 2½-inch squares for the sawtooth edging. *From the green fabric,* cut seventy-two 2½-inch squares. *From the red fabric,* cut one hundred twenty-four 2½-inch squares. Also trace, without cutting, seven small (dotted line) hearts ½ inch apart.

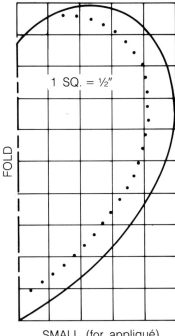

FIG. V, 14A HEARTS

1 SQ. = ½"

FOLD

···· SMALL (for appliqué)
— LARGE

3. Block A: Following the diagram in FIG. V, 14B, sew the 2½-inch squares side by side to make five horizontal rows. Sew the rows from top to bottom, seams matching, to make the block. Make eight blocks.

Continued on page 192

FIG. V, 14B QUILT BLOCKS
BLOCK A

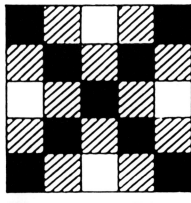

 GREEN   RED ☐ WHITE

Hearts & Checkers Quilt

FIG. V, 14C BLOCK B

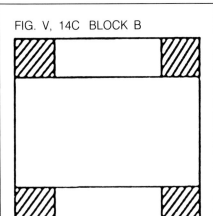

4. Block B: Sew a red square at each end of a 2½ x 6½-inch white strip *(see* FIG. V, 14C*)*. Sew this row to one long edge of a 10½ x 6½-inch white rectangle. Repeat at the opposite edge. Make seven B blocks.

5. Assembling: Following the diagram in FIG. V, 14D, sew five horizontal rows of three blocks each. Sew the rows one below the other, seams matching.

6. Borders: Sew a 52-inch-long border at each side of the assembly *(see* FIG. V, 14D*)*, and trim the ends flush. Sew the 7-inch-wide border to the top and the 9-inch-wide border to the bottom of the assembly.

FIG. V, 14D

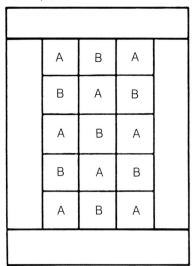

FIG. V, 14E

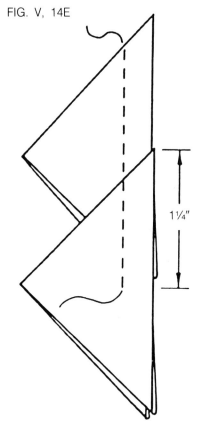

1¼"

7. Sawtooth Edging: Fold each 2½-inch white square in half diagonally, then in half again, raw edges even, to make a triangle; press. Repeat. Lap one tooth 1¼ inches over another, with each single fold at the top and raw edges even *(see* FIG. V, 14E*)*. Repeat to make 33 points. Stitch the points together a scant ¼ inch from the raw edges to make the top edging. Make a second row of 33 points the same way for the bottom edging. Make two rows of 47 points each for the side edgings. With right sides together and raw edges even, stitch the sawtooth strips to the top and bottom edges of the quilt top, then to each side edge; remove excess teeth if necessary. Press the edging outward.

8. Quilt Back: Sew the two quilt back pieces together along a long edge, and press the seam to one side. Spread out the quilt back, wrong side up, on a

clean, flat surface, and tape down the corners. Cut a piece of batting to fit the quilt back. Spread the batting and then the quilt top, right side up and centered, on top of the quilt back. Using the darner needle, white sewing thread and long stitches, baste from the center diagonally outward to each corner, and straight out to the center of each edge. Add more basting rows about 6 inches apart.

9. Quilting: Place the quilt in the quilting frame or hoop (work from the center outward if you use a hoop). Using the between needle and quilting thread, sew running stitches through all the layers about ¼ inch from each seam. At the inner edge of the borders, quilt ½ inch outside the seam.

10. Appliquéing: Spread a piece of batting on the back of the red fabric on which the appliqué hearts are traced. Machine-stitch over the traced heart outlines. Cut out the hearts ¼ inch *outside the stitch lines.* Trim the batting close to the stitching. Pin a heart to the center of each Block B, all points toward the bottom. Turn the appliqué edges under on the stitch lines, clipping the curves, and slipstitch each heart in place through all the layers. Quilt a smaller heart about an inch inside each appliqué heart.

11. Border Quilting: Using the hard pencil, trace a large heart diagonally at each corner. Trace more large hearts, spaced evenly, along the border, points toward the quilt edges *(see photo, page 191)*. Quilt over the traced lines, and again about an inch inside them to make smaller hearts. Baste through the quilt ½ inch inside the sawtooth edging.

12. Quilt Back Edges: Turn the quilt wrong side up. Trim the batting flush with the outside seamline. Trim the quilt back ½ inch outside the sawtooth seamline. Turn under ½ inch at each quilt back edge, and slipstitch the fold to the seamline all around the quilt.

CARING FOR QUILTS

Whether you own an antique quilt, handed down through the generations, or have created your own heirloom-quality quilt, the following will provide you with what you need to know to care for your quilts so you can enjoy them for years to come.

AIRING QUILTS

The safest method for airing a quilt 50 or more years old is to place it in the shade on a nice, breezy day.

Never hang a quilt on a clothesline; this weakens the stitches.

To air a quilt indoors, drape the quilt over a chair for half a day.

CLEANING QUILTS

Vacuum Cleaning a Quilt
(this method should not be used more than once a year)

Lay the quilt flat on a bed or other clean surface. On top of the quilt, place a 24-inch square of fiberglass screening with its edges taped. Slowly and gently vacuum over the screen using a low-power, hand-held vacuum with a clean brush attachment. Carefully move the screen to another part of the quilt, and repeat the vacuuming. When the top of the quilt is done, turn back half the quilt and vacuum the bed or surface under it. Repeat the vacuuming on the other side of the quilt. **Never** vacuum a quilt with beading on it.

Dry Cleaning a Quilt
Wool, velvet or silk quilts must be dry cleaned by an expert cleaner who specializes in antique garments. There is no guarantee that dry cleaning will work, or that it will not damage the quilt.

Wet Cleaning
Like dry cleaning, washing a quilt should be done by an expert. It is too easy to damage a quilt if you wash it yourself at home.

HOW TO DISPLAY QUILTS

Quilts can be displayed for up to three months at a time. Then allow them to "rest" for four months by storing them as suggested below.

Never display a quilt in direct sunlight, reflected sunlight, near a heat source, or under fluorescent lights. This also is true for heirloom needlework.

Never place an object on top of an heirloom quilt, even if the quilt is under glass.

THE DO'S & DON'TS OF STORING QUILTS

Do store quilts in a cool area that is clean, dry, dark, and well-ventilated. Relative humidity should be about 50%.

Do wrap quilts in acid-free tissue paper, washed muslin, washed cotton, or cotton/polyester-blend sheets. Acid-free products are available at craft stores or by mail order. If your quilt has a metal part attached to it, remove the metal, if possible, before wrapping the quilt for storage.

Do place wrapped quilts in acid-free boxes. If you are going to store a quilt in a bureau drawer, first line the drawer with acid-free tissue paper, washed muslin, washed cotton, or cotton/polyester sheets. For extra protection, coat the bureau drawer with a polyurethane varnish before lining the drawer with the tissue paper or sheets. If your home gets a lot of dust, line the drawer with heavy polyethylene sheets, Mylar® or fiberfill.

Don't store a quilt in the attic or basement. These rooms tend to be damp, and the quilt will mildew.

Don't wrap quilts for storage in plastic, styrofoam, or any product made from wood, such as cardboard or regular (not acid-free) tissue paper.

FOLDING A QUILT FOR STORAGE

To prevent soil buildup, discoloration and wear along fold lines, fold the quilt into thirds, placing a roll of acid-free tissue paper along and under each fold. Fold the quilt again into thirds, toward the center. Place a roll of crumpled acid-free tissue paper along and under each of these two fold lines. If you wish, you may substitute washed cotton, cotton/polyester sheets, or washed unbleached muslin for the acid-free tissue paper.

GRANNY SQUARE AFGHAN & PILLOW TOP

*(afghan: 45 x 60 inches;
pillow top: 13 inches square)*
*This is a great portable project for
people on the go, because you make
each square separately.*

AVERAGE: For those with some
experience in crocheting.
MATERIALS: Three-ply sport weight
yarn (3-ounce ball): 7 balls of
Vermilion (A) and 5 balls of Ecru (B);
size F crochet hook, OR ANY SIZE HOOK
TO OBTAIN GAUGE BELOW; tapestry
needle; sewing needle; 13-inch square
knife-edge ecru pillow form.
GAUGE: Each Motif = 7½ inches
square.

DIRECTIONS:

1. Afghan Motif (make 48): With A,
ch 6. Join with sl st to form ring. **Rnd
1:** Ch 3, make 2 dc in ring, ch 3, * make
3 dc in ring, ch 3; rep from * 2 more
times. Join to top of ch-3. **Rnd 2:** Sl st
in next 2 dc, sl st in next sp, ch 3, in
same sp make 2 dc, ch 3, 3 dc, * ch 1,
in next sp make 3 dc, ch 3, 3 dc; * rep
from * 2 more times; ch 1. Join. **Rnd
3:** Sl st in next 2 dc, sl st in next sp,
ch 3, in same sp make 2 dc, ch 3, 3 dc,
* ch 1, 3 dc in next ch-1 sp, ch 1, in
corner ch-3 sp make 3 dc, ch 3, 3 dc;
rep from * 2 more times; ch 1, 3 dc in
last ch-1 sp, ch 1. Join. Cut A and end
off. **Rnd 4:** Attach B with sl st in next
ch-3 sp at beg of last rnd, ch 3, in same
sp make 2 dc, ch 3, 3 dc, * * ch 1, 3 dc
in next ch-1 sp; rep from * * to next
corner ch-3 sp, ch 1, in corner ch-3 sp
make 3 dc, ch 3, 3 dc. Work remaining
3 sides in same way, starting at * *. Join
last ch-1 to top of ch-3. Cut B and end
off. **Rnds 5 to 7:** Attach A with sl st in
next ch-3 sp at beg of last rnd and rep
Rnd 4. Cut A and end off. **Rnd 8:**
Attach B as before and rep Rnd 4.
Fasten off.

2. Blocking: Pin each motif to
measure 7½ inches square on a
padded surface. Cover the motifs with
a damp cloth, and allow them to dry.
Do not press the motifs.
3. Joining Motifs: From the right
side, sew the motifs together, working
through the back lp *only* of each st
and keeping the seams as elastic as the
crocheted motifs. Sew the motifs
together from the center of a ch-3
corner sp to the center of the next
corner sp, matching sts. Join eight
rows of six motifs each.
4. Edging, Rnd 1: With the wrong
side facing, attach B to any ch-3 corner
sp, ch 1, make 3 sc in the same corner
sp, * sc in each st across to next corner,
3 sc in corner; rep from * around. Join.
Rnd 2: With the right side facing, sl st
in each st around. Join. Fasten off.
5. Pillow Top: Work the same as the
Afghan motif through Rnd 8. **Rnds 9
to 12:** Attach A as before and rep Rnd
4. Cut A and end off. **Last Rnd:** Attach
B as before and rep Rnd 4. Fasten off.
Edging: Follow the directions in
Step 4.
6. Pillow Top Finishing: Block the
Pillow Top to measure 13 inches
square, following the directions in
Step 2. Slipstitch the Pillow Top edges,
right side up, to the seamline of the
pillow form.

Granny Square Afghan & Pillow Top

Twisted-Rib Pullover

TWISTED-RIB PULLOVER

A simplified version of the classic Aran Isle sweater.

AVERAGE: For those with some experience in knitting.
Directions are given for Men's Size Small (36-38). Changes for Sizes Medium (40-42) and Large (44) are in parentheses.

MATERIALS: Caron Wintuk yarn (3½-ounce skein): 8 (8,10) skeins of Bone; one pair each size 13 and size 17 knitting needles (14-inch length), OR ANY SIZE NEEDLES TO OBTAIN GAUGE BELOW; stitch markers; stitch holder; tapestry needle.

GAUGE: On size 17 needles with two strands of yarn in Reverse Stockinette Stitch (p on right side, k on wrong side), 9 sts = 4 inches; 3 rows = 1 inch.

SIZES:	SMALL	MEDIUM	LARGE
	(36-38)	(40-42)	(44)
BODY CHEST:			
	38″	42″	44″
FINISHED MEASUREMENTS:			
CHEST:	39″	42½″	46″
WIDTH ACROSS BACK OR FRONT AT UNDERARMS:			
	19½″	21¼″	23″
WIDTH ACROSS SLEEVE AT UPPER ARMS:			
	18½″	19″	20″

DIRECTIONS:

1. Back: With size 13 needles and two strands of yarn held together, cast on 37 (41, 45) sts. **Row 1 (wrong side):** P 1, * k 1, p 1; rep from * across. **Row 2:** K 1, * p 1, k 1; rep from * across. Rep these 2 rows for ribbing for 2 inches, ending with Row 2. K 1 row, inc 9 sts evenly across — 46 (50, 54) sts. Change to size 17 needles and pattern.
Row 1 (right side): P 3 (5, 7), *k next st going through back loop — k 1b made;* (p 1, k 1b) 3 times, * p 4, k 1b, (p 1, k 1b) 3 times*; rep between *'s 2 times more, p 3 (5, 7). **Row 2:** K 3 (5, 7), p 1, (k 1, p 1) 3 times, * k 4, p 1, (k 1, p 1) 3 times;

rep from * 2 times more, k 3 (5, 7). Rep these 2 rows for pattern. Work until 14 inches from beg. ***Mark beg and end of next row for start of armholes.*** Work even until armholes measure 10 (10½, 11) inches, ending with a k row. **Shaping:** Keeping to the pattern, bind off 6 (7, 7) sts at beg of next 2 rows, then bind off 6 (7, 8) sts at beg of next 2 rows — 22 (22, 24) sts. Bind off rem sts for Back neck.
2. Front: Work the same as the Back until the armholes measure 4½ (5, 5½) inches, ending with a right-side row — 46 (50, 54) sts. **Neck Shaping:** Keeping to the pattern, work 18 (20, 21) sts, sl these sts to the stitch holder, bind off center 10 (10, 12) sts loosely, and complete the row. Working on one side ***only,*** dec at neck edge 1 st every right side row 6 times — 12 (14, 15) sts. Work even in the pattern until the armhole measures the same as the Back to the shoulder, ending at the armhole edge. **Shoulder Shaping:** Keeping to the pattern, bind off 6 (7, 7) sts once. Work 1 row, bind off rem 6 (7, 8) sts. Sl sts from the stitch holder to the size 17 needle. Work to correspond to the other side, reversing the shaping.
3. Neckband: Sew the left shoulder

seam. With the right side facing, using size 13 needles and two strands of yarn held tog, beg at the right Back neck, pick up and k 53 (53, 57) sts around the neck. K 1 row on wrong side. Work in k 1, p 1 rib for 4 rows. Bind off loosely in ribbing. Sew the right shoulder and neckband seams.
4. Sleeves: With the right side facing, using size 13 needles and two strands of yarn held tog, beg at one armhole marker, pick up and k 43 (45, 47) sts to other armhole marker. K 1 row. Change to size 17 needles and pattern.
Row 1 (right side): P 18 (19, 20), k 1b, (p 1, k 1b) 3 times; p 18 (19, 20). **Row 2:** K 18 (19, 20), p 1, (k 1, p 1) 3 times; k 18 (19, 20). Rep these 2 rows for pattern. Work even for 6 inches from beg. Keeping to the pattern, dec one st each end of next row, then every 1½ inches 6 times more — 29 (31, 33) sts. Work to 18 inches from beg, or 3 inches less than the desired length, ending with a right side row. Change to size 13 needles and k 1 row, dec 3 sts across each k section (***do not*** dec across panel) — ***6 sts dec*** — 23 (25, 27) sts. Work in k 1, p 1 rib for 3 inches. Bind off in ribbing. Sew the side and sleeve seams. ***Do not*** block the sweater.

Checkerboard Pullovers

CHECKERBOARD PULLOVERS

One for her, one for him. The perfect gift for your favorite couple!

AVERAGE: For those with some experience in knitting.
Directions are given for Women's Size Small (6-8). Changes for Sizes Medium (10-12) and Large (14-16) are in parentheses ( ). Immediately following the Women's Sizes are the Men's Sizes in brackets [ ]: Small [36-38], Medium [40-42] and Large [44-46]. See chart on page 200 to determine sizing.
MATERIALS: Worsted weight yarn (1¾-ounce/ 50-gram ball): **WOMEN:** 3 (4, 5) balls of Turquoise (A), 2 (3, 4) balls each of Dark Blue (B), Purple (C), Green (D), Green Tweed (E) and Red Tweed (F); **MEN:** 4 (5, 6) balls each of Turquoise (A) and Purple (C), 3 (4, 5) balls each of Dark Blue (B), Green (D), Light Blue (E) and Medium Green (F); 1 pair each size 6 and size 8 knitting needles, OR ANY SIZE NEEDLES TO OBTAIN GAUGE BELOW; 1 set size 6 double-pointed needles (dp) for Women's Collar; stitch markers; tapestry needle.
GAUGE: On size 8 needles in Stockinette Stitch (st st), 5 sts = 1 inch; 6 rows = 1 inch.
Note 1: The pullover has no armhole shaping.
Note 2: When changing colors while working the Checkerboard design (see Fig. V, 15, page 201), pick up the color to be used under the color previously used, twisting the yarns on the wrong side to prevent holes in the work. Carry the unused color loosely on the wrong side of the work.

DIRECTIONS:
1. Back: Starting at the lower edge with size 6 needles and A [A], cast on 86 (92, 104), [92 (104, 116)] sts. Work in k 1, p 1 ribbing for 2 inches, increasing 10 sts evenly spaced across the last row—96 (102, 114),

[102 (114, 126)] sts. Cut A [A]; attach C [D]. Change to size 8 needles and with C [D], work in st st (k 1 row, p 1 row) until the total length is 10 (11, 12) inches, [11 (12, 13) inches] from beg, ending with a p row. Beg the Checkerboard design for both Women and Men, following Fig. V, 15, as follows: **Rows 1, 3, 5, 7:** * With A k 6 (6, 6), [6 (6, 6)], B k 6 (6, 6), [6 (6, 6)]; rep from * across, ending with A k 0 (6, 6), [6 (6, 6)]. **Rows 2, 4, 6, 8:** With A, p 0 (6, 6), [6 (6, 6)], * B p 6 (6, 6), [6 (6, 6)], A p 6 (6, 6), [6 (6, 6)]; rep from * across. Continue to follow Fig. V, 15 as established until Row 24 is completed. Cut A and B; attach D [C]. ***Mark each end of last row worked for beg of armhole.*** With D [C], work in st st until 8 (9, 10) inches, [9 (10, 11) inches] from marked row, ending with a p row.

2. Shoulder Shaping: Bind off 32 (35, 38), [35 (38, 42)] sts at beg of next 2 rows for shoulders. Bind off rem 32 (32, 38), [32 (38, 42)] sts for back of neck.

3. Front: Work the same as for the Back until 4½ (5½, 6¼) inches, [5½ (6¼, 7) inches] from marked row, ending with a p row.

4. Neck Shaping: Work across first 42 (44, 49), [44 (49, 54)] sts; join second ball of yarn and bind off center 12 (14, 16), [14 (16, 18)] sts for front of neck; work to end. Working both sides at once, dec one st at each neck edge every other row 10 (9, 11) times, [9 (11, 12) times]—32 (35, 38), [35 (38, 42)] sts. Work even in st st until the same length as the Back from the marked row, ending with a p row.

5. Shoulder Shaping: Bind off 32 (35, 38), [35 (38, 42)] sts at each side for the shoulders.

6. Sleeve One: Starting at the lower edge with size 6 needles and B [B], cast on 48 (50, 56), [54 (56, 62)] sts. Work in k 1, p 1 ribbing for 2 inches, increasing 6 (6, 8), [6 (6, 8)] sts evenly spaced across last row — 54 (56, 64),

[60 (62, 70)] sts. Cut B [B]. Change to size 8 needles and work in st st. Inc one st each end every 7th (6th, 6th) row, [7th (6th, 6th) row] until there are 80 (90, 100), [90 (100, 110)] sts on needle, working as follows: With F [E], work for 6 (6½, 7) inches, [7 (7½, 8) inches.] Beg Checkerboard design following Fig. V, 15, working additional stitches into design. With E [F], work for 6 (6½, 7) inches, [7 (7½, 8) inches] more. Bind off all sts.

7. Sleeve Two: Work the ribbing the same as for Sleeve One. Continue to work the same as for Sleeve One in the following sequence: Work E [F] for 6 (6½, 7) inches, [7 (7½, 8) inches], Checkerboard design, and then F [E] for 6 (6½, 7) inches, [7 (7½, 8) inches] more. Bind off all sts.

8. Finishing, Women's Collar (overlapped): Sew both shoulder seams. With the right side facing and A, beg 2 rows below the front neck bound-off sts and starting to the right of the center Front 3 sts from start *(see photo, pages 198-199)*, with dp needles pick up and k 9 (10, 11) sts,

working across the rows, moving up until you are at the bound-off front neck edge. **Tapering Right Edge:** Pick up and k 75 (76, 87) sts around the remainder of the neck edge, ending to the left of the center Front so that 3 sts will overlap at the center Front — 84 (86, 98) sts. Divide sts evenly among 3 needles. Work back and forth in rows in k 1, p 1 ribbing for 4 inches. Bind off loosely in ribbing. Sew in Sleeves from marker to marker. Sew the side and Sleeve seams.

9. Men's Collar: Sew the left shoulder seam. With the right side facing, using size 6 needles and [A], starting at the right back neck edge, pick up and k the following sts: [32 (38, 42)] sts along the back neck edge, [13 (15, 17)] sts down the left front neck edge, [14 (16, 18)] sts along the front neck edge and [13 (15, 17)] sts up the right front neck edge — [72 (84, 94)] sts. Work in k 1, p 1 ribbing for 6 rows; bind off loosely. Sew the right shoulder and neckband seams. Sew in the Sleeves from marker to marker. Sew the side and Sleeve seams.

WOMEN'S SIZES			
SIZES:	SMALL (6-8)	MEDIUM (10-12)	LARGE (14-16)
BODY BUST:	31½"	34"	38"
FINISHED MEASUREMENTS:			
BUST:	38"	41"	46"
WIDTH ACROSS BACK OR FRONT AT UNDERARMS:	19"	20½"	23"
WIDTH ACROSS SLEEVE AT UPPER ARMS:	16"	20"	22"

MEN'S SIZES			
SIZES:	SMALL (36-38)	MEDIUM (40-42)	LARGE (44-46)
BODY CHEST:	38"	42"	46"
FINISHED MEASUREMENTS:			
CHEST:	41"	46"	50"
WIDTH ACROSS BACK OR FRONT AT UNDERARMS:	20½"	23"	25"
WIDTH ACROSS SLEEVE AT UPPER ARMS:	18"	20"	22"

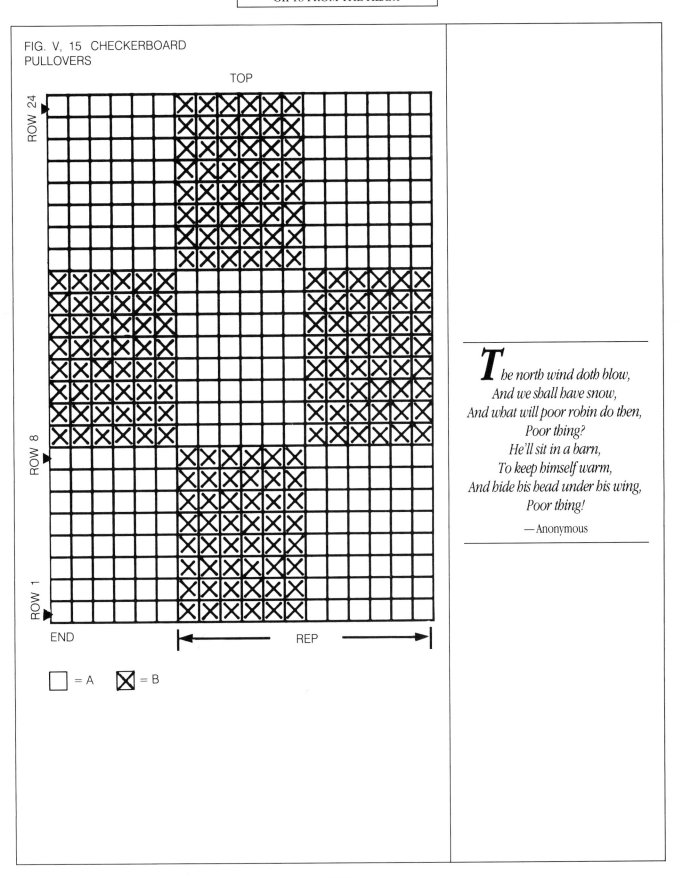

FIG. V, 15 CHECKERBOARD PULLOVERS

*The north wind doth blow,
And we shall have snow,
And what will poor robin do then,
Poor thing?
He'll sit in a barn,
To keep himself warm,
And hide his head under his wing,
Poor thing!*

—Anonymous

SOMETHING FOR EVERYONE

Floral Fabric Accessories; Rice Paper Jars

FLORAL FABRIC ACCESSORIES

These handy — and lovely — organizers make perfect presents for a co-worker or your child's teacher.

AVERAGE: For those with some experience in sewing.

LINGERIE CASE

MATERIALS: 15 x 36 inches each of floral fabric, lining fabric and synthetic batting; matching threads; snap or Velcro® closure *(optional).*

DIRECTIONS:

1. Cut one 15 x 27-inch rectangle each of floral fabric, lining fabric and batting. Cut two 3½ x 8½-inch strips each of floral fabric, lining fabric and batting for the side boxing. Curve the corners at one end of each strip.
2. Baste the batting to the wrong side of the floral fabric rectangle and boxing strips. Quilt around the flowers or other motifs, if you wish. Sew the strips to the rectangle, starting at one end of a 27-inch edge; this will form the pouch. Sew the lining fabric rectangle and boxing strips together in the same way.
3. With right sides together, pin the flap end of the floral fabric to the flap end of the lining. Stitch around the three flap edges. Turn the flap right side out, and poke the lining pouch into the bag pouch. Turn in the raw edges of the lining and pouch, and slipstitch the lining to the pouch around the top edges. Press.
4. Topstitch ½ inch from the flap edge and continue, through all the layers, around the boxing edges. Sew on a snap or Velcro® closure, if you wish.

POCKET TISSUE CASE

MATERIALS: Two 6 x 8-inch pieces of floral fabric; bias tape or 1-inch-wide fabric in coordinating color; matching thread; 6 x 8 inches of synthetic batting; pocket pack of tissues.

DIRECTIONS:

1. Place the floral fabric pieces wrong sides together, and place the batting between them. Baste along the edges. Using the bias tape or 1-inch-wide fabric, bind the two 6-inch edges.
2. With right sides together, fold the bound edges inward to meet at the center. Stitch each short end using a ¼-inch seam allowance. Turn the case right side out. At each end of the case opening, slipstitch the bound edges from the ends in for ½ inch. Fill the case with the pack of tissues.

EYEGLASS CASE

MATERIALS: 7 x 8 inches each of floral fabric, lining fabric and synthetic batting; matching threads.

DIRECTIONS:

1. Pin the batting to the wrong side of the floral fabric, and quilt along the flower outlines. Fold the piece in half, right sides together, to 7 x 4 inches. Using a ¼-inch seam allowance, sew the side and bottom edges. Sew the lining the same way.
2. Turn the quilted piece right side out, and slip the lining inside. Turn in the lining and quilted case ¼ inch at the top edges, and slipstitch the lining to the case.

RICE PAPER JARS

You also can use this technique on a bottle with an attractive shape, or to pretty-up a vase that's past its prime.

EASY: Achievable by anyone.
MATERIALS: Glass jar with cork top; 24 x 36 inches of textured rice paper; Mod Podge® matt (available in craft supply stores); sponge brush; wax paper; floral paper cutouts; spoon.

DIRECTIONS:

1. Cut the rice paper 1 inch taller than the jar height, and ½ inch wider than the jar girth. Place the rice paper on the wax paper. Mix 1 part Mod Podge® with about 2 parts water. Using the sponge brush, paint the rice paper with the Mod Podge mixture.
2. Place the wet rice paper around the jar, overlapping the edges of the paper. Turn the paper ½ inch to the bottom, and ½ inch to the inside. Mold the paper around the jar neck. Let the paper dry.
3. Turn the jar upside down, and cover the bottom with rice paper following the directions in Steps 1 and 2.
4. Using full-strength Mod Podge®, glue the paper flowers to the jar. Press the flower edges with the spoon to prevent them from curling. Let the flowers dry. Dampen the sponge brush and paint four or five coats of Mod Podge over the jar; let the Mod Podge dry between coats.

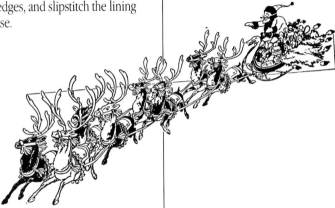

Stencil Magic

STENCIL MAGIC

Here's a great way to customize store-bought items in a snap!

EASY: Achievable by anyone.
GENERAL MATERIALS: Accent Country Colors Self-Adhesive Stencil No. 2053 "Gift of Spring Borders," from the Victorian Collection, or the stencil of your choice; Accent Country Colors fabric painting dyes: Crimson Moiré, Coral Chintz, Green Taffeta and white tint medium, or the colors of your choice; ¾-inch stencil brush; two No. 6 scrubber stencil brushes; cardboard; paper toweling; iron.

GENERAL DIRECTIONS:

1. Cover the cardboard well with paper toweling. Place the padded cardboard between the front and back of the garment, or underneath the fabric to be stenciled.

2. Remove from the stencil those areas that will be painted, and peel off the paper backing. Using the photo and individual project directions as placement guides, smooth the stencil onto the fabric.

3. Mix an equal part of the white tint medium with each color you use. Use the ¾-inch brush for the leaves and vine, and the No. 6 scrubber brushes for the roses and baskets. Select a different brush for each color you use.

4. Dip a dry stencil brush in the paint, and rub the brush on paper toweling in a circular motion until the brush is nearly dry. Either gently dab the brush in an up and down, stippling motion, or use a circular motion, to brush the paint through each stencil cutout. Start at the edges of each cutout and work toward the center. Change the paper towel padding on the cardboard each time you peel off the stencil to reposition it and continue the design. When you are finished stenciling, clean the brushes with soap and water until the rinse water runs clear, and dry them with paper toweling. Clean the stencils in hot water for 5 minutes, and wipe off the loosened paint.

5. Let the stenciled fabric dry overnight. Cover the fabric with paper toweling, and set the iron one step above the setting for the fabric. Apply heat with a circular motion for one minute. Cool the iron to one step below the setting for the fabric, and iron for one minute.

CAMISOLE AND HALF SLIP

MATERIALS: Purchased poly/cotton blend white camisole and half slip; General Materials.

DIRECTIONS:

1. Using the photo as a color and placement guide, and following the General Directions, stencil a rose border along the bottom edge of the camisole and the half slip. Continue the border up the sides of the slip.

2. To launder the stenciled garments, machine-wash them on the gentle/delicate cycle, and machine-dry them on the low/cool setting.

SHEETS AND PILLOWCASES

MATERIALS: Purchased poly/cotton blend white sheets and pillowcases; 2-inch-wide lace edging; white thread; General Materials.

DIRECTIONS:

1. Using the photo as a color guide, and following the General Directions, stencil a basket at the center of each pillowcase border. Stencil a rose on each side of the basket.

2. Stencil a basket at the center of each sheet border, and a rose border on

each side of the basket. Repeat to the edges of the sheet.

3. Edgestitch the lace edging to the sheets and pillowcases above the stenciled borders, turning under the lace's raw ends.

TOWELS

MATERIALS: Purchased poly/cotton blend finger, hand, and bath towels with at least a 40% polyester content; General Materials, substituting No. 4 fabric brushes for the stencil brushes, and omitting the white tint medium.

DIRECTIONS:

1. Wash the towels, using fabric softener in the rinse cycle, and machine-dry them.

2. Use the fabric painting dyes full strength, and follow the General Directions. On the finger towel, stencil a basket at the center of each short edge. On the hand towel, stencil a rose border along each short edge. On the bath towel, stencil a basket at the center of each short edge, and a rose border on each side of the basket. Use the photo as a color guide.

3. Machine-wash the stenciled towels in cold water with a mild detergent. Additional washings can be done in warm water with a warm rinse. Machine-dry the towels on the permanent press/medium setting for 45 minutes.

PILLOW

MATERIALS: ½ yard of white poly/cotton blend fabric; 2 yards of lace and ribbon trim; white thread; synthetic stuffing or a 17-inch square pillow form; General Materials.

DIRECTIONS:

1. Cut two 18-inch squares from the white fabric. Place one square on the padded cardboard.

2. Using the photo as a color and placement guide, and following the

General Directions, stencil a rose border across the center of the square. Leaving a ¾-inch space between rows, stencil a row of three baskets above and below the rose border. Then stencil a rose border above and below the baskets, leaving a ¾-inch space between rows.

3. Topstitch the lace and ribbon trim between the stenciled rows (see photo). Using a ½-inch seam allowance, sew the stenciled pillow front to the pillow back, right sides together, around three sides and four corners. Turn right side out. Stuff the pillow, turn in the open edges, and slipstitch the opening closed.

BASKET

MATERIALS: Purchased basket with handle; Accent clear acrylic spray sealer; Accent Designer spray paint: Soft White; Accent Instant Finish Clear Gloss Alkyd Varnish; General Materials, substituting the following Accent Country Colors acrylic paints for the fabric painting dyes: Roseberry, Apricot Stone, Village Green and Off White, or the colors of your choice.

DIRECTIONS:

1. Spray the basket with the acrylic sealer. When the sealer has dried, spray one or two coats of the Soft White paint over the entire basket, letting the paint dry between coats.

2. Use an equal amount of the Off White acrylic paint with each acrylic paint color you use. Using the photo as a color and placement guide, and following the General Directions, stencil a rose design on the sides of the basket with the acrylic paints.

3. When the paints have dried, apply a coat of the clear gloss alkyd varnish over the entire basket.

FOLK ART HEART SHELF

AVERAGE: For those with some experience in staining and decorative painting.

MATERIALS: Unstained wood shelf with heart cut-out on backboard (available at country craft stores); oil paints: leaf green light, leaf green medium, leaf green dark, cadmium red light, burnt alizarin, burnt umber and black; white acrylic paint; palette; palette knife; odorless turpentine; wide mouth container for turpentine; soft rags; clear oil-based antiquing glaze; oil-based varnish; wood sealer; clear acrylic spray; brushes: PH Red Sable small 6 or 8, PH Red Sable medium 10 or 12, PH Red Sable large 14 or 16, No. 1 liner or scroll brush, and sponge brush; tracing paper; graphite paper; stylus or old ballpoint pen; masking tape; medium-fine sandpaper.

DIRECTIONS:

1. Stain the shelf with the burnt umber paint mixed in turpentine. Spread the paint on the shelf with a clean rag, and wipe it off with another clean rag. Repeat to make the stain darker, if you wish. Let the stain dry, then apply a coat of wood sealer. When the sealer is dry, sand the shelf lightly.

2. Using the sponge brush and white acrylic paint, paint the backboard with the heart cut-out. Let the paint dry. Seal the background by spraying on several light coats of clear acrylic.

3. Enlarge the pattern in FIG. V, 16 onto tracing paper, following the directions on page 239. Center the design around the shelf heart cut-out *(see photo)*, tape the design in place, and slip a sheet of graphite paper between the design and the prepared surface. Be sure the right side of the graphite is facing the shelf. Neatly and *lightly* go over the lines on the tracing paper with the stylus or old pen to transfer the design to the wood.

4. Squeeze the oil colors onto the palette. Use turpentine to thin the reds to the consistency of soft butter, and the greens to the consistency of heavy cream. Using the large brush, paint the tulips cadmium red light. Wipe the brush and, if you wish, apply a little burnt alizarin to the left side of each tulip, blending the two colors together where they meet each other.

5. The large green strokes are painted in thinned leaf green dark, the

FIG. V, 16 HEART SHELF

1 SQ. = 1"

HALF PATTERN

FOLD

medium strokes in leaf green medium and the small strokes in leaf green light. The inside edges of the heart cut-out are painted cadmium red light. Use the liner or scroll brush and black paint to outline the edges of the painted designs. Also use the black paint to cover the bottom edge of the shelf *(see photo)*.

6. When you have finished painting, allow the paint to dry thoroughly. This will take several days depending upon the temperature, humidity and air circulation. When the paint is completely dry, apply a coat of oil-based varnish to the entire shelf.

7. To antique the shelf, mix a little burnt umber oil paint into a tablespoon of oil-based antiquing glaze. Brush the mixture over the shelf and painted design. Use a soft rag to wipe off as much of the antiquing glaze as you wish. Let the glaze dry well, and apply a final coat of varnish.

Folk Art Heart Shelf

Cross Stitch Jar Covers

CROSS STITCH JAR COVERS

AVERAGE: For those with some experience in counted cross stitch.
MATERIALS: 20-count white Aida cloth; 1¼-inch-wide lightweight beaded lace edging; matching sewing threads; embroidery floss: 1 skein each of Purple, Rose, Salmon, Lime, Yellow, Dark Blue, Green, Olive and Light Blue; No. 26 tapestry needle; scraps of thin fabric for lining; ¾ yard of silk macramé cord.

DIRECTIONS:

1. Draw 6-inch-diameter circles on the Aida cloth. Using 2 strands of floss in the needle, and following the charts in Fig. V, 17, cross stitch the motif of your choice centered in each circle *(see Embroidery Stitch Guide, page 240)*. When the design is completed, place a damp cloth on each motif and press on the wrong side of the motif to block it. Cut out the circles.
2. Cut out the same number of 6-inch-diameter circles from the lining fabric. With right sides together, and using a ¼-inch seam allowance, stitch each Aida cloth circle to a lining circle, leaving an opening for turning.

Turn the circles right side out, turn in the open edges, and slipstitch the openings closed.
3. For each circle, lap the beaded part of the lace edging over the Aida cloth and slipstitch the inner edge in place, holding it in slightly so the edging lies flat. Sew the raw ends of the edging together. Slipstitch the edging to the Aida cloth a second time, near the cloth edge.
4. Thread a length of macramé cord through the beading on each cover, and knot each end of the cord. Place the cover over a jar top, draw up the cord, and tie it into a bow.

FIG. V, 17 CROSS STITCH JAR COVERS

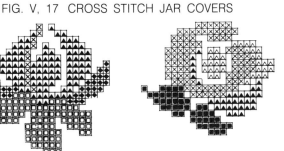

⊞ = PURPLE   ▲ = ROSE   ◮ = SALMON   ◪ = LIME   ⊠ = YELLOW   ◉ = DK. BLUE   ▣ = GREEN   ◨ = OLIVE   ◎ = LT. BLUE

Folk Art Frames

FOLK ART FRAMES
(about 7³⁄₈ x 9¼ inches and
10½ x 12¼ inches)

AVERAGE: For those with some experience in woodworking.
MATERIALS FOR ONE SMALLER FRAME:
¾ x 1½ x 36-inch pine; scrap of ¼-inch pine; ½-inch and 1½-inch brads; wood glue; miter box; hammer; saw; router; acrylic paints: red and dark green; sandpaper; masking tape; antiquing stain; sponge; soft cloths; 5 x 6⅞-inch piece of glass; 5 x 6⅞-inch piece of cardboard; 5 x 7-inch photograph; screw eyes; picture wire.
Note: *To make the larger frame, increase all the dimensions proportionately, and follow the directions below.*

DIRECTIONS:
1. Use the router to cut a ⁵⁄₁₆ x ¼-inch deep groove along one edge of the ¾-inch pine.
2. Using the miter box, cut two pieces from the ¾-inch pine with an outside edge of 7⅜ inches, and two pieces with an outside edge of 9¼ inches (the grooved edge is the inside edge and the cutting angle is 45°). Glue the mitered edges of the frame together, securing them with the 1½-inch brads.
3. Cut several hearts from the ¼-inch pine. Round their edges with sandpaper, and paint them red. Paint the frame dark green. Glue the hearts in place, using the photo as a placement guide.
4. For painted corners, use a sponge to get a soft effect. For checkerboard corners, use masking tape to mark off the checks, and a sponge to apply the paint. To antique, brush the front and sides of the frame with the antiquing stain, and wipe off as much of the stain as you wish with a soft cloth.
5. Place the glass in the frame opening, then the photograph and cardboard. Fasten them in place with the ½-inch brads.
6. Hang the frame using the screw eyes and picture wire.

PATCHWORK PIG PILLOW
A whimsical country accent pillow.

AVERAGE: For those with some experience in sewing.
MATERIALS: 12-inch square from an old quilt, or patch and quilt a new square; 12-inch square of fabric for pillow back; 3-inch square of cotton print to coordinate with quilt colors; 1 x 7-inch bias strip of coordinating fabric; matching threads; chenille stem; embroidery needle; Black embroidery floss; synthetic stuffing; paper for patterns.

DIRECTIONS:
1. Enlarge the patterns in Fɪɢ. V, 18 onto paper, following the directions on page 239. Cut out the patterns.
2. Place the body pattern on the right side of the quilted square, and pin it in place. Cut out the quilted body front piece. Unpin the pattern, and place it, right side down, on the right side of the pillow back fabric. Pin them together, and cut out the pillow back.

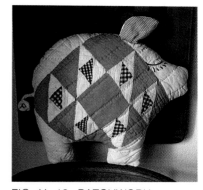

FIG. V, 18 PATCHWORK
PIG PILLOW

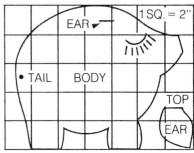

Repeat with the ear pattern on the 3-inch print square. Unpin the pieces.

3. Mark the eyelid and lashes on the right side of the pillow front. Embroider the features, using the embroidery needle and 3 strands of the Black floss.

4. Pin the ear pieces right sides together. Sew the ear pieces together, using a ¼-inch seam allowance and leaving the straight edge open. Cut off the excess fabric, and slash the curved edges to ease the seams. Turn the ear right side out, turn under the open edges, and pin the straight edge to the body at the line indicated on the pattern. Stitch through all the layers to close the opening and attach the ear to the body.

5. For the tail, fold the bias strip in half lengthwise. Fold each long raw edge in to the first fold, and press. Fold the strip in half again, and overcast stitch the two folded long edges together. Insert the chenille stem into the resulting tube. Pin one end of the wired tube to the body at the dot marked on the pattern, with the wired tube extending across the right side of the body. Stitch at the marked point, catching the chenille stem. Cut off any excess stem. Fold under the cut end of the stem to prevent a sharp point. Turn under the open edge of the tube, and slipstitch the opening closed.

6. Pin the pillow front to the pillow back, right sides together. Beginning at the tail, sew the pieces together, leaving a 3-inch opening under the tail. Trim the seam, and slash the curves and corners. Turn the pillow right side out, stuff it firmly, turn under the open edges, and slipstitch the opening closed.

Country Kitten Towel Rack

COUNTRY KITTEN TOWEL RACK

AVERAGE: For those with some experience in sewing.

MATERIALS: ½ yard of calico fabric; ¾ yard of toweling; matching threads; heart-shaped lace appliqué; 1 yard of ribbon; one 12-inch dowel with knobs; synthetic stuffing; 1 yard of cluny lace; ¾-inch-diameter bone ring; paper for patterns.

DIRECTIONS
(¼-inch seams allowed):
1. Towel: Hem each end of the toweling fabric. Cut a 3-inch-wide strip from the calico fabric long enough to fit the width of the towel. Make a ¼-inch hem around the calico strip, and sew the strip to the towel 3 inches from the towel's bottom hem, inserting the cluny lace close to the calico hem as you sew *(see photo)*. Fold the towel into thirds, and press.

2. Kitten: Enlarge the patterns in FIG. V, 19 onto paper, following the directions on page 239. Pin the paper patterns to the calico fabric. Cut out a kitten front, and turn over the pattern to cut out a kitten back. Cut out a tail front and back.

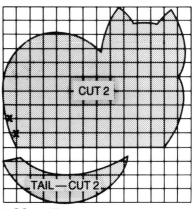

FIG. V, 19 COUNTRY KITTEN TOWEL RACK

CUT 2

TAIL — CUT 2

1 SQ. = 1"

3. From the calico fabric, cut out two 2½ x 7-inch tabs. Fold each tab in half, right sides together, and sew the long edges together. Turn the tabs right side out, and press them. Sew the tail front and back right sides together, leaving an opening where the tail will connect to the body *(see the X's on the pattern)*. Turn the tail right side out, and stuff it. Sew the body front and back right sides together, inserting the tail between the X's on the pattern, and the tabs into the seam on the bottom edge. Leave about a 4-inch opening on the bottom. Turn the kitten right side out, stuff it firmly, and slipstitch the opening closed. Place the lace heart appliqué as shown in the photo and stitch it in place. Tie the ribbon in a bow around the kitten's neck.

4. Finishing: Sew the bone ring on the back of the kitten for a hanger. Slide the dowel through the tabs.

CHRISTMAS
IN A FLASH

Animal Farm Sweatshirts

ANIMAL FARM SWEATSHIRTS

EASY: Achievable by anyone.

MATERIALS: Red or white cotton or poly/cotton sweatshirt; sheet of No. 10 acetate, or stencil-acetate with adhesive side; acrylic or fabric paints: black, and red or white *(see photo)*; 2 stencil brushes; masking tape; cutting board; utility knife; tracing paper; thumbtacks; pushpins; basting thread; cardboard; paper toweling; rubbing alcohol *(optional)*.

DIRECTIONS:

1. Pattern: You will need two stencils for each of the two patterns. Cut a piece of acetate at least 6 inches square for each stencil.

2. Stencil No. 1: Trace the full-size figures in FIG. V, 20 onto tracing paper. Thumbtack the traced figures to the cutting board. Center an acetate square over one of the figures, and tape down the corners of the square. Using the utility knife, cut along the outlines of *only* the dark portions of the figure (do not cut out the eye or

other striped areas). Carefully lift off the acetate square. Stencil No. 1 is used for the principal color.

3. Stencil No. 2: Tape a second acetate square over the traced figure on the board. Cut out *only* the striped areas of the figure (bow for the dog; 4 spots, 4 hooves and an eye for the cow). Stencil No. 2 is used for the second color.

4. Placement: Baste a vertical line on the sweatshirt to mark the center front. Measure the figure to be stenciled, to find the space needed for each row. Baste horizontal guidelines across the sweatshirt to mark the bottom of each row. You now can stencil a centered figure on alternate rows, then stencil a figure on either side of it. On the intervening rows, it will be easy to stagger figures between those above or below them.

5. Stenciling: Spread out the sweatshirt, and place the cardboard inside it between the front and back. Keep the fabric taut with pushpins. Tape Stencil No. 1 to the sweatshirt, and apply the principal color. Use the paints just as they come, straight from

FIG. V, 20 STENCILED SWEATSHIRTS

🌿 🌿 🌿 🌿 🌿 🌿

DID YOU KNOW . . .

The bright red and green colors of the poinsettia have made it a cherished part of Christmas celebrations. This native of the Americas was discovered in Mexico in 1828 by Dr. Joel Roberts Poinsett. The Mexicans refer to the colorful plant as the "Flor de la Noche Buena" — the Flower of the Holy Night — believing that the leaves resemble the Star of Bethlehem.

■ STENCIL NO. 1   ▨ STENCIL NO. 2

the jars or tubes. *Don't* mix them with water. Pick up some of the first color paint on the end of a dry stencil brush. Gently pounce the brush, in an up and down, stippling motion, on paper toweling to remove excess paint and distribute the paint evenly through the bristles. Then gently pounce the brush through the stencil openings, working from the outside inward, to apply a thick, even covering of color; white paint may require another coat after the first one has dried. Lift the stencil straight up, and let the paint dry before applying the second color. Tape Stencil No. 2 over the first color so the spaces match and the design registers. Using the second stencil brush, apply the second color paint. If you wish to reverse the colors, as we did for the cows, or the position of the animals

(see photo, page 210), cut a second set of stencils, or wash the first set *(see Step 6)* and turn over the stencils.
6. Clean the brushes, before the paint gets hard, with soap and water until the rinse water runs clear. Dry them with paper toweling. The stencils can be cleaned in hot water for 5 minutes, and the loosened paint wiped off, or they can be cleaned with paper toweling soaked in rubbing alcohol.
7. Acrylic paint is water-soluble when it is wet. When it dries, it becomes permanent and washable if you follow the manufacturer's directions. Turn the sweatshirt inside out before laundering it. Wash and rinse the sweatshirt with cold water, using the permanent press cycle. Do not dry clean the sweatshirt.

SUGARPLUM PAJAMAS

The perfect attire for your little one on Christmas morning.

AVERAGE: For those with some experience in sewing.
MATERIALS: Scrap fabric: one 9-inch square each of red, white, green, brown, yellow, and striped red and white; matching threads; ⅓ yard of fusible interfacing; store-bought sleeper pajamas; sewing machine; iron; ruler; fabric marking pencil; paper for patterns.

DIRECTIONS:
1. Enlarge the patterns in Fig. V, 21 onto paper, following the directions on page 239. Use the paper patterns to cut two red lollipops, three green lollipops, three brown gingerbread boys, one yellow horn, one striped candy cane, one stocking (red foot and white cuff), and a fusible interfacing piece to match each appliqué.
2. Pin the stocking to the bottom of the left pajama leg. Pin goodies along the left front of the pajamas, using the photo as a placement guide. Pin a gingerbread boy and a green lollipop to the right front. Fuse the appliqués to the pajamas, following the fusible interfacing manufacturer's directions. Using the ruler and fabric marking pencil, draw a 2½-inch-long "stick" on each lollipop.
3. Set the sewing machine on a medium-width satin stitch. Using thread to match each appliqué, sew around the appliqués. Sew along each fabric pencil line with thread to match its lollipop.

FIG. V, 21 SUGARPLUM PAJAMAS

1 SQ. = 1"

Sugarplum Pajamas

Bath Buddies Sponges, Bath Mitts and Pouch

BATH BUDDIES SPONGES

Quick and easy stocking stuffers the kids will love to use!

EASY: Achievable by anyone.
MATERIALS: Bag of colored sponges; scissors; paper for patterns.

DIRECTIONS:

1. Enlarge the patterns in FIG. V, 22 onto paper, following the directions on page 239.
2. Trace the paper patterns lightly onto the sponges in pencil. Cut out the novelty shapes.

BATH MITTS AND POUCH

EASY: Achievable by anyone.
MATERIALS: Washcloth for each mitt or pouch; ¼ yard of narrow elastic for each mitt. **FOR DRAWSTRING POUCH:** ½ yard of lace trim; ¾ yard of grosgrain ribbon. **FOR CREATURE MITT:** Scrap of red fabric; embroidery floss: Black and White.

DIRECTIONS
(½-inch seams allowed):
1. Rectangular Mitt: Cut 8 inches of

narrow elastic, and sew it to wrong side of washcloth 3 inches from one (wrist) edge. Fold washcloth in half, right sides together, so elastic also folds in half. Seam long edges and short end. Turn mitt right side out.
2. Creature Mitt: Cut a 3-inch square from red fabric for tongue. Fold in half, right sides together. Stitch a curved short edge; stitch long edges together. Turn tongue right side out. Follow directions in Step 1, inserting tongue between right sides of the folded washcloth's short end, straight edges matching. Take a 1-inch tuck an

inch above the tongue. Turn mitt right side out. Use Black floss to embroider round satin stitch eyes, and White floss to outline eyes with chain stitches *(see Embroidery Stitch Guide, page 240).*
3. Drawstring Pouch: Fold the washcloth in half; seam one short (bottom) end. Stitch long edges together, stopping 3 inches from top. Turn pouch right side out. At the top end, turn down a cuff 2½ inches to the outside; stitch lace to edge. Topstitch ½ inch from fold to make a casing; insert grosgrain ribbon for drawstring.

FIG. V, 22 BATH BUDDIES SPONGES   1 SQ. = 1"

Cook's Cover-Up

COOK'S COVER-UP

Whip up this apron in an evening. Pair it with matching potholders, and you've got the perfect gift for your favorite cook.

AVERAGE: For those with some experience in sewing.

MATERIALS: Two linen dish towels with decorated borders on the long edges; 2 coordinating terry cloth potholders; matching threads; scissors; 1½ yards of 2-inch-wide ribbon or fabric to match towels (*optional*).

DIRECTIONS:

1. Waistband: Cut the border design from the two long edges of one towel. Sew the borders together along one short end; if the borders have a top and a bottom, be sure they match up. Or, if you wish, use a 2-inch-wide ribbon or fabric scrap for the waistband. If necessary, fold over the top edge and short ends of the waistband and hem them.

2. Apron: Gather the top long edge of the other towel with a long running stitch. Center the gathered edge on the wrong side of the waistband (*see photo*), and stitch.

3. Pockets: Using the photo as a placement guide, place the terry cloth potholders on the apron. Stitch around three sides to make pockets; the pocket opening may be at the top or the outside edge of each potholder.

*N*o Santa Claus! Thank God! he lives, and he lives forever. A thousand years from now, Virginia, nay, ten times ten thousand years from now, he will continue to make glad the heart of childhood.

—*New York Sun, 1897*

Gifts from the heart, wrapped with love.

Wrapping It Up

Beautifully wrapped bundles, peeking out from under the tree—this is the magic of Christmas morning, a vision of the mysterious goodies that await us.

Perfect gift wrapping is more than just buying pretty paper at the store. First decide on the "look" you want to create: dramatic, Victorian, country. Then select containers (you don't have to limit yourself to boxes!), choose the papers, create beautiful bows and extra-special trims to personalize your presents.

Sometimes your gift won't fit in a box. Not to worry. We help you wrap *anything*! With our easy, step-by-step guide, you can tackle any size and shape object. Bottles, umbrellas, even canisters full of homemade goodies can be wrapped in a snap when you know the right tricks.

This year, let your holiday greeting cards be as personal as your lovingly crafted gifts. Using simple techniques, such as hole punch and paper quilting, we show you how to create beautiful, unique, and sometimes just plain fun, Christmas cards.

We want to make sure your special packages arrive safely and on time to those loved ones far away. So we tell you everything you need to know about sending gifts by mail: when, where and how.

The wrapping of Christmas gifts is the icing on the cake. And, with our great gift wrap ideas, your precious packages will be picture-perfect.

BOXES 'N

PAPER POINTERS

To wrap holiday gifts, you'll need both coated gift wrap and colored tissue paper. Use the coated wrap for standard boxes; it makes very sharp, neat corners. Use the colored tissue paper for odd-shaped packages, such as canisters, bottles or stuffed toys. Tissue paper, being soft, often rips on the sharp corners of a box, but works beautifully around the curves and folds of a round or soft package.

Buy coated gift wrap on rolls rather than folded flat. A roll allows you to measure the wrap more accurately to avoid wasting paper.

Buy special holiday-patterned gift wrap after the season ends. After the holidays, many stores reduce the prices of holiday wraps, cards, ornaments and trims by as much as 50 percent. That's the time to stock up for the next holiday season!

Never underestimate the power of a solid color. When buying gift wrap, include at least one solid color wrap that you can dress up with ribbons or trims. Red always is a winner. Deep green can be very elegant. Aluminum foil wrap in silver or gold is great for a glamorous gift. Choose a rich royal blue for Hannukah gift wrap. Leftover solid color gift wraps can be used throughout the year, making them very economical.

Look for solid color gift wrap among the "all-occasion" wraps at card stores. When holiday-patterned wraps are priced at a premium, all-occasion gift wraps often are more reasonably priced. Other good choices include pin dot, plaid or striped wrapping paper in holiday colors. Gifts wrapped in simple patterned paper will complement solid color boxes for a smashing look under the tree.

For wonderfully unique gift wrap, buy a roll of white or off-white butcher-type paper, supply your kids with crayons, marking pens, or water color or poster paints, and let them go wild! The kids will have a ball creating their own Christmas scenes or designs. Then let them wrap some of the presents (have lots of solid color ribbons and bows on hand). Good fun and spirited packages will abound.

Create a "look" with the wrappings you select: Brown or off-white paper trimmed with yarn, gingham ribbons, or calico fabric cut into strips or shapes with pinking shears lend a country look. Opulent velvet ribbons, gold cord, or fountains of lace on brocade-like or floral-patterned paper is reminiscent of Victoriana. Geometric patterns with solid color ribbons add a contemporary note. And a sprig of evergreen, holly or mistletoe tucked into a bow is always a nice touch.

If you run low on a favorite patterned wrapping paper, wrap the gift in a solid color, and cut out holiday shapes (Christmas trees, bells, hearts, gingerbread boys, angels) from the patterned paper to use as package trims.

If you're using tissue paper for wrapping, you'll need at least a two sheet thickness to disguise a package. Tissue paper is so sheer, usually you can see through one sheet!

Buy tissue paper in several different colors. There are red, green and white tissue papers packaged together for Christmas, as well as solid color tissue paper decorated with glitter.

When wrapping a gift, use one sheet each of different colors placed one on top of the other. Gather the tissue with a ribbon or yarn tie at the top of the package, and fluff out the tissue so the different color layers show at the top (see Bottle Beauty, page 220).

Use tissue paper to make paper flower gift trims. Cut different color tissue paper into 4 x 5-inch rectangles. Stack five or six rectangles, alternating the colors. Fold over one short end of the stack ½ inch. Continue folding the stack into ½-inch pleats as you would for a fan. Round each end of the folded stack with scissors. Straighten a small paper clip. Bend one end of the paper clip wire over the center of the folded stack, and secure the wire end by wrapping it around the rest of the paper clip wire. Carefully lift the top sheet of tissue paper away from the others on one side of the wire. Do the same on the other side. Fluff up the tissue for the center of the flower. Repeat for each sheet of tissue until all are fluffed out to form the flower. Attach the flower to the package with the paper clip wire stem.

REVIVING GIFT WRAP AND BOWS

To take the wrinkles out of gift wrap, spray the underside of the paper with starch, and iron it.

Perk up a bow by running a curling iron in and out of each loop.

STORING GIFT WRAP

Store rolls of gift wrap in long cardboard boxes used to deliver long-stemmed roses. Or reroll gift wrap tightly, and insert it inside its cardboard tube.

BUNDLES

FOXY BOXES

Disguise packages to look like something they're not. A big box can conceal a small present. Large, hard-to-wrap gifts, such as tricycles, giant stuffed animals or wagons, fit neatly into jumbo plastic bags. Stuff tissue paper in the bags to disguise the shapes.

If you're giving several small gifts to one person, try the "needle in the haystack" approach to wrapping. Wrap the gifts individually, then place them all in a carton filled with crumpled or shredded paper. Wrap the carton and present it. The receiver will have a great time digging through the paper "haystack" to find her or his gifts.

For a small gift, such as jewelry or tickets to a show, try the "box within a box" approach. Place the gift in an appropriate-size box, and wrap it. Place the wrapped box in a slightly larger box, and wrap it. Continue two or three times more with increasingly larger containers. Vary the box shape and gift wrap, if you can. Watching the receiver unwrap this gift will keep everyone entertained!

Vary package shapes by wrapping some gifts in cylindrical containers, others in handle bags or cube-shape boxes. Posters and prints can be wrapped inside cardboard tubes.

Wrap an oversize or unusually shaped gift — such as a cuddly teddy bear — in a designed gift bag. Add a tag, and draw the top closed with a yarn bow.

For crazy shapes — bottles, baseball bats, footballs — tissue paper is perfect. Or go to your local fabric store and search the remnants bin. Fabric can make great gift wrap for oddly shaped items.

Package small toys that come without containers in tin banks or canisters that can be used to store the "treasures" later on.

"NEWS-WORTHY" GIFT WRAPS

For the young (or young-at-heart), use the Sunday comics as wrapping paper. Trim with ribbons, and red and green lollipops.

Give a crossword buff a treat by wrapping her gift in the puzzle page. Trim it with green pencils and red erasers.

Wrap a new homeowner's gift in the real estate section. Trim with a house-shaped ornament.

Impress a financial whiz with the stock listings, or the front page of The Wall Street Journal. Top with a bag of chocolate gold coins.

Use the society page of your hometown newspaper to wrap a gift for a loved one who's far away from home. Mark the juiciest items with a highlighter pen. He'll be able to enjoy the gift and catch up on local news at the same time.

CLEVER COVER-UPS AND CONTAINERS

Wrap a magazine subscription card in the cover of an old issue.

Point your favorite jogger in the right direction with a map of the city; tie it up with a pair of shoelaces.

Strike the right note for the musician in your life with sheet music wrapped around a compact disc or concert tickets.

Turn on the holiday glow by wrapping a bottle of wine or champagne (or sparkling cider!) in aluminum foil. Put confetti inside the foil, and tie with paper streamers.

Appeal to a lawyer with a blank legal form closed with gold notary seals. Use graph paper for an architect or engineer.

Fill a canister or apothecary jar with a batch of your best cookies. Top with a cookie cutter.

Put cash or gift certificates in old-style tins or piggy banks.

Give a casserole dish along with some of your favorite recipes and a few of the herbs and spices needed. Tie the dish with a big bow.

QUICK-FIX GIFT WRAPS

Brown Bag It. Recycle those brown paper grocery bags as unique gift wraps. Turn them over to your resident artists (the kids) to decorate with holiday drawings. Drop a gift in each bag, and tie the bags with pretty ribbon or yarn. Or punch a couple of holes at the top on each side, and knot ribbons through for handles.

Bandanna It. Bandannas are colorful, inexpensive, and make jiffy wraps for smaller gifts. Knot the bandanna ends, and you've got two gifts in one. For larger presents, make a "Santa Sack," using pieces of fabric in red, green, or a seasonal print. Pull up the edges, tie with yarn, and trim with pinking shears.

Basket It. Buy inexpensive baskets, fill them, and tie a pretty bow on the handle, or attach the bow to the side of the basket. Breakfast treats (jams, teas, muffins), party snacks (cheeses, pâté, crackers, cocktail napkins), fresh fruit, bath accessories, hair accessories, and pine cones for sweet-smelling kindling, all are good basket gifts.

Bottle It. Many grocery and cosmetic products come in attractive bottles. When they're empty, wash them in hot, sudsy water and refill them with Christmas gifts — potpourri, bath salts, Christmas candy, spices, coffee beans, your own homemade spaghetti sauce. A bow at the neck and they're wrapped!

Foil It. Aluminum foil wrapping paper adds sparkle to gifts. Foil-wrapped packages underneath the tree will reflect the lights and colors of your holiday decorations.

SPECIAL SHAPES

CLEVER CANISTER

MATERIALS: Gift wrap; 1-inch-wide red velvet gift ribbon, or snowball bow or yarn bow *(directions, page 223)*; miniature ornaments *(optional)*; transparent tape; glue stick.

DIRECTIONS:

1. Trace the top and bottom of the box onto the back of the gift wrap, and cut out the two circles.

2. Wrap the side of the box, allowing the gift wrap to extend beyond the top and bottom edges *(see illustration)*. Fold over the long free end of the gift wrap, and tape it to secure it.

3. Fold the extending gift wrap over the edge at each end of the box, and tape the folded wrap to the top and bottom of the box.

4. Affix the gift wrap circles to the top and bottom with the glue stick.

5. Make a multi-loop bow from the red velvet ribbon, and tape it to the top of the box. Or decorate the box with a snowball bow or yarn bow. Add miniature ornaments, if you wish.

BOTTLE BEAUTY

MATERIALS: Tissue paper or fabric scrap; gift wrap cord, ribbon or yarn.

DIRECTIONS:

1. Measure the height of the bottle, and double the number. Cut the tissue paper or fabric into a square whose measurements are a few inches longer than the doubled height of the bottle.

2. Fold the square into a triangular shape three times *(see illustration)*. Round off the edge of the triangle, and unfold the paper or fabric circle.

3. Place the bottle in the center of the circle. Draw up the sides of the circle, and tie them together with the cord, ribbon or yarn. Flare the top of the paper or fabric for a ruffled look.

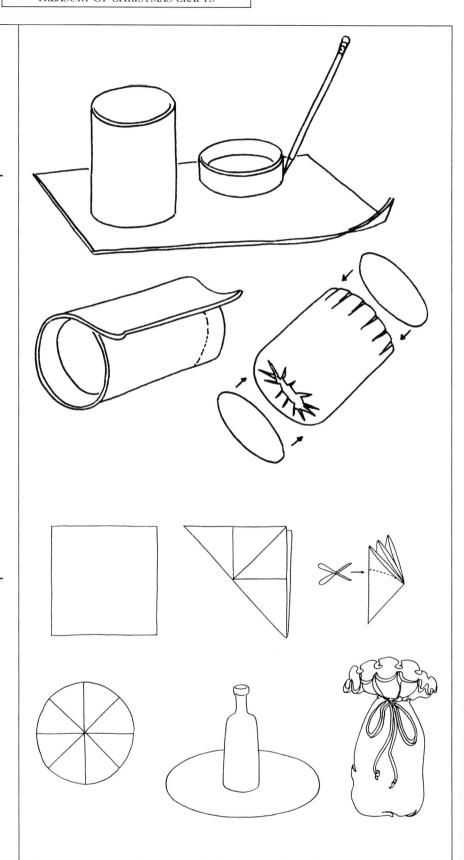

CANDY CANE UMBRELLA

MATERIALS: White tissue paper; 2-inch-wide red velvet gift ribbon; transparent tape; small piece of garland with berries *(optional)*.

DIRECTIONS:

1. Cut the tissue paper 6 inches wider than the circumference of the umbrella. Place the umbrella on one edge of the paper and roll up both together, leaving the umbrella handle free. Tape the paper in place.

2. Twist the ends of the paper around the handle, and tape to secure them.

3. Tape one end of the ribbon to the bottom of the wrapped umbrella, and wrap the ribbon around and up *(see photo)*. Cut the ribbon and tape the end to the handle.

4. Make a multi-loop bow from the ribbon, leaving the ends free. Trim the ends and, if you wish, add some garland with berries to the bow.

CHRISTMAS JAR

MATERIALS: Scrap of print fabric; yarn or ribbon; ornament *(optional)*.

DIRECTIONS:

1. Cut out a fabric circle 5 inches wider than the diameter of the jar lid.

2. Place the fabric circle on top of the jar. Fold down the fabric edges and tie the yarn or ribbon around the neck. If you wish, add an ornament.

CYLINDER TWIST

MATERIALS: Gift wrap; transparent tape; gift ribbon; tiny ball ornaments.

DIRECTIONS:

1. Cut a piece of gift wrap twice the length of the cylinder. Fold over one long edge of the wrap, center the cylinder on the raw edge, and roll up both together. Tape to secure.

2. Twist the wrap at either end of the cylinder, and tie with the ribbon. Curl the ribbon, and add the miniature ball ornaments *(see photo)*.

TAKE A BOW!

❦ ❦ ❦ ❦ ❦ ❦

TRIMMING TRICKS

Try placing ribbons slightly off center on gift boxes. Split a ribbon to varying widths for a decreasing stripe effect. Two colors or shades of ribbon can be woven easily into a nostalgic basket-weave pattern.

Use gift wrap for trimming as well as wrapping. Make a bow by stapling strips of gift wrap together like the spokes of a wheel. Draw the strips over a dull scissor or knife edge to create curls.

Ordinary items, such as small toys, candy or old greeting cards, make eye-catching trims, and can be used to hint at the contents of the packages.

GATHERED RIBBON BOW

MATERIALS: One spool each of red, green and white ¾-inch or 1¼-inch-wide self-sticking ribbon; scissors; curling ribbon or string.

DIRECTIONS:

Using all three colors of self-sticking ribbon, cut thirteen to fifteen 12-inch-long ribbon strips. Fold each strip in half, then unfold it. Moisten the ends only of one strip, fold the ends into

the center crease without overlapping them, and press to form a double bow.

Repeat for all the strips. Dry for 10 minutes. Cut a small triangle on one

side in the center of each double bow *(see photo)*. Do the same on the other side, leaving ¼ inch in the center. Cut a 54-inch length of curling ribbon or string, and lay it on a flat surface. Alternating the colors, place all the double bows on top of the curling ribbon, close together but not touching *(see photo)*. Bring up both ends of the curling ribbon, cross one end in front of the other, and pull quickly and tightly. Knot the curling ribbon, and cut off the excess.

YARN BOW

MATERIALS: Yarn.

DIRECTIONS:
1. Loop the yarn back and forth until you have the desired number of loops.
2. Using a separate piece of yarn, tie the loops very tightly in the center and flare them out to form the bow. Tie knots in the four loose yarn ends.

TAILORED BOW

MATERIALS: Shiny ribbon; transparent tape.

DIRECTIONS:
For a 6-inch-long bow, cut a 2-foot length of ribbon. Form a 3-inch-long loop, and secure it with tape. Add a matching loop to the other side (do not cut the ribbon), and secure it with tape. Make a slightly smaller loop over the first loop, secure it, and repeat over the second loop. Continue to make slightly smaller loops each round, and secure each loop with tape. End with a small loop in the center.

SNOWBALL BOW

MATERIALS: Curling ribbon; scissors.

DIRECTIONS:
1. For a 3-inch-diameter snowball, cut an 8-foot length of ribbon. Draw the entire length over a dull scissor edge to curl it.
2. Gather the curls into a ball and tie them with a separate piece of ribbon, catching stray curls into the ball.

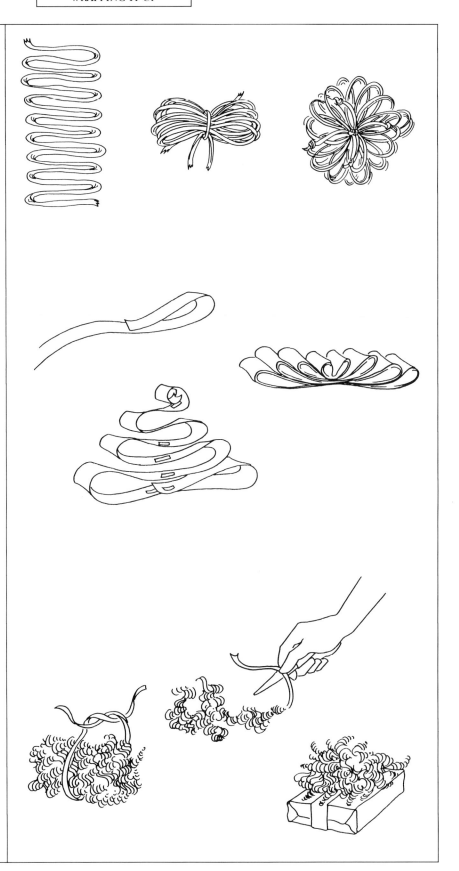

HOMEMADE CHRISTMAS CARDS

Dot Designs Cards and Stationery

🌸 🌸 🌸 🌸 🌸 🌸

SHARE THE SPIRIT OF THE SEASON

Christmas cards and letters are a wonderful way to keep in touch with far-away friends and relatives. But this year, why not try something a bit different? Take a series of photographs of your caroling and tree-trimming festivities, or videotape them, if possible. Your distant loved ones will feel as though they actually spent the season with you.

Patchwork Christmas Cards

DOT DESIGN CARDS AND STATIONERY

Use this simple hole punch technique to jazz up your holiday notes and cards; we've seen high priced stationers do much the same thing!

EASY: Achievable by anyone.
MATERIALS: Sheets of paper in various sizes and colors; ⅛- and ¼-inch paper punches; ribbon, yarn or metallic cord.

DIRECTIONS:
Fold some sheets of paper into cards, and leave some flat to use as stationery. Use the photo as a design guide, or create your own decorative designs. Lightly sketch the desired designs on the paper. Punch out the designs with the paper punches. Carefully erase any design lines still showing. Thread lengths of ribbon, yarn or metallic cord through holes on some of the sheets *(see photo)*, and tie them into bows.

PATCHWORK CHRISTMAS CARDS

EASY: Achievable by anyone.
MATERIALS: Tracing paper; fabric scraps, fabric printed with a quilt motif, or gift wrap; construction paper; glue stick; colored fine-point permanent felt-tip pens.

DIRECTIONS:
1. Choose geometric shapes, or a patchwork quilt motif, and draw these on the tracing paper. Cut out the tracing paper shapes for patterns.
2. Using the tracing paper patterns, cut out the shapes from the fabric scraps or gift wrap, or cut out an entire quilt motif from the printed fabric.
3. Fold the construction paper into cards. Glue the fabric or gift wrap shapes onto the cards in a patchwork motif, or glue the quilt motif onto a card. Allow the glue to dry completely.
4. Write your Christmas greetings on the front or inside the cards with the felt-tip pens.

Christmas Kid-Cards

CHRISTMAS KID-CARDS

A perfect project for snowy or rainy days. Your kids will have a wonderful time cutting and pasting these cards.

EASY: Achievable by anyone.
MATERIALS: Tracing paper; fabric scraps; string, ribbon, cotton and other trimmings; construction paper; white glue.

DIRECTIONS:

1. Choose designs to be cut out from the fabric, and draw them on tracing paper. Cut out the tracing paper designs to make patterns.
2. Using the tracing paper patterns, cut out the designs from the fabric scraps.
3. Fold the construction paper into cards. Glue the designs cut from the fabric scraps onto the front of the cards. Let the glue dry completely.
4. Decorate the cards with string, ribbon, cotton and other trimmings.

EASY GIFT TAGS

Once all your gifts are wrapped, you'll have a hard time telling them apart. To avoid confusion, label the packages as you wrap them.

EASY: Achievable by anyone.
MATERIALS: Unlined white index cards; scraps of gift wrap, yarn and ribbon; paper punch or pointed scissors; colored fine-point permanent felt-tip pens; glue or glue stick; pinking shears *(optional).*

DIRECTIONS:

1. Cut the index cards into 1½-inch squares. Using the paper punch or scissors, punch a hole in one corner of each square to make a tag.
2. Decorate one side of each tag with the scraps of gift wrap, yarn and ribbon: Cut gift wrap into a heart, star or tree shape, glue the shape to a tag, and decorate with ribbon. Outline a shape on a tag with glue, and fit yarn around the outline. Cut out a motif from patterned gift wrap, and glue it to a tag. If you wish, cut around the edges of some tags with pinking shears.
3. Write who a gift is for and who it is from with a felt-tip pen on the other side of each tag. Thread a scrap of yarn or ribbon through the hole in the tag, and attach the tag to the gift.

"SPECIAL DELIVERY" GIFTS BY MAIL

SELECT THE PROPER CONTAINERS

Fiberboard containers (commonly found in supermarkets or hardware stores) generally are strong enough to mail items of average weight and size—up to 10 lbs. Paperboard cartons (similar to suit boxes) also can be used for items weighing up to 10 lbs. Some boxes have a "test board" rating, which tells you how strong they are, and is indicated by a round imprint on a bottom corner of each box. A corrugated fiberboard box (125-lb. test board) is good for mailing items weighing up to 20 lbs. High density items, such as tools, require a stronger container.

HOW TO PACKAGE YOUR GIFTS

Soft goods, such as clothing, pillows or quilts, should be placed in a self-supporting box or tear-resistant bag. Seal with reinforced tape.

Perishables, such as cheese, fruit, vegetables, meat, or any food with an odor, must be placed in an impermeable container that is filled with absorbent cushioning and sealed with filament tape.

Fragile items, such as glasses, dishes or photography equipment, are safest packaged in a fiberboard container (minimum 175-lb. test board), and cushioned with plastic foam or padding. Seal and reinforce the package with filament tape.

Shifting contents, such as books, tools and nails, should be packaged in a fiberboard container (minimum 175-lb. test board). Be sure to use interior fiberboard separators or tape to prevent the contents from shifting in transit. Seal and reinforce the package with filament tape.

Awkward loads, such as umbrellas, pipes or odd-shaped tools and instruments, require special packaging. Use a fiberboard tube or box with length not more than 10 times its girth. Cushion the items with preformed fiberboard or plastic foam. The closure should be as strong as the box or tube itself.

USE ADEQUATE CUSHIONING

If you are mailing several gift items in one package, wrap the items individually, and protect each gift from the others with padding or plastic foam. Fill the mailing box completely with cushioning material, leaving no empty spaces. Polystyrene, "bubble" plastic, fiberboard, and shredded, rolled or crumpled newspaper all are good cushioning materials. You also can use packing straw, plastic foam chips, or plastic foam egg cartons cut into pieces. Commercially available foam shells or air pocket padding also can be used. Padded mailing bags are good for small items.

BE SURE A WRAPPED GIFT ARRIVES SAFELY

Always mail a wrapped gift inside another box. Many gift boxes just aren't meant to be shipping boxes. Be sure to choose a mailing box that is sturdy enough to support its contents, and withstand the wear and tear of delivery.

Use a heavy gift wrap. Thicker, heavier wrapping paper has a better chance of arriving without being torn.

Consider using a designed gift box. Many gift boxes come printed with holiday motifs.

Bows don't travel well. Instead, decorate wrapped gifts with flat trims, stickers, yarn or tinsel tie.

SEAL THE PACKAGES PROPERLY

Use one of three recommended types of tape to secure your parcels: pressure-sensitive filament tape, nylon-reinforced Kraft paper tape, or plain Kraft paper tape. All three types are available in stationery stores or dime stores. The Postal Service will not accept parcels sealed with ordinary transparent tape or masking tape.

Do not wrap packages with brown paper or tie them with twine. Paper sometimes rips in handling, and twine often gets entangled in mail processing equipment.

REQUEST SPECIAL MARKINGS

Certain phrases printed on the outside of your parcels will alert Postal Service employees to the nature of their contents. Mark breakable objects FRAGILE in three places: above the address, below the postage, and on the reverse side. Packages of food or other items that can decay should be marked PERISHABLE in the same locations. The words DO NOT BEND on packages will signal fragile items. Be sure to protect such items with stiffening material, such as cardboard. When you take your packages to the post office for mailing, ask the clerk to stamp them appropriately.

INSURE THE PACKAGES

Any gifts sent by mail should be insured. You can insure each package in varying amounts for up to $400. The cost is minimal, and you have the added security of knowing that you will be reimbursed if the package is lost or damaged. If you are mailing something that is worth more than $400, or if you are sending cash or an irreplaceable item through the mail, send it by registered mail or via an air courier service.

USE ZIP CODES

The easiest ways to delay delivery of mail are to forget to use the ZIP Code, or to use the wrong one. When addressing each package, be sure to include the ZIP code in both the recipient's and your return address.

TIME IT RIGHT

The Postal Service offers a wide range of delivery options for mailing packages, depending on the amount of money you want to spend and the time you've allowed for delivery. A good general rule to follow is to mail early in the day and early in the month. First-class letters and cards sent coast-to-coast should arrive within three to four days. Greetings sent within a state should arrive within two to three days, and those mailed to an address within a city should reach their destination in two days. However, the Christmas season is the busiest time of the year for the Postal Service. Just to be on the safe side, it's best to allow at least two weeks for domestic delivery of holiday cards and gifts.

DOMESTIC MAIL SERVICES

You can choose one of three services to send packages up to
70 lbs. and 108 inches (length plus girth) by mail.

SERVICE	DESCRIPTION	COST	TIME
PRIORITY MAIL	Packages receive the same attention as first-class letters. Shipped by air, these parcels can be sent from any post office station or branch to any address in the U.S.	Determined by weight and distance traveled. A 2-lb. package from New York to Chicago: $2.40; a 5-lb. package: $4.86. A 2-lb. package from New York to Los Angeles: $2.40; a 5-lb. package: $6.37.	3 to 4 days
PARCEL POST	Takes longer than priority mail, but costs less. Packages can be mailed from any post office station or branch and are delivered directly to the addressee.	Determined by weight and distance traveled. A 2-lb. package from New York to Chicago: $2.24; a 5-lb. package: $3.29. A 2-lb. package from New York to Los Angeles: $2.35; a 5-lb. package: $6.25.	8 days
EXPRESS MAIL	Guaranteed delivery to the addressee by 3 P.M. the following business day. Packages are insured automatically for up to $500. If the mail is late, a full refund may be obtained by applying to the originating post office.	For direct delivery anywhere in the U.S., a ½-lb. package: $8.75; a 2-lb. package: $12.00; a 5-lb. package: $15.25. For recipient pick-up at post office, a 2-lb. package: $9.85; a 5-lb. package: $13.10.	Overnight

Note: Prices are accurate at time of press.

INTERNATIONAL MAIL

DESTINATION	AIR PARCELS	AIRMAIL LETTERS/CARDS
North and Northwest Africa	24 Nov	1 Dec
Australia	24 Nov	24 Nov
Caribbean and West Indies	12 Dec	12 Dec
Central and South America	5 Dec	5 Dec
Europe	1 Dec	5 Dec
Far East	1 Dec	5 Dec
Middle East	24 Nov	28 Nov
Southeast Asia	24 Nov	24 Nov
Southeast Africa	24 Nov	1 Dec
West Africa	24 Nov	1 Dec

Note: These dates are for mailing from the continental U.S. only.

Crafts Basics & Abbreviations

HOW TO KNIT

THE BASIC STITCHES

Get out your needles and yarn, and slowly read your way through this special section. Practice the basic stitches illustrated here as you go along. Once you know them, you're ready to start knitting.

CASTING ON: This puts the first row of stitches on the needle. Measure off about two yards of yarn (or about an inch for each stitch you are going to cast on). Make a slip knot at this point by making a medium-size loop of yarn; then pull another small loop through it. Place the slip knot on one needle and pull one end gently to tighten (FIG. 1).

FIG. 1

• Hold the needle in your right hand. Hold both strands of yarn in the palm of your left hand securely but not rigidly. Slide your left thumb and forefinger between the two strands and spread these two fingers out to form a triangle of yarn.

• Your left thumb should hold the free end of yarn, your forefinger the yarn from the ball. The needle in your right hand holds the first stitch (FIG. 2).

FIG. 2

You are now in position to cast on. See ABBREVIATIONS (at right) for explanations of asterisk (*).

• *Bring the needles in your right hand toward you; slip the tip of the needle under the front strand of the loop on left thumb (FIG. 3).

FIG. 3

• Now, with the needle, catch the strand of yarn that is on your left forefinger (FIG. 4).

FIG. 4

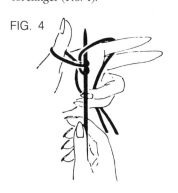

• Draw it through the thumb loop to form a stitch on the needle (FIG. 5).

FIG. 5

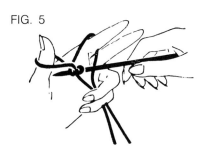

• Holding the stitch on the needle with the right index finger, slip the loop off your left thumb (FIG. 6). Tighten up the stitch on the needle by pulling the freed strand back with your left thumb, bringing the yarn back into position for casting on more stitches (FIG. 2 again).

FIG. 6

• **Do not cast on too tightly.** Stitches should slide easily on the needle. Repeat from * until you have cast on the number of stitches specified in your instructions.

KNIT STITCH (k): Hold the needle with the cast-on stitches in your left hand (FIG. 7).

FIG. 7

• Pick up the other needle in your right hand. With yarn from the ball in **back** of the work, insert the tip of the right-hand needle from **left to right** through the front loop of the first stitch on the left-hand needle (FIG. 8).

FIG. 8

• Holding both needles in this position with your left hand, wrap the yarn over your little finger, under your two middle fingers and over the forefinger of your right hand. Hold the yarn firmly, but loosely enough so that it will slide through your fingers as you knit. Return the right-hand needle to your right hand.
• With your right forefinger, pass the yarn under (from right to left) and then over (from left to right) the tip of the right-hand needle, forming a loop on the needle (FIG. 9).

FIG. 9

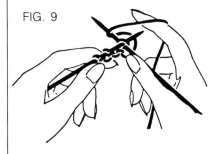

• Now draw this loop through the stitch on the left-hand needle (FIG. 10).

FIG. 10

KNITTING ABBREVIATIONS AND SYMBOLS

*Knitting directions are always written in standard abbreviations. They look mysterious at first, but you'll soon know them: **beg** — beginning; **bet** — between; **bl** — block; **ch** — chain; **CC** — contrasting color; **dec(s)** — decrease(s); **dp** — double-pointed;" or **in(s)** — inch(es); **incl** — inclusive; **inc(s)** — increase(s); **k** — knit; **lp(s)** — loop(s); **MC** — main color; **oz(s)** — ounce(s); **psso** — pass slipped stitch over last stitch worked; **pat(s)** — pattern(s); **p** — purl; **rem** — remaining; **rpt** — repeat; **rnd(s)** — round(s); **sk** — skip; **sl** — slip; **sl st** — slip stitch; **sp(s)** — space(s); **st(s)** — stitch(es); **st st** — stockinette stitch; **tog** — together; **yo** — yarn over; **pc** — popcorn stitch.*

***(asterisk)** — directions immediately following * are to be repeated the specified number of times indicated in addition to the first time — i.e. "repeat from * 3 times more" means 4 times in all.*

() (parentheses) — directions should be worked as often as specified — i.e., "(k 1, k 2 tog, k 3) 5 times" means to work what is in ( ) 5 times in all.

• Slip the original stitch off the left-hand needle, leaving the new stitch on the right-hand needle (FIG. 11).

FIG. 11

Keep the stitches loose enough so that you can slide them along the needles, but firm enough so they do not slide when you don't want them to. Continue until you have knitted all the stitches from the left-hand needle onto the right-hand needle.

• To start the next row, simply pass the needle with the stitches on it to your left hand, reversing it, so that it is now the left-hand needle.

PURL STITCH (p): Purling is the reverse of knitting. Again, keep the stitches loose enough to slide, but firm enough to work with. To purl, hold the needle with the stitches in your left hand, with the yarn in ***front*** of your work. Insert the tip of the right-hand needle from ***right to left*** through the front loop of the first stitch on the left-hand needle (FIG. 12).

FIG. 12

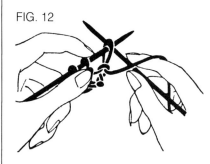

• With your right hand holding the yarn as you would to knit, but in ***front*** of the needles, pass the yarn over the tip of the right-hand needle, then under it, forming a loop on the needle (FIG. 13).

FIG. 13

• Holding the yarn firmly so that it won't slip off, draw this loop through the stitch on the left-hand needle (FIG. 14).

FIG. 14

• Slip the original stitch off the left-hand needle, leaving the new stitch on the right-hand needle (FIG. 15).

FIG. 15

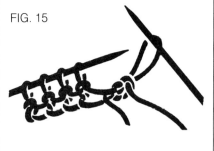

SLIPSTITCH (sl st): Insert the tip of the right-hand needle into the next stitch on the left-hand needle, as if to purl, unless otherwise directed. Slip this stitch off the left-hand needle onto the right, ***without working it*** (FIG. 16).

FIG. 16

BINDING OFF: This makes a finished edge and locks the stitches securely in place. Knit (or purl) two stitches. Then, with the tip of the left-hand needle, lift the first of these two stitches over the second stitch and drop it off the tip of the right-hand needle (FIG. 17).

FIG. 17

One stitch remains on the right-hand needle; one stitch has been bound off.

• *Knit (or purl) the next stitch; lift the first stitch over the last stitch and off the tip of the needle. Again, one stitch remains on the right-hand needle, and another stitch has been bound off.

Repeat from * until the required number of stitches have been bound off.

• Remember that you work two stitches to bind off one stitch. If, for example, the directions read, "k 6, bind off the next 4 sts, k 6 . . ." you must knit six stitches, then knit **two more** stitches before starting to bind off. Bind off four times. After the four stitches have been bound off, count the last stitch remaining on the right-hand needle as the first stitch of the next six stitches. When binding off, always knit the knitted stitches and purl the purled stitches.

• Be careful not to bind off too tightly or too loosely. The tension should be the same as the rest of the knitting.

• To end off the last stitch on the bound-off edge, if you are ending the piece of work here, cut the yarn leaving a six-inch end; pass the cut end through the remaining loop on the right-hand needle and pull snugly (FIG. 18).

FIG. 18

SHAPING TECHNIQUES

Now that you know the basics, all that's left to learn are a few techniques which will help shape whatever it is you are making.

INCREASING (inc): This means adding stitches in a given area to shape your work. There are several ways to increase.

1. To increase by knitting twice into the same stitch: Knit the stitch in the usual way through the front loop (FIG. 19), but ***before*** dropping the stitch from the left-hand needle, knit ***another*** stitch on the same loop by placing the needle into the back of the stitch. (FIG. 20). Slip the first stitch off your left-hand needle. You have made two stitches from one stitch.

FIG. 19

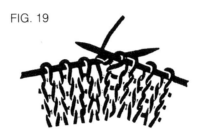

FIG. 20

2. To increase by knitting between stitches: Insert the tip of the right-hand needle under the strand of yarn ***between*** the stitch you've just

worked and the following stitch; slip it onto the tip of the left-hand needle (FIG. 21).

FIG. 21

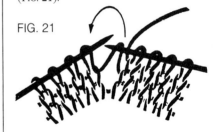

Now knit into the back of the loop (FIG. 22).

FIG. 22

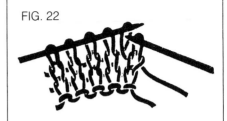

3. To increase by "yarn-over" (yo): Pass the yarn over the right-hand needle after finishing one stitch and before starting the next stitch, ***making an extra stitch*** (see the arrow in (FIG. 23). ***If you are knitting,*** bring the yarn under the needle to the back. ***If you are purling,*** wind the yarn around the needle once. On the next row, work all of the yarn-overs as stitches.

FIG. 23

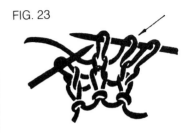

DECREASING (dec): This means reducing the number of stitches in a given area to shape your work. Two methods for decreasing are:

1. To decrease by knitting (FIG. 24) **or purling** (FIG. 25) **two stitches together:**

FIG. 24

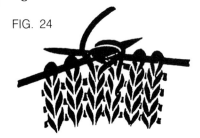

FIG. 25

Insert the right-hand needle through the loops of two stitches on the left-hand needle at the same time, and complete the stitch. This is written as "k 2 tog" or "p 2 tog."
• If you work through the **front** loops of the stitches in the usual way, your decreasing stitch will slant to the right. If you work through the **back** loops of the stitches, your decreasing stitch will slant to the left.

2. Slip 1 stitch, knit 1 and psso: Insert the right-hand needle through the stitch on the left-hand needle, but instead of working it, just slip it off onto the right-hand needle (go back to FIG. 16). Work the next stitch in the usual way. With the tip of the left-hand needle, lift the slipped stitch over the last stitch worked and off the tip of the right-hand needle (FIG. 26).

FIG. 26

Your decreasing stitch will slant to the left. This is written as "sl 1, k 1, psso."
Pass Slipped Stitch Over (psso): Slip one stitch from the left-hand needle to the right-hand needle and, being careful to keep it in position, work the next stitch. Then, with the tip of the left-hand needle, lift the slipped stitch over the last stitch and off the tip of the right-hand needle (FIG. 26).

ATTACHING THE YARN
When you end one ball of yarn or wish to change colors, begin at the start of a row and tie the new yarn with the previous yarn, making a secure joining. Continue to work (FIG. 27).

FIG. 27

HOW TO CROCHET

DIRECTIONS FOR RIGHT-HANDED AND LEFT-HANDED CROCHETERS

Most crochet stitches are started from a base of chain stitches. However, our stitches are started from a row of single crochet stitches which gives body to the sample swatches and makes practice work easier to handle. When making a specific item, follow the stitch directions as given.

Holding the crochet hook properly (FIG. 1), start by practicing the slip knot (FIG. 2) and base chain (FIG. 3, page 236).

FIG. 1 HOLDING THE HOOK (BASIS FOR CHAIN STITCH)

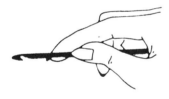

FIG. 2 THE SLIP STITCH

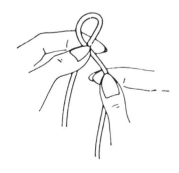

FIG. 2a

FIG. 2b

FIG. 2c

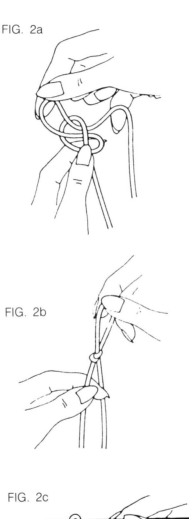

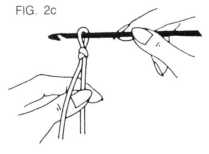

CROCHET ABBREVIATIONS

The following is a crochet abbreviations listing, with definitions of the terms given. To help you become accustomed to abbreviations used, we have repeated them through our stitch instructions. **beg** — *begin, beginning;* **ch** — *chain;* **dc** — *double crochet;* **dec** — *decrease;* **dtr** — *double treble crochet;* **hdc** — *half double crochet;* **in(s)** *or* **"** — *inch(es);* **inc** — *increase;* **oz(s)** — *ounce(s);* **pat** — *pattern;* **pc** — *picot;* **rem** — *remaining;* **rnd** — *round;* **rpt** — *repeat;* **sc** — *single crochet;* **skn(s)** — *skein(s);* **sk** — *skip;* **sl st** — *slip stitch;* **sp** — *space;* **st(s)** — *stitch(es);* **tog** — *together;* **tr** — *triple crochet;* **work even** — *continue without further increase or decrease;* **yo** — *yarn over;* * *(asterisk) — repeat whatever follows * as many times as indicated;* ( ) — *do what is in parentheses as many times as indicated.*

CHAIN STITCH (ch): Follow the steps in FIG. 3. As you make the chain stitch loops, the yarn should slide easily between your index and middle fingers. Make about 15 loops. If they are all the same size, you have maintained even tension. If uneven, rip them out by pulling on the long end of the yarn. Practice making chains and ripping out until you have a perfect chain.

FIG. 3 CHAIN STITCH (CH)

YARN OVER (YO)

FIG. 3a

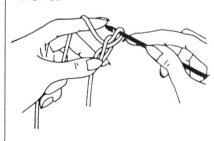

FIG. 3b

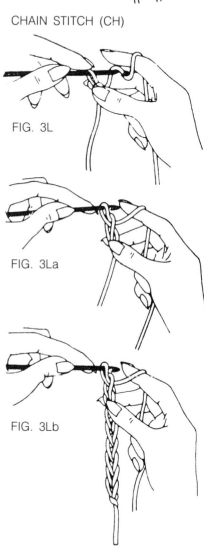

FOR LEFT-HANDED CROCHETERS

FIGS. 1 to 3 are for right-handed crocheters and are repeated in FIGS. 1 Left to 3 Left for left-handed crocheters.

LEFT-HANDED CROCHETERS
FIGS. 1 LEFT TO 3 LEFT

FIG. 1L
HOLDING THE HOOK

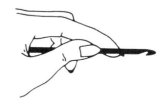

FIG. 2L

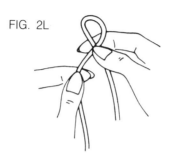

FIG. 2La

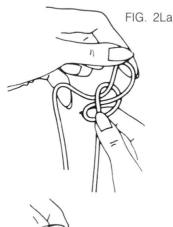

FIG. 2Lb

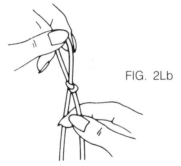

FIG. 2Lc

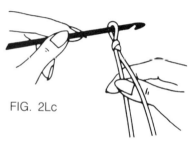

CHAIN STITCH (CH)

FIG. 3L

FIG. 3La

FIG. 3Lb

From here on, we won't be showing hands — just the hook and stitches. Left-handed crocheters can use all of the following right-handed illustrations by simply turning the book upside down and using a mirror (with backstand) that will reflect the left-handed version.

SINGLE CROCHET (sc): Follow the steps in FIG. 4. To practice, make a 20-loop chain (this means 20 loops in addition to the slip knot). Turn the chain, as shown, and insert the hook in the second chain from the hook (see arrow) to make the first sc stitch. Yarn over (yo); for the second stitch, see the next arrow. Repeat to the end of the chain. Because you started in the second chain from the hook, you end up with only 19 sc. To add the 20th stitch, ch 1 (called a turning chain) and pull the yarn through. Now turn your work around (the "back" is now facing you) and start the second row of sc in the first stitch of the previous row (at the arrow). Make sure your hook goes under both of the strands at the top of the stitch. Don't forget to make a ch 1 turning chain at the end before turning your work. Keep practicing until your rows are perfect.

ENDING OFF: Follow the steps in FIG. 5. To finish off your crochet, cut off all but 6 inches of yarn and end off as shown. (To "break off and fasten," follow the same procedure.)

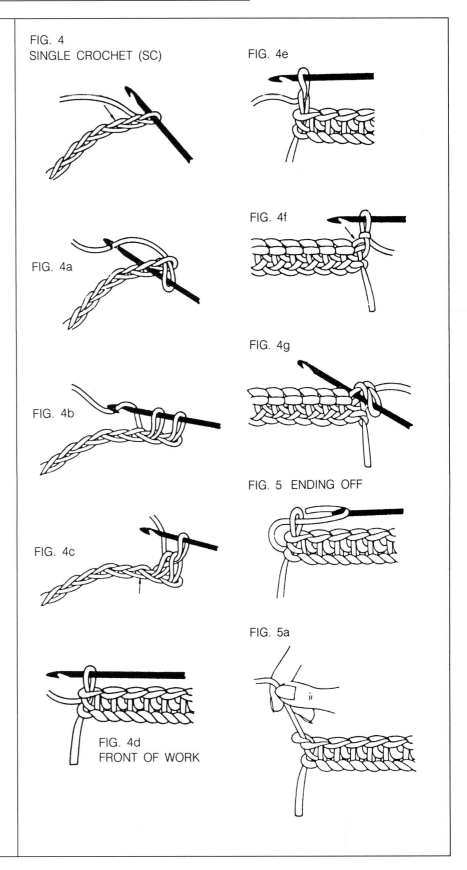

FIG. 4
SINGLE CROCHET (SC)

FIG. 4a

FIG. 4b

FIG. 4c

FIG. 4d
FRONT OF WORK

FIG. 4e

FIG. 4f

FIG. 4g

FIG. 5 ENDING OFF

FIG. 5a

DOUBLE CROCHET (dc): Follow the steps in Fig. 6. To practice, ch 20, then make a row of 20 sc. Now, instead of a ch 1, you will make a ch 3. Turn your work, yo and insert the hook in the second stitch of the previous row (at the arrow), going under both strands at the top of the stitch. Pull the yarn through. You now have three loops on the hook. Yo and pull through the first two, then yo and pull through the remaining two—one double crochet (dc) made. Continue across the row, making a dc in each stitch (st) across. Dc in the top of the turning chain (see arrow in Fig. 7). Ch 3. Turn work. Dc in second stitch on the previous row and continue as before.

FIG. 6
DOUBLE CROCHET (DC)

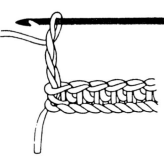

FIG. 6a

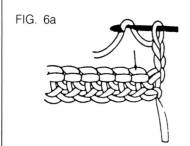

FIG. 6b

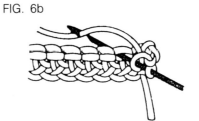

FIG. 6c

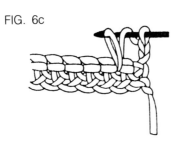

FIG. 6d

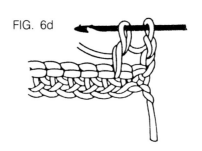

FIG. 6e

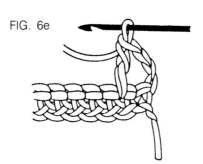

FIG. 7

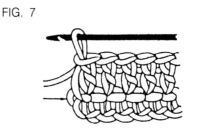

FIG. 8

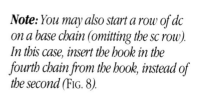

STARTING FROM A CHAIN

Note: *You may also start a row of dc on a base chain (omitting the sc row). In this case, insert the hook in the fourth chain from the hook, instead of the second (Fig. 8).*

SLIPSTITCH (sl st): Follow the steps in Fig. 9. This is a utility stitch you will use for joining, shaping and ending off. After you chain and turn, **do not yo.** Just insert the hook into the *first* stitch of the previous row (Fig. 9A), and pull the yarn through the stitch, then through the loop on the hook—the sl st is made.

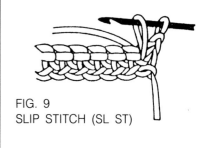

FIG. 9
SLIP STITCH (SL ST)

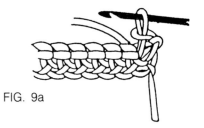

FIG. 9a

HALF DOUBLE CROCHET (hdc):
Follow the steps in FIG. 10 and 10A.

FIG. 10
HALF DOUBLE CROCHET (HDC)

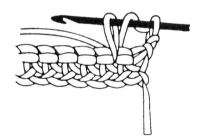

FIG. 10a

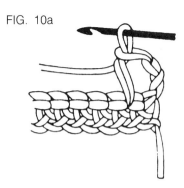

To practice, make a chain and a row of sc. Ch 2 and turn; yo. Insert the hook in the second stitch, as shown; yo and pull through to make three loops on the hook. Yo and pull the yarn through *all* three loops at the same time — hdc made. This stitch is used primarily as a transitional stitch from an sc to a dc. Try it and see — starting with sc's, then an hdc and then dc's.

TECHNIQUES OF CROCHETING
Now that you have practiced and made sample squares of all the basic stitches, you are ready to learn about adding and subtracting stitches to change the length of a row whenever it's called for. You do this by increasing (inc) and decreasing (dec).

To increase (inc): Just make two stitches in the same stitch in the previous row (see arrow in FIG. 11). The technique is the same for any kind of stitch.

FIG. 11   INCREASING (INC)
FOR SINGLE CROCHET

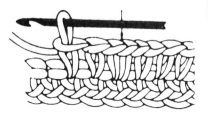

To decrease (dec) for single-crochet (sc): Yo and pull the yarn through two stitches to make three loops on the hook (see steps in FIG. 12). Pull the yarn through all the loops at once — dec made. Continue in regular stitches.

FIG. 12   DECREASING (DEC)

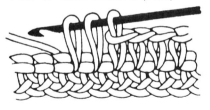

FIG. 12a   FOR SINGLE CROCHET

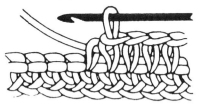

To decrease for double crochet (dc): In a dc row, make the next stitch and stop when you have two loops on the hook. Now yo and make a dc in the next stitch. At the point where you have three loops on the hook, pull yarn through all loops at the same time. Finish the row with regular dc.

HOW TO ENLARGE DESIGNS
If the design is not already marked off in squares, make a tracing of it. Mark the tracing off in squares: For a small design, make squares ¼ inch; for larger designs, use ½-inch or 2-inch squares, or the size indicated in the directions. Decide the size of enlargement. On another sheet of tracing paper, mark off the same number of squares that are on the design or original tracing. For example, to make your design, each new square must be six times larger than the original. Copy the outline from your original tracing to the new one, square by square. Use dressmaker's carbon and a tracing wheel to transfer the design onto the material you are decorating.

EMBROIDERY STITCH GUIDE

BLANKET STITCH

Work from left to right, with the point of the needle and the edge of the work toward you. The edge of the fabric can be folded under or left raw. Secure the thread and bring it out below the edge. For the first and each succeeding stitch, insert the needle through the fabric from the right side and bring it out at the edge. Keeping the thread from the previous stitch *under* the point of the needle, draw the needle and thread through, forming a stitch over the edge. The stitch size and spacing can be uniform or varied.

BLANKET STITCH

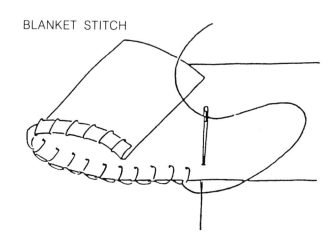

CHAIN STITCH

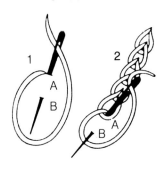

CROSS STITCH

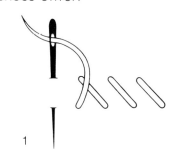

FEATHER STITCH

FRENCH KNOT

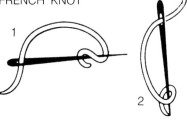

FLY STITCH

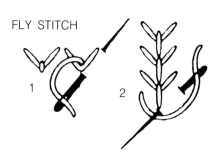

STRAIGHT STITCH

BLIND STITCH

TENT OR CONTINENTAL STITCH
OR PETIT POINT

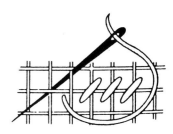

MOSAIC STITCH

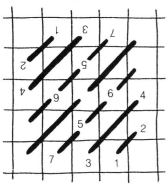

SLANTED GOBELIN STITCH
(worked vertically)

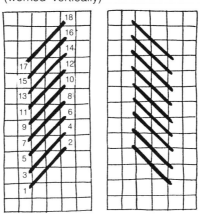

LONG AND SHORT STITCH

INTERLOCKING GOBELIN STITCH

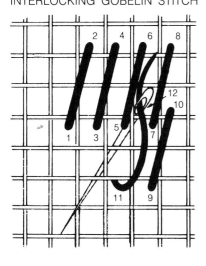

SCOTCH STITCH

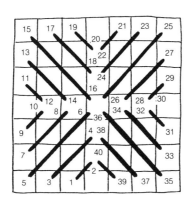

SCOTCH STITCH VARIATION

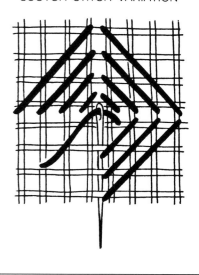

Index

Italicized Page Numbers Refer to Photographs

· D ·

· E ·

· F ·

· G ·

· T ·

· U ·

· V ·

· Y ·

· W ·

PHOTO CREDITS

Robert Ander

David Bishop

Ralph Bogertman

John Bonjour

John Galuzzi

Ronald G. Harris

James Kozyra

Taylor Lewis

Bill McGinn

Chris Mead

Maris/Semel

Jeff Niki

Leonard Nones

Bradley Olman

Carin Riley

Gordon E. Smith

William Steele

Bob Stoller

Theo

Rene Velez

Comments? Questions? Complaints? Praise?
We value your thoughts on our books. If you'd like to write to us
about this book, please address your letter or postcard to: Christmas Craft Comments,
Family Circle Books, 110 Fifth Avenue, New York, NY 10011.